— Syrian Episodes —

Figure 1. In October 2004, the Syrian government confiscated more than six hundred photographs and other works of art at the Le Point Gallery in Aleppo, including the above installation, and closed the International Photography Gathering and the Women's Art Festival of which this exhibition was a part. This closure was rare, and the reasons for it remain mysterious, though Issa Touma, festival organizer and gallery owner, suspected they were personal, tied to his long struggle to exhibit international and "modern" art. While attending an Arab-Dutch poetry reading at the gallery, I was impressed with this installation by Dutch artist Richtje Reinsma. Bread symbolizes *kheir*—everything good that can come to you—and is treated as sacred in all Arab countries. It stands for abundance and is considered a blessing of Allah. You never step on bread and never throw it away, and if you find it on the ground, you should pick it up and kiss it.

⁓ Syrian Episodes ⁓

Sons, Fathers,
and an
Anthropologist in Aleppo

John Borneman

PRINCETON UNIVERSITY PRESS

PRINCETON AND OXFORD

Library of Congress Cataloging-in-Publication Data

Borneman, John, 1952–
Syrian episodes : sons, fathers, and an anthropologist in Aleppo / John Borneman.
p. cm.
Includes index.
ISBN-13: 978-0-691-12887-0 (hardcover : alk. paper)
ISBN-10: 0-691-12887-1 (hardcover : alk. paper)
1. Ethnology—Syria—Aleppo. 2. Kinship—Syria—Aleppo. 3. Patriarchy—
Syria—Aleppo. 4. Fathers and sons—Syria—Aleppo. 5. Philosophy, Arab.
6. Aleppo (Syria)—Social life and customs. I. Title.
GN635.S95B67 2006
306.874'20956913—dc22
2006022436

British Library Cataloging-in-Publication Data is available

This book has been composed in Jansen and Centaur MT display

Printed on acid-free paper. ∞

press.princeton.edu

Printed in the United States of America

1 3 5 7 9 10 8 6 4 2

— Contents —

✧

─ Illustrations ─

✦

⟿ Preface ⟿

✧

Oriental Encounters

I suppose I went to Syria for enchantment, reenchantment, or some kind of magic unavailable to me in America, my home, and in this motivation I share something with the now largely discredited desires of some of my Orientalist predecessors: Gustave Flaubert, Ernest Renan, Richard Burton, T. E. Lawrence, Rudolf Virchow, Alexander von Humboldt, and all people from the West who go to the East—in this case, Near East or Middle East—for an encounter with difference. But in this encounter we do not all have the same kind of experience, and the apparent unity of the Orientalists dissolves quickly: there are the textualists (whom I neglect totally here) for whom experience is at best anecdotal, for whom the activity of reading and intuiting from written material yields authoritative understandings of that topos called the "Orient"; and there are the experientialists.

Even those Orientalists primarily drawn to experience surely were motivated by different interests—pure knowledge, science, policy, domination, adventure, love; and they surely acted within radically different social contexts—colonialism, rebellion, hot war, Cold War—which in turn shaped the kinds of encounters to be had. But what they share with each other, and I with them, is both a commitment to experience itself, to sensual experience in face-to-face interactions as a privileged mode of encounter, one that may ultimately lead to knowledge unattainable through other means; and an interest in difference itself, in the exotic, strange, foreign, unassimilable.

This shared commitment to experience of the exotic, to the pursuit of knowledge not as an accessory of power but as integral to enjoyment, is what led me, a sociocultural anthropologist, a tenured professor, known as a scholar of Europe, author, coauthor, or editor of nine books, to begin research in the Levant. Having hit the half-century mark, I needed some impulse, some disturbance in the comfortable existence of my American middle class—as well as a new fieldsite. I had already invested several decades in studying the Cold War, its dual organization and its symbolically most pregnant site, Germany, when the Berlin Wall opened. Then I witnessed (and wrote about) the dissolution of these very same Cold War structures in Germany and Europe. But ultimately, at the end of all this, at the end of the twentieth century, I found myself observing a similar set of fears and phobias; a similar Manichean cognitive dualism had indeed reasserted itself as a global organizing force, though the symbolic site of its operation had shifted from Europe to the Middle East. Moreover, the new divisions were often either attributed to, or expected to lead to, a "clash of civilizations"—a gloss that most professional anthropologists reject.

So in 1999, I switched gears and began studying Arabic; reading novels, travelogues, ethnographies, and histories of the Middle East; visiting Lebanon and Syria in the summers; and preparing for a sabbatical year when I could live there for a longer period of fieldwork. In 2001, the momentous attack and massacre in New York City—the event now known as "9/11"—happened, and with that the American president and the American media proclaimed a new era and assented to its new name: a perpetual and global "War on Terror"—which, again, uncannily resembled the Cold War processes and structures that I had spent the prior two decades studying. "Arab terrorists" and "nondemocratic states" in the Middle East and Central Asia replaced Communists as the source of evil, the enemy against whom an eager and brawny world power, the United States, and a reluctant but self-absorbed Europe, would define themselves. In 2004, I was awarded a Fulbright scholarship to teach and do research in Aleppo, Syria, and subsequently a Wenner-Gren Foundation grant. These, then, are the personal conditions and desires that led me to begin the research and to write *Syrian Episodes*, the reasons I give myself, which are, of course, only those reasons I can presently make conscious to myself.

There are, to be sure, other reasons, more purely intellectual and more generally anthropological, and in the larger scheme of things more significant, more narrowly political, to go to this place called Syria. It is the home of the Fertile Crescent and known as the Cradle of Civilization; its largest cities, Aleppo and Damascus, are two of the oldest continuously inhabited cities in the world—places of mythic stature; Syria is the place where the Gospel was first preached and it was an Arab kingdom long before the Arabs achieved their glory under Islam; it is the home of Arab nationalism. As for today, Syria still understands itself as the "beating heart" of the Arab, and, bordering strategically on Turkey, Iraq, Jordan, Israel, and Lebanon, it is on the frontlines of the U.S.-led "war on terror." Moreover, with the overthrow of the Iraqi regime in 2003, the secular ideology of Ba'athism is now practiced only in Syria and is unlikely to survive in its present form. In contrast to European secular ideologies, which were responses to religious wars and to the delegitimation of inherited monarchic authority, Ba'athist ideology had its origins in a national socialist, pan-Arab response to European colonialism and the collapse of the Ottoman Empire. Although the days of Syrian Ba'athism may be numbered, this ideology—largely egalitarian and pragmatic, encouraging of religious pluralism—has not left Syrians unaffected. Situated in the center of the major geopolitical battles of the present and indulged with a surfeit of history, then, Syria's diverse peoples are summoned by competing, often contradictory siren songs. Yet for most people in the West, Syrians still do not have a face.

Most scientists, including ethnographers such as myself, go to a place with a set of questions; they ask these questions, in some form, and write up the responses. Partly due to limited linguistic skills (four years of intermittent Arabic at my age is not enough!) and a conscious choice to let people define themselves to me, I ended up answering more questions than I asked. It is not that I had no questions—in any case, a theoretically naïve and untenable position—but that my major interest was in the curiosities and self-definitions of the residents of Aleppo. That said, I want to stress that the success of my project, its potential for insight, depended upon sharing with the people I met this curiosity about difference, about the exotic foreigner, upon a mutual orientation to knowledge as a form of pleasure in an encounter with the extraordinary. To give readers a full sense of these interactions, I include a great deal of unabridged dialogue—fieldnotes translated into English and written-up evenings, recordings of what was said as close as I can recall. I took along a tape recorder but used it only in language lessons. Because the U.S. government, my government, considers the Syrian Arab Republic a hostile "rogue state," I thought it best not to foster suspicions of me as a CIA agent, for which I have a perfect profile. Thus I also dropped my initial plan to sketch scenes in public to capture visual impressions, and instead resorted to my digital camera, ubiquitous in present-day urban life and unlikely to draw undue attention.

Throughout this book I use the present tense—the "ethnographic present"—to lend the text more of a sense of the immediacy of situations. Writing in the 1980s and 1990s, I had thought of the past tense as more honest. There was something about the use of the eternal present that seemed to arrest artificially if not to deny time's flow, to reduce scenes to wide-angle snapshots. This thought was a response to a critique of the use of present tense in earlier ethnographic accounts and a product of the growing dominance of historical narratives within anthropology in the 1980s.

In retrospect, I have come to think that the quality of writing as well as our interpretive skills has been compromised by subsuming all listening, viewing, observation, interaction, comparison, and contextualization into historical narratives. Lost is the accidental, incidental, and occasional; the serendipitous, fateful, and irregular; events and scenes that don't always hang together, that resist facile inclusion in a temporal development or argument. Lost is the episodic: experience that is personal, tied to a particular time and place, a part that does not always readily fit into the whole.

Due to the present dominance of History—the code of before and after—there is a tendency within anthropological writing to reduce encounters and interactions during a period of fieldwork to anecdote, before the mass of pastness—the temporal depth and solidity of texts, citations, archives, erudition—is brought to bear on a question. This book argues for the insight from the rawness and brevity of a momentary exchange, an unusual taste, an overheard comment or direct gaze; from the feel of a hand or play of light in a room; from linguistic errors, slights, misunderstandings; from obscure glances and desires that seem to go nowhere.

Most sustained fieldwork happens in condensed time (three to six years of preparation, one or two years of being there), though in writing, several such short sustained periods over a number of years or decades are often strung together as part of a longer historical narrative. How, then, do we recover the irreducible vividness of ethnographic episodes from each of these sustained periods of fieldwork without relegating them to mere prologues or supplements to History? Can we present fieldwork episodes themselves as forms of knowledge that stand in a complementary relation to larger and longer historical narratives? In writing such episodes, I hope to present a descriptive art, a storytelling, that both contributes to the documentary function of the ethnographic encounter and to its analytical potential. Along these lines, I also include my snapshots of people and places, some of the faces of Syria that evoke other stories only partially explicated in the text. The faces in photos do not match the named people in the episodes described, and because of the intimacy of most episodes, I have changed the names of people (except for public persons and the two individuals, Majid and Jihad, who explicitly gave me permission)—a measure I take to prevent harming those about whom I write.

This book is primarily about Syrian men—their relations with each other; their hopes, dreams, everyday experiences and rhythms; their victories and defeats; their understandings of secular authority—and their relations with me. All this reveals, above all, a range of communicative possibilities among men themselves, through and with me. Women are of course present—foremost as mothers, and to a lesser extent as wives, mistresses, sisters, and daughters—but the focus is on men. Arabs generally tend to define themselves patrilineally, by descent through the father, and in the Near East the ultimate source of authority is the relation of the father to the son. For this, among other reasons, Western scholars have traditionally neglected women (and their relations with other women and men), a focus that anthropologists, in particular, have reversed in the last several decades. But as a consequence of this new emphasis on women, there is very little recent ethnography of the same texture, quality, and political significance on men's relation to men within the Arabic-speaking world.

Among men, I concentrate mostly on sons, specifically—a decision not a matter of conscious research design alone. Fathers are certainly not absent from the episodes, but in daily encounters, it seemed, they were more reticent about reflecting on the authority they exercise over their children. Also, the need to ask fathers to explain to me their authority was somewhat obviated by the fact that I could actually see them exercise it in practice, in public. In addition, though, I suspect that fathers were reticent to explain themselves at length because the conditions of paternal authority in Syria have been severely compromised—in terms of an inability to procure jobs for their sons and daughters; an inability to reverse a trend in contemporary representation to reduce Arab men to terrorists, Islamic extremists, and ineffectual victims of Israeli politics; and an inability to assert any influence over the political sphere in their own country. Who, under these conditions, would want to explain himself? Faced with the obvious, to ask for explanations would have been to add insult to injury. Nonetheless, I found no evidence of what some observers call "Muslim or Arab rage," no anger at the West or wholesale rejection of "modernity" or of the doctrine of secularism, despite the fact that I continually put myself in the position to hear or become the object of such sentiments. This rage may indeed exist, among Arabs or Muslims elsewhere, but my experience suggests it is not nearly so widespread as pundits lead us to think.

Most young men, by contrast, were still seeking to understand the nature of paternal authority, the conditions under which they should submit to it, and the cost of its inheritance. They generally also had more free time and therefore were more readily available to hang out with. Married men—most men over thirty—felt an obligation, even intense pressure, to spend evenings with their families; during the days most worked. Those in the souk, the grand bazaar where I lived, were generous with their time while working. Of the few adult men and fathers whom I got to know more intimately, most are not merchants but members of the small class of professionals—artists, architects, doctors, journalists—along with a few businessmen; I have not written about them here for reasons of parsimony alone.

Primarily, also for reasons of parsimony, I did not write much about the women whom I got to know well. In fieldwork, women were generally not as readily available for me to meet, and with respect to these encounters I envied my fellow female ethnographers. It seemed as if all doors—of men and women alike—were open to foreign women traveling, studying, or doing research in Syria. Men and women of all ages went out of their way to guide them, protect them, spend time with them, adopt them into their families—and usually without asking anything in return.

Additionally, I am, in the Middle East, frequently identified both as a man who could be a father, hence someone already known, and, because I am not married, as a grand ambiguity, something unknown and perhaps unknowable. In Syria, what provokes the most incomprehension is the nonmarried man who does not marry even though he would be able to, or who says he does not want to marry. Most people would have readily understood and perhaps even sympathized with me if I had identified myself as an American Christian fundamentalist, an atheist, a Jew, a hippie, or a poor person—all identifications to which Syrians do not aspire. But to not marry, who in their right mind would even consider it? In fieldwork, then, I embodied some of the roles I was studying; I was frequently identified as one of my own objects of study.

In sum, this is an ethnography more of my subjects' questions than of mine, and it is a reflexive ethnography of the transference and countertransference in relationships between an American and some of the people of Syria: how, in our encounters, do expectations and counterexpectations shape the questions we ask each other and the dynamics of our interaction? No two anthropologists are alike in the way they ask or answer questions, in the kinds of interactions open to them, or in the varieties of experience they allow themselves to explore. This makes our studies partial and nontypical, but the singular facts, if properly contextualized, make for more unpretentious and accurate representations. During fieldwork, moreover, I was not a disinterested fly-on-the-wall ethnographer but actively engaged in inciting and interpreting responses, in seeking out a wider range of experiences than most anthropologists might deem permissible. Given that I aroused such a wide range of ambivalences—from American national to father-substitute to foreign friend to nonmarried man to professional anthropologist, it might surprise some readers that men, young men or "sons" in particular, did indeed even bother to talk to me. Why submit oneself to the intellectual, emotional, political, cultural, and religious doubts introduced through an encounter with an anthropologist?

My explication demands a degree of honesty and disclosure that may make some readers uncomfortable. I do not patronize Syrians by assuming that certain differences between us are beyond their understanding. I record less the "native's voice" than that voice used to address me. I expose less the macro "conditions of possibility" than the micro conditions in a fieldwork encounter that lead to a specific "native" self-representation. I give equal weight to description of employment activities, political orientations, religiosity, erotic and imaginary investments, culinary habits, and dreams—if such activity evokes or yields insight into the significance of patterns of authority in everyday life generally.

I write this at a time when in the United States knowledge generally and academic knowledge specifically is dismissed if politically, religiously, or cognitively inconvenient. This book, in response, is an attempt to write a no-spin or anti-spin monograph. It does not repeat propaganda; it does not attempt to hide or twist anything said or done, observed or overheard, nor does it attempt to serve ideological ends or to support a particular theory. My goal is simple:

to render the experience of fieldwork and the insights gained in it vivid, accessible, and understandable.

The larger and timely intellectual question raised in this study is how to anticipate possible scenarios of regime change in Syria, what I have elsewhere called the question of the "death of the Father," and a methodological stance of "anticipatory reflection." How, from top to bottom and bottom to top, do different levels of authority interact and how are they changing in the secular Syrian state? The Souk al-Atarin in Aleppo is one site for my ethnographic encounters, and I chose it because of its reputation as a commercial center that cultivates the traditional, a center of secular activity but also one dominated by majority Sunni (meaning orthodox) Muslims—a place that theoretically should be both pragmatic and conservative as well as resistant to the changes in authority I hope to track. The other site is the University of Aleppo, where I worked with a mixed group of students for a semester as a Fulbright scholar.

In the second part of this preface, I provide a set of condensed reflections on the gestalt of authority in Syria today, the relation of contemporary political history to the episodes in this book. If readers are familiar with this history, I encourage them to simply jump into chapter 1. *Syrian Episodes* is divided into three parts: city, souk, and country, though these are somewhat arbitrary distinctions. A postscript reflects on the experience of teaching and learning in Syria. And because I omit footnotes and references, the academic scaffolding on which most similar accounts are built, I provide suggestions for orientation and further reading in a final bibliographical essay.

Reflections on Authority in a Secular Dynasty

Syria is a secular republic ruled by the Arab Socialist Renaissance (Ba'ath) Party, whose President, Bashar el-Assad, inherited his authority in March 2000 upon the death of his father, Hafez el-Assad, who had taken control of the government through a putsch within the Party in November 1970. There are two crucial facts about this secular dynasty, about the meaning of this form of authority in this

Figure 2. Father and Son. Officer's Club, Damascus

time and place: first, that the current leader is not the father but the father's son, and neither the eldest nor favorite son but an accidental heir; and second, that the Assad family rules as part of a non-Sunni minority sect, the Alawites, which, while claiming to be Muslim (and Bashar is married to a Sunni Muslim), eschew any organization of power (other than, in many ways, their own) along the lines of religious, sectarian, or regional loyalties.

As to the first fact, Bashar's brother Basil was the heir apparent before his death in a speeding accident in January 1994 left only Bashar, an ophthalmologist with advanced training in England, to inherit the presidency. Bashar, then, has no basis other than patrilineage on which to claim legitimacy to rule. Although both president of the republic and secretary general of the Ba'ath Party, which ideologically and administratively leads the Syrian state and society, he must loosen the controls of the state and Party in order to spur economic growth. This loosening, of course, risks undermining the rule of his family and sect. And that is the second fact: the Alawite sect to which the Assad family belongs operates as a clan, amassing wealth and centralizing power through a clientilistic system that rewards disproportionately other members of the Alawite sect, who comprise only 12 percent of all Syrians. Alawites control the military and hold key positions in various bureaucracies, and through the dominance of the Party and distribution of government licenses and granting of perks, they have largely co-opted the majority Sunni merchants (over 70 percent of the population) and much of the leadership of the various other minority communities.

In his thirty years of rule, President Hafez el-Assad constructed an authoritarian state, represented by a Stalin-like cult of personality regime but with no all-encompassing ideology. Still today, the attention of the entire Syrian media is directed solely to events surrounding the president and his immediate circle: whom they meet, opinions, pronouncements, decrees, edicts. Posters of Hafez el-Assad with his two sons, in military uniforms and dark glasses, Roman bustlike from the chest up, are ubiquitous; the chinless Bashar, who rules, and the lightly bearded and handsome Basil, who is deceased, are displayed behind the father. Bashar has stated publicly that he wishes to discontinue this cult, but people nonetheless continue to put his photo everywhere—on the streets, in public buildings, restaurants, and homes, properly framed on walls or desks—though he is increasingly portrayed alone with his father, or even without the father and brother but instead with his wife or wife and children.

Formerly a part of the Ottoman Empire, Syria initially came into existence as a French mandate following the carve-up of the Middle East by the victorious and imperial European powers after the First World War. It declared independence in 1943, but the French left only three years later, in 1946. A series of military coups and a short period of parliamentary democracy followed independence before, in 1958, Syria united with Egypt in an ill-fated pan-Arab republic. This republic lasted until 1961, when a rightist putsch in Damascus broke with Egypt. In 1963, the Ba'ath Party seized power under the slogan, "Unity, Liberty, Socialism," which it retains to this day.

The founding of the state of Israel in 1948 presented each post-independence Syrian regime with a set of intractable problems, as well as a reason for pan-Arab unity. Foremost among these problems are the several waves of Palestinian refugees who fled to Syria (representing 10.5 percent of all Palestinian refugees worldwide, 3 percent of all Syrian residents), and who continually implicate Syria in Israeli geopolitics. Palestinians are denied Syrian citizenship (largely to keep open the "right to return" to their Palestinian homelands in Israel), but they are allowed to work and in fact, unlike in all of the other Arab states, enjoy nearly all of the rights granted to citizens. Also, the pro-Israeli/anti-Palestinian tilt of the U.S. government led Syria during the Cold War to rely more on the Soviet bloc, whose dissolution after 1989 confronted Syria with potential isolation and another economic-political crisis. Israeli presence is, therefore, the dominant political factor for contemporary Syria, setting many of the parameters of both foreign and domestic policies.

Israel inflicted three major defeats on Syria: the preemptive strike against Egypt, Jordan, and Syria in the Six-Day War of 1967, in which Israel occupied (and still occupies) the Golan Heights; the defeat of the Egyptian-Syrian surprise attack (with Iraqi help) in the Yom Kippur (Ramadan) War of 1973; and the invasion of Lebanon from 1982 to 1984 (which followed a brief, unsuccessful five-month invasion in 1978), after which Israel occupied southern Lebanon until 2000 (Lebanon and Syria were not separate political units until 1947–48), and Syria stationed troops in the rest. All of these wars have different names in Arabic and English (I am following the Western convention, which also corresponds to the Israeli naming), and Syria does not acknowledge losing any of them. Still, the collective defeat and humiliating experience of the many soldiers who fought in these wars haunts the official declaration of victories, ultimately producing resentment among Syrians not merely against Israel, the enemy, but against their own government and military, and perhaps themselves for the way they deny this reality.

Following the 1973 war, Hafez el-Assad transformed Syria into a national security state, increasing the size and power of the security apparatus (Mukhabarrat), and further centralizing authority within the Party and in his person. After 1976, he sent troops into Lebanon to intervene in ongoing sectarian wars, in 1990 bringing about peace but also exercising hegemony over the northern two-thirds until

2005. The spoils from Lebanon quickly became one of the central perks for the ruling elites, but the common soldiers who have served in Lebanon take little pride in this "occupation." In fact, for those I met who had served in Lebanon, that occupation was simply another experience that led them to disrespect their own army. From 1976 to 1982, the Syrian government battled a violent internal rebellion, spearheaded by the (Sunni) Muslim Brotherhood, which eventually ended with an uprising in several cities, including Aleppo, and an army massacre of Sunnis in Hama in 1982. Subsequently, the government has been less confrontational and more accommodating with Islamic institutions in Syria, building hundreds of mosques in many cities and encouraging pious but not militant or political Muslims.

The political instability of this recent history—the wars with Israel, internal sectarian and religious rebellions, settlement of Palestinian refugees, collapse of their patron the Soviet Union and its markets, the increased power of Arab Gulf states through their oil wealth and influence on the fundamentalist Islamic movements they support—has meant an ongoing legitimation crisis for Syrian rulers that is also, to some extent, perversely ameliorated by the specter of Israel (and its continued occupation of Syria's Golan Heights). The Israeli threat, in other words, both destabilizes the country and unites the Syrians in the same way that Israel is destabilized but Israeli Jews are united by the specter and hostility of the Arabs around them. In addition to the Israeli threat, the Syrian public has also united collectively around another issue, or set of relations, which the political leadership has used to prop up its authority, and that is Syria as the leader or voice of both pan-Arabism and secularism in the Middle East, two "titles" Syria took over from Egypt following the death of Gamal Abdel Nasser in 1970.

In 1971 Assad replaced the collective leadership of the Party with his personal rule, and in 1973 a new constitution granted the Ba'ath Party additional powers in the state and society, and the president ultimate power in all fields. Subsequently, there was an expansion of Party membership, leading to a current membership that is more opportunistic and less ideological. All of these changes have been top-down, and have had the effect of arresting the development of independent professions and accountable institutions as well as discouraging initiative of any sort.

But individual initiative is desperately needed to reverse dire economic conditions, which in the near future may get worse, for many reasons. First, the population growth of Syria is one of the highest in the Middle East: in 1985 the population totaled around ten million; in 2005 around eighteen million; in 2025 it is predicted to be twenty-six million. One of the major responses of Syrians historically has been labor migration, not only to Lebanon and the Gulf States, which have in the last several decades absorbed many of Syria's unskilled as well as highly skilled workers, but also to Europe, Africa, and the Western Hemisphere. As the numbers of young Syrians grow, however, neither the economy of Syria nor of neighboring countries can absorb them into their labor forces.

Second, since 1980 per capita GDP has remained fairly constant, approximately $1,000, meaning that economic growth consistently lags behind population growth. Therefore, youth unemployment is bound to grow precipitously, creating an ideal dynamic for domestic unrest.

Third, Syria has few resources or export products to compete internationally. Oil reserves, which account for fifty percent of the state budget and two-thirds of all exports, are running out (a dramatic drop is predicted by 2008), and within a decade or two Syria is expected to be a net importer of oil. Agricultural goods (cotton is the major export product) require water, but changes in global climate patterns make it unlikely that precipitation will increase, and with increased global demands for clean water, it will not become cheaper to import. Moreover, Syrian universities are largely sites of mediocrity that are not reproducing the elites, and even when the universities do excel, such as in medicine and engineering, they lose many of the most talented individuals to out-migration. (Germany alone, for example, employs approximately six thousand Syrian-trained doctors.) Intense global competition makes it difficult for Syria, already behind comparably sized countries in all high-growth sectors, to establish itself or remain competitive in the global economy.

Fourth, support for Palestinians and opposition to Israel is part and parcel of the regime's internal legitimacy, but because of these positions, both principled and opportunistic, the regime also suffers relative international isolation. Consequently, unable to submit to American demands to reverse these positions, Syria may be forced in order to survive to turn away economically from Europe and the United States and move closer toward Iran, China, and Saudi Arabia.

Fifth, a general increase in support and sympathy among the youth for political Islamic leaders (including a renewed Muslim Brotherhood), partly attributable to opposition to the American occupation of neighboring Iraq, shadows current political arrangements. In the short run, the regime is trying to contain "political Islam" through surveillance and by preventing much spill-over from Iraq. In the long run, this threat is likely to manifest itself in violent, antiregime activities led by a new generation of insurgent leaders who are now being trained in fighting the Americans in Iraq but will eventually return to Syria.

Sixth, and finally, as mentioned above, the Alawite-dominated regime and the Ba'ath Party appear unwilling to give up advantages obtained through closed networks and political controls, but those very controls make both domestic and foreign investment unattractive. The Party still dominates most institutions, or at least tries to, but it is largely a rubber-stamp organ for the president and his circle, and therefore irrelevant for ruling or creating initiative. To some degree it can block power and redistribute wealth, but even President Bashar el-Assad is reported to go around rather than through the Party to get things done. Hence, the reformist intentions that many attribute to Assad can only be realized by negating—or, as one friend said, "smashing"—the Party, the very instrument that mediates the regime's power.

Indeed, in my own limited observations, the Party seems to have a more pernicious influence on social life—blocking institutional and personal initiatives, promoting mediocrity—than does the Mukhabarrat. In 1999, on my first visit to Damascus, then under the presidency of Hafez el-Assad, the city had an omnipresent security apparatus, and I noticed a palpable fear of mixing in public areas, especially mixing with foreigners. Even today Syrians are not allowed to enter into the hotel rooms of foreigners. Aleppo, at that time, was more relaxed than Damascus, the fear in public places much less marked. Now people tell me that since Bashar el-Assad took over the presidency, the state security has relaxed its grip in Damascus, leading to an opening of the city to a cosmopolitan mix of foreigners and Syrians from every part of this very diverse land. Conversely, the "traditional conservatism of Aleppo," as Syrians call it, a conservativism not of politics or religion (as in Damascus) but of economics, has asserted itself. My own experience tends to confirm this difference: the liberalization of the political-religious center of Damascus, the conservatism of an economically centered Aleppo.

Yet even in Aleppo, I was free to move about without interference, and agents of the Mukhabarrat contacted some of the people I saw regularly only after I left. While living in the souk, agents did follow me several times. Three weeks into my stay, an old, tired-looking and slow-moving man approached a merchant whom I had visited and asked, "What is John's last name?"

"I don't know," he replied, insouciantly, "You should find these things out before they come into this country, not after." The person who told me this story was reassuring that I should not let it concern me.

About eight weeks into my stay, another friend outside the souk told me that a man had followed me to his office near a meat market in another part of city. He entered the office and asked for a copy of an interview about human rights that I had given to the independent Beiruti newspaper *An-Nahar*, published about four weeks earlier. Syrian authorities forbid the sale of *An-Nahar* because of its critical coverage of Syria (and at the time, of Syrian's presence in Lebanon). I had given this friend a copy of the interview, but his reply to the agent's query was, "I read it on the Internet—as do most intellectuals in Aleppo. You have to download it yourself."

In a third case, about four months into my stay, the Mukhabarrat sought out the owner of my apartment (and her son at the Belgian Consulate), to inquire not about me but about an American woman who was living in Damascus and visiting me. Their response: he is a free man, and we know nothing about who visits him.

It is clear that the use of fear to control public expression has lessened considerably, though fear is still everywhere and manifests itself unevenly over time and in more subtle ways. (In my last visit to Syria, January 2006, the Mukhabarrat was more systematic in following me, interviewing the people I talked to within minutes of our meetings. A general paranoic atmosphere seemed to pervade public life, as the regime was actively mobilizing patriotism in reaction to international pressures resulting from the assassination of Rafiq Hariri in Lebanon.) Yet people offer critical political opinions all the time in public, in cafés, restaurants, parks, walking on the street, though they usually express these in a slightly hushed voice. If a conversation critical of local politics continues for more than a few minutes, I notice other people listening in, and most likely it gets reported to the appropriate offices. People have learned to disassociate their opinions—whether of solidarity with Palestine or opposition to the Ba'ath Party—from their own action. If I ask people what they might do, given a certain opinion, the conversation usually drifts to another topic and not to the consequences of their opinion. Hence, in my own discussions, I find most people politically astute but depoliticized. At another level, people's shrewdness about politics—the assumption that behind every political action is some concealed or unseen interest, or in the extreme view, conspiracy—is generally counterbalanced by a faith in Islam that permits no doubt or questioning of interests.

In any case, Syrian newspapers cover mostly political events (in the narrower sense of the term "political"), and it takes less than five minutes to read any of them from front to back. (One journalist confided in me that he writes most of his articles from home—once he has the story they want, he simply plugs in the names and places.) People read the local papers more for omissions—what is not covered—than for "the news." Only a small group of intellectuals regularly read foreign newspapers, among which the people I know read mostly the liberal *An-Nahar* and critical leftist *As-Safir* (both from Beirut), and conservative *Al-Hayat* (Saudi-funded from London). A much wider public listens to the new pan-Arabic cable television stations (to which everyone indeed has access; in Syria satellite TV is free), the favorites among these include al-Jazeera (from Qatar), al-Arabiya (from Dubai), al-Manar (the Hezbollah station from

Lebanon), the LBC (from Beirut), and the BBC (from London). The competition for viewership among these stations is intense, and most of the people I know channel surf rather than remain loyal to one station—meaning they are exposed to a very wide spectrum of opinion and diverse pictorial representation of the world, much wider than they are presently able to verbalize or make use of.

Despite access to a world press (largely through the Internet) and visual media that is often extremely critical of the Syrian government, I hear much formal support for the person of Bashar el-Assad. Sunni, Kurdish, or Christian resentment at Alawite corruption and dominance is often tempered by fears of instability: that there will be bloody reprisals should the Sunni majority assume control. People are also generally frightened by the dangers of sectarian violence—Lebanon and Iraq are neighbors. Many sense that rule by a minority sect is the best guarantee against majority tyranny. Perhaps that is the reason for the prominent display of the new president's picture despite his own disavowal of this tradition. Pictorial ubiquity may in fact be an expression of another kind of fear: that without affirmation of this secular dynasty, the one symbol of Syrian unity, there is little that holds the Syrian people together.

The many Alawites that I got to know personally are not part of the wealthy elite and do not seem to have gained much personally from the dominance of their sect in the political system. They also tend to be consistently undogmatic: for example, fasting but not saying the requisite prayers, and not bothered by other Muslims who do not fast; drinking alcohol and not concerned about whether others drink; relatively relaxed about inter-sect dating and marriage; relatively unconcerned about the sect membership of others; curious about alternative perspectives. They point out that Islam is differently practiced in Syria than in most Arab states, and that this is at least partly due to the secularizing influence of the Assad dynasty. And many of them, along with many non-Alawites I meet, adamantly identify Bashar el-Assad as Syrian rather than Alawite.

Still, the vast majority of young people—across sect, region, and religion—want to leave Syria, at least temporarily; they want to leave primarily because most do not see an economic future for

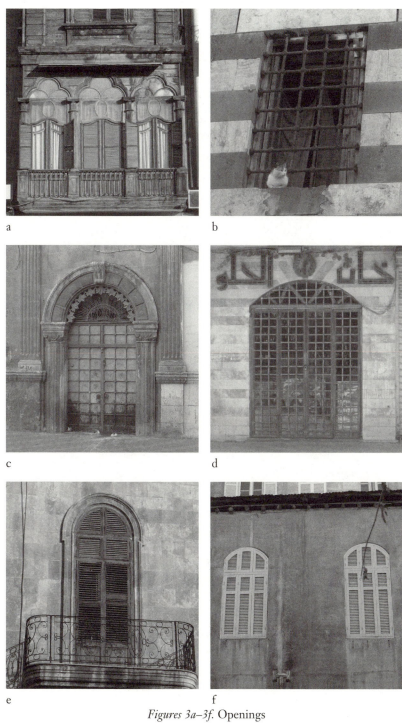

Figures 3a–3f. Openings

themselves. And there is no economic future because the fathers—
from Bashar el-Assad to family fathers—despite often good intentions and for reasons largely beyond their control, are unable to
reproduce the economic and political conditions that might generate the growth needed to employ their sons and daughters mean-
ingfully. Moreover, for many young Muslim men, Islam—its many
representatives, institutions, and community—promises to fill this
void created by the general decline in paternal authority. If, somehow, any of the conditions were to change that contribute to the
political strangulation of Syria—a democratic rapprochement with
Lebanon, peace with Israel, American withdrawal from and peace
within Iraq—and if a free internal labor market and the economic
possibilities for self-sufficiency were created, I suspect that the people of Syria, who have in the last several centuries been oriented as
much or more to Turkey and Europe than to Saudi Arabia and the
Gulf, would largely reject the appeal of Islam in its present more
radical forms.

— Acknowledgments —

Many thanks for research support from the Fulbright Scholar Program and the Wenner-Gren Foundation for Anthropological Research. I thank Princeton University for language study; Mona Zaki, who so patiently tutored me in Arabic; many Lebanese friends for schooling me of the politics and history of the Levant; and especially Tarek el-Ariss for his friendship and an intellectual exchange of the type most anthropologists can only dream of. My colleague at Princeton Abdellah Hammoudi very perceptively commented on a draft, and I thank him dearly. I had the opportunity to present parts of this manuscript for the Monroe Lecture at the University of Edinburgh, as well as at the New School for Social Research and the University of Chicago; I thank these audiences for the interactions. Above all, I thank Parvis Ghassem-Fachandi for patience and love while doing the research and writing this book. Finally, I thank the many people in Aleppo, most of whom I fear to name personally, for all their generosity and assistance. The three that I can name personally—Dr. Nabil Ades, Dr. Assem Faress, and Dr. Fouad Mohammed Fouad—you have my deepest gratitude. The cover photo is based on three paintings by Saad Yagan, which he painted specifically for the theme of this book, and I also thank him for in particular for our many Sunday dinners at Challal and Wanes that raised to new heights my own already high culinary standards.

— Syrian Episodes —

Chapter I

Aleppo

"Prayer is better than sleep"

Summer days are long, noisy, exhausting, and at the end of each I often feel as old as the souk itself, inevitably covered head to foot with a thin coat of dust. I awake at dawn to the Islamic "call to the good," the *Fajr* prayer (where the crier calls out twice, "Prayer is better than sleep"), though loud catfights also punctuate the still of the night. Four hours later I awake again to the clanging of cast-iron locks and the rumble of rolling aluminum doors. Sometime after midnight I fall asleep to a resounding pitter-patter of shoes rhythmically pounding against the large stone-paved streets. In between, I am immersed in the sounds of muttering, milling customers and the shrieks of merchants who lure them into their shops. Then there are the vendors without shops, with merely a tray or a table or an open suitcase tied to their necks or a mule-drawn wagon; they must be more aggressive—block the aisle, cry out as loudly as possible—to entice someone to buy their merchandise.

From about 10:00 a.m. until noon, the loudest sound on the busy intersection near my apartment is "*Abufaaaas, Abufas! Abufaaaas, Abufas! Abufaaaas, Abufas!*"—the baritone call of a middle-aged man. For the longest while, I had no idea what he was selling. Then someone explained: *abufas* is a general purpose cream that works, especially for arthritis.

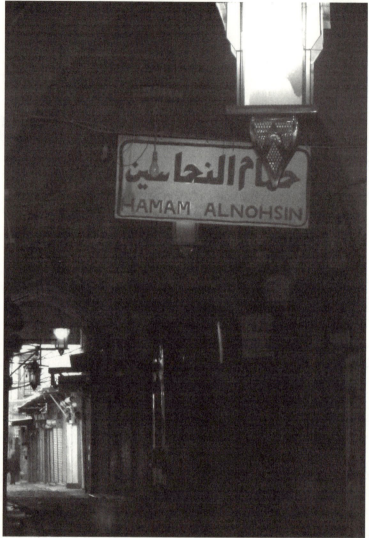

Figure 4. Bathhouse in the Souk al-Atarin

Whereas days the souk is congested, nights it is nearly empty except for rowdy men and boys entering and leaving the Hammam Alnahosin across from my apartment—wedding parties, men's nights out, friends on a lark, patrilineal cleansings. There, especially on the evening before Friday—or the Muslim Holy Day—

they enjoy a scrub, massage, and collective bath. On the streets outside my living room until about 2:00 a.m., the sounds of animated talk, singing, and shoes-against-pavement bounce off the vaulted stone ceilings.

I live in the middle of my research, in the Souk al-Medina in Aleppo, Syria, where I rent an apartment that is the former Venice Consulate in Khan al-Nahasin (the "Khan of Coppersmiths," though now a shoe market), right off the famous Souk al-Atarin (the "Spice Souk," now mixed with textiles), running north and south from the impressive Citadel, which successfully resisted waves of Crusaders and now rises above and anchors the city, to Bab Antakya, one of the original gates, both dating from the same period. The Venetians had financed the fourth and final crusade from 1202 to 1204 and enriched their city-state with the plunder of Constantinople, then capital of the Byzantine Empire. Later in the thirteenth century they were the first of the many European traders to arrive and build a khan—a caravanserai, or inn, for commercial travelers— as part of the Silk Road linking the Orient and Occident.

For most people who work in the souk, the day begins at nine or ten, and ends at six. During Ramadan, the holy month of the Islamic lunar calendar (which, being eleven to twelve days shorter than the Gregorian solar calendar, falls on a different date each year), Muslims are forbidden to eat, drink, smoke, or have sex during daylight. Therefore days during the holy month begin at ten or eleven, break at five in the afternoon for an hour or two to eat *iftar* (literally, "breakfast"), every day a few minutes earlier, then resume until 9:00 or 9:30 p.m., until the last week of Ramadan, when most shops lock up closer to eleven. The last several days of Ramadan the workers in the courtyard of the khan where I live are active until three the following morning. Most people go home to eat *iftar*, but some stay and have a meal prepared by one of the local bakeries, or their wives have something delivered from home.

At the invitation of several of eight brothers who work together in the souk, I occasionally join the men and boys in their family— fathers, uncles, sons, nephews—for this breakfast. Since I have already eaten (I do not fast along) I merely nibble, but for the others, after about fourteen or fifteen hours of fasting, they are edgy, and desperate, especially for water. Even people who are not particularly religious fast; some give health as a reason, others that it teaches patience. I tell a friend that the people in Aleppo do not look particularly patient at five o'clock, but more like animals, using the Arabic word *hiyawan*, which is more antithetical to the human than its English counterpart, more disparaging in tone. He finds this amusing and now often jokingly accuses his relatives of being *hiyawan* as they stuff their mouths with food. Yet they smile and call out, "*Tfaddl! Tfaddl!*" (Welcome! Welcome!), to any stranger who happens by, an obligatory display of generosity. On more than one occasion, the strangers, usually tourists, take them up on this offer, which means less food for themselves and, because they have fasted the whole day, a tinge of unacceptable resentment at not being sated.

One friend starts to pray during Ramadan after not having prayed for three months. I tell him, "You have found a good balance, three to one: Aristotle insisted balance was the most difficult and important principle in life. Even better would be four to one: four months off, one month of prayer. Religion is dangerous!"

At the time, he does not react to my comments. I thought perhaps it was because I had overreached in my humor and offended his religious sensibility. In the 1970s Aleppo had been one of the major sites for the organization of the Muslim Brotherhood, a Sunni-based, antisecular movement engaged in assassinations and bombings, and it was rumored that they had been active in the Souk al-Medina also. In 1982, the Syrian state under Hafez al-Assad crushed them in a massacre many recall with a roll of the eyes and nervous change of topic. Now, more than twenty years later, I am unable to see any trace of this former radicalism in the souk. Later that evening, in front of a small group of men, my friend blurts out, "You are really intelligent, you know."

In this majestic old bazaar I meet only Muslim shop owners, renters, and workers, all Sunni Muslim, as are, officially, 74 percent of Aleppo's residents. In fact, 90 percent of Aleppo's residents belong to some Muslim sect, and the city itself is famous for the number of its mosques; some people say it has the third largest number of any city in the world. There are still a few Christian owners left in the Souk al-Medina, and indeed, Christians from Austria, dealers in Bohemian porcelain, originally built the khan where I live, which had served the caravans linking Europe to the Far East for nearly five hundred years. Christians had already arrived in Aleppo at the time of Christ, and although Christianity originated with Christ's birth in Jerusalem, men in Syria were the first to call themselves "Christians" and to develop the organizational structure of what we now call the Church. Today, officially, 10 percent of Aleppo's residents are Christians, but their numbers have been in steady decline the last quarter century, as is the case throughout the Near East, and most people say this figure is closer to 6 percent. Within Aleppo, many Christians left the Souk al-Medina in the chaos that followed the end of the French Mandate, around 1944, and moved to modern apartments in newer sections of the city. During the mandatory period, many persecuted groups—such as Armenians and Kurds from Turkey and Assyrians from Iraq—found refuge in Syria, and each of them has a souk in Aleppo. Across the street, on the east side of the Souk al-Medina, is the Russian souk, apparently with all Christian Orthodox owners and workers: in Jdeideh, a ten-minute walk northeast, is an Armenian souk; and near the Pullman bus station, a twenty-minute walk southeast, there is a large Kurdish souk.

Customers in the souk where I live, in contrast to the merchants, are of mixed confessions and nationalities, with tourists making more than half of the purchases of carpets and fine textiles; the tourists are mostly from Europe, although I see the occasional Australian, Malay, Japanese, Iraqi, Lebanese, Turk, Kuwaiti, and Saudi. Within Syria, Aleppo's Muslims are known as business-oriented but culturally conservative; they generally do not permit women to work with them in public. Some of the men and boys in the souk tell me that their mothers, wives, or sisters have never even visited them there. They see these women—their female relatives—only in the evenings, though even then they often eat separately or entertain in separate rooms, and on Fridays, the Holy Day when the souk is closed. For the boys, to spend all day with other men would mean nothing special—historically in nearly all parts of the world day activities and frequently nights, too, have been strictly segregated by gender—except for the fact that nowadays the influence of Western advertising and film is so prevalent that nearly all of these men imagine they should be obsessed with desire for women, and this obsession begins long before they have any opportunity to have sex.

There are many women customers in the souk, however, and I find particularly delightful the sight of men and boys, without embarrassment, selling women fancy bras, slips, and underpants in specialty shops, in improvised stalls, on wagons, or simply in piles on the ground. Merchants give foreign women, most of whom are tourists, special attention. Anytime I bring a woman to the souk, questions about her presence, her status, my relations to her, her future, her intentions, follow for weeks after the visit.

"When is Katherine coming back?"

"Jean-Marie, did you see her today?"

"Lucy, she's my cup of tea."

"Ah, Katherine, you going to visit her in Damascus? Can I go in your suitcase?"

All of these women happen to be younger than me, sometimes much younger—students, recent graduates, journalists, filmmakers. Interest in their age has little to do with attraction, however, but with the attempt to understand my relation to them. So at first, they ask me if these women are my daughters. After about six weeks, they stop asking, since they all know my response, I think, since I have repeated it a zillion times: I AM DIVORCED WITH NO CHILDREN. Usually this response is followed by the question, "Are you going to remarry?" "No," I say, "why should I?" "Why not not marry?" "Once is enough for me, but you should marry several times." This they find hysterically funny to the point of being absurd, though it usually stops this line of questioning for the time being. The point is, most men not only in Aleppo's Souk al-Medina but also in Syria generally think adult life begins with marriage, and they obsessively fantasize about these absent women and their presumed availability.

Imad's Japanese Girlfriend

"You wouldn't believe today—I knew what was coming," says Imad as I enter his shop in the afternoon. "A woman"—he always tells me a version of the same story—"came in from Australia, shorts up to here," he points his fingers two inches below his crotch—"and on top, everything spilling over," his hands cascade down from his chest to his navel, and then swerve to make an hourglass shape.

"So why is this new to you, Imad? You know what women look like, you have seen them before."

"But she is special!" he pleads, forever confused by my lack of enthusiasm.

"This is just what your mother looks like. You've seen her hundreds of times."

"But she is different," he twists his head away and scoffs dismissively, "and anyway, I don't look at my mother like that."

"Then you should look at her sometime, so you know what you are talking about."

Imad, at seventeen, is a boy desperately wanting to be a man but with no intimate experience. Of average height and build, he dresses about twenty years older than he is, wearing long-sleeved, striped shirts in conservative colors, buttoned at the collar and at the sleeves, his hair cut short, perfectly parted on the side, and too-neatly combed. His mother and her brothers, for whom he works in the souk, are raising him. His father wanted the divorce, which is still uncommon but not unknown, but he also wants no contact with his son, which is very unusual and predisposes Imad to a very ambivalent relationship with men. He aggressively inserts himself into the center of all adult conversations, and he unreflectively questions the authority of men older than him, which I have seen no other boy his age do.

Regarding women, however, Imad talks a very straight line. One of his uncles told me he chases after "anything with a crack, she can be ninety years old and it doesn't matter." With me, however, anytime sex or sexual experience comes up, he refers to his Japanese girlfriend.

"Oh yes, I have had sex," he insists, "for a week with my Japanese girlfriend."

"Then you must know it is nothing out of the ordinary. What was it like?"

"Wonderful! First, she is beautiful, and willing to do anything. Then," his loud voice becomes a whisper, "we go to her hotel room, she takes me inside, and"—he pumps his hips back and forth and sniggers loudly. "She really liked it."

"If it was so wonderful, why don't you keep contact with her?"

"Well," he sighs, perturbed by my doubts, "she's in Japan, I am here. But she wants to keep in touch."

I take to teasing Imad about his Japanese girlfriend, especially since he seems relentlessly eager to tell me about any foreign woman he talks to in the souk.

"When is your Japanese girlfriend coming back to visit?"

"She wants to, she leaves messages all the time, but I don't answer."

"How many messages, twenty?"

"Eighteen."

"Why do you avoid her when she is so nice?"

"But really, first, she is not nice. And second, her eyes"—and he stretches the skin on the side of his big round eyes so they appear slanted.

"What do you mean, she is not nice? Japanese eyes are beautiful, the opposite of yours, and opposites attract."

He ignores my bait. "And then, down here"—he points to his crotch—"she is like this"—and he makes a triangle with his hands and tips it on its side, indicating her vagina has a horizontal rather than a vertical opening.

"That just means you have to be more flexible."

"I know youuuuu. You'll always say the opposite of what I say."

"You should respond to her calls. I'd like to meet her."

"Why do you want to meet her?"

"She sounds like an interesting person."

I ask Imad to tell me his dreams. "I cannot remember them," he says.

"Just try. The first thing in the morning when you wake up, think of what was on your mind."

The next day, I ask again. "I dream I marry a woman with long blonde hair and blue eyes, medium-sized breasts. We have sex, and then I sleep with her a whole day and night. We do not leave the bed."

"But that is a daydream, Imad. I am interested in your night dreams."

"I'll give those to you later," he promises.

Several days later, Imad says he was on the top of a tall building and fell off, but he woke up just before he reached the bottom.

"Everywhere he goes people remember him," another uncle tells me. "Even in the most remote places of Syria. Imad has been there, and he leaves behind a black stain."

That is indeed what happens when, after work, we meet a group of Belgian tourists at a café outside the souk, and Imad joins us. He sits himself in the very middle of the table, with the Belgian men on one end, the Syrian on the other, and proceeds to loudly question the Belgians in very vulgar English about their sexual lives.

I am acquainted with the cashier, who takes me aside as we are leaving and asks, "WHO is he?"

"You mean the Belgian tourists?" I ask, wanting to evade responsibility for this gathering. "No, HIM," he says, pointing to Imad, "NEVER bring him again."

Although Imad seems to irritate everyone I know in the souk, or at least they direct toward him much of the anger resulting from their daily frustrations, this does not seem to bother him much. He carries on in public as if aggressively oblivious to any offense he causes.

I am sitting in a small shop with several people, including an older uncle, whom Imad tells, "There is a customer waiting for you in your shop," as he wiggles his way in between us. The uncle bellows at him, *"Rooh! Rooh!"* (Get out! Get out!), and chases him down the aisle, beside himself at his nephew's lack of respect. Others tell Imad to leave for the day, but he just makes himself scarce for a half hour before resurfacing. Frequently someone takes him aside for a chat, and Imad then agrees to stop the behavior in question—only to do the same thing the next day. What Imad lacks, of course—and everyone is aware of this—is a father who cares—who acts like one—and all the quiet confidence and security that comes with this authority.

His mother and her brothers are his only protectors, but they are proxies, not the real thing.

To tourists, however, Imad is quick with languages and can be clever and charming. One friend who visited me from Damascus loved it when he said to her, "I want to come back in my next life as your necklace." Reference to sex is also one way men in the souk get tourists to stop and look at their merchandise, and many sellers, including Imad, tend to make no distinction between male and female partners, often deliberately creating ambiguity. But when Imad speaks about sex to tourists, his vocabulary is limited to phrases like, "Did you fuck him (or her)?" or *Willst Du mir Ein' blasen?*" (Want to give me a blow job?), which he yells down the corridors.

"Nobody understands," he says.

"But I do," I say, "and if anyone else does they will be offended." Imad takes great pleasure in sex talk, finding it genuinely funny, and it does get people's attention, though they do not, on the whole, find it humorous. He tells me that the Catholic priest from France who visits the young men in the souk regularly warns him not to use this language when talking about sex between men, that he should restrict his talk about sex to relations between men and women alone.

During the last five days of Ramadan, a man of about thirty, retarded, unwashed, legs too mangled to walk, shoeless, with one foot bandaged, is planted early each morning before most people arrive, ostensibly by his parents but nobody is sure, in the middle of the aisle of the al-Atarin Souk. When vehicles need to pass, someone drags him over to the side, after which he inevitably finds his way back to the middle. A tin bowl for coins sits next to him, and I see people give him figs and bread and tea. One friend approaches and asks him if he would like a prostitute, and though he cannot speak intelligibly, he seems to understand and laughs heartily. Then one of the many overweight Muslim women dressed in an all-black burqa, everything covered except the hands, who young people in the souk refer to as "moving tents," stumbles and falls on top of him, scattering the money from his tin bowl. She picks herself up, her black robe dirtied on the side, and someone I take to be her daughter appears and ushers her forward. They leave without looking back at the man, now tipped over on his side, rolling in laughter. A friend says, "This is black humor." Another, "He is sadistic." And Imad, "He is laughing because it is the first time a woman has laid on him, and it will be the last time."

Farce

In portraying Imad's desires as farcical, I wonder if I enact a sort of violence on him. Would it not be preferable to solicit his agreement and arrive at a collaborative representation? His meticulous attention to being straight—buttoned-down collars, long-sleeve shirts, polished shoes with pointed toes, hair never out of place—suggests that he takes his life seriously; he is what he appears to be, a boy preternaturally a man; he is already what he will become, or, minimally, wants us to think so.

But there is a perverse complicity in this portrayal, as Imad stubbornly ignores the advice of others (including myself) to desist with the Clean Gene look. His public assiduousness may be just a cover for a private world he wants someone to crack. Perhaps he wants his hair messed up, his shirt torn, his shoes scuffed, his virginity taken away, by whomever, whenever. The absence of his father makes him desperate for sensuality, for the automatic touching and giving most Syrian boys like him enjoy. A father may withdraw his affection, occasionally, purposefully, but a permanent absence is unthinkable. "In the Middle East," a professor friend here confides in me, "the father never dies." Imad is forced to make do without.

What could I possibly be for Imad? He consistently rejects or ignores the advice of his grandfather and uncles, treating them more as equals than as father substitutes. In his own mind, he bridges, or in his more aggressive moments, negates, the differences that separate them, and he does the same with me. Not only age (I am older) and education (I know more) but, equally important, desire separates us, for I cannot (or am unwilling to) give him what he most wants. I, therefore, do not submit to his insistence on equality: I query his

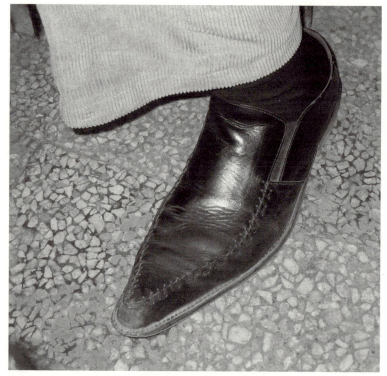

Figure 5. Imad's Shoe

motives, mock his fantasies, fashion his stories to unflattering ends—I admit, without risking much of anything myself.

Yet, while most of our exchanges may be unequal, we greet each other daily, a kiss and handshake in the middle of the souk, which confers on him the public recognition he longs for—the acquaintance of an exotic foreigner; and for me, even more crucially, it signals to the public that the merchants accept me, that I am integrated into their complex relationships, that I am solicitous of one of their odd ones. On another level, although my humor may not harm him, it is *his* vulnerabilities and deceptions and fabrications that are revealed. Nothing about me is exposed, while I reveal and dissect his motives and entire appearance. Is revelation, though, not part of a process of human recognition, of bringing to consciousness, and with respect to Imad and myself, an intrinsic quality of the adult-child dichotomy?

The basis of our relationship, it seems to me, is an ambiguity within this process of revelation. I am to him neither father, brother, uncle, nor sex partner—in large part, because of my own resistance to his claims. Nor am I much of a teacher, a relation I have with other young men and women, since Imad is not eager to learn the sort of things I teach. Perhaps I am merely an *adult stranger*, with all the vagueness, danger, and possibilities for projection that implies.

The dichotomy between adult and youth has largely broken down in many circles in the West, especially among the professional middle classes in which I am usually situated, yet here I am, in Aleppo, in situations where this dichotomy is alive. In the United States, as an adult stranger interacting with children or youth, I am frequently reduced to a sign of danger, and the differences between us are largely understood as predispositions for coercion and exploitation in encounters. Those predispositions exist, for sure, and so do the opportunities to carry them out. And Imad is at some level aware of this, even desiring the forbidden exchange for which we both would risk punishment. But I resist thinking of our encounters as reducible to a mutual exchange, exploitative or liberatory, requiring an ethics of agreement or collaborative representation, and instead prefer to characterize them as mere episodes, experiences without closure.

"I would rather have children than fly"

Back in Princeton, I was told that classes in Aleppo begin in mid-September, so I arrive two weeks early, even making a detour through Damascus to pick up the books and articles that I had shipped for teaching. I am to serve as Senior Fulbright Professor of Social Anthropology, as a cultural ambassador, a gift from the U.S. government to Syria's Ministry of Education. My professorship is for one semester of half-time teaching and half-time research in Aleppo.

I am not new to the Fulbright Program, as I had been awarded a Fulbright professorship in 1995 in Berlin, Germany. Formally independent though financially and administratively supported by the Department of State, the Fulbright is the oldest U.S. government–

Figure 6. Coffee, but No Break

sponsored academic exchange program, one of the few relics of the
Cold War that has not been discredited and disassembled. It was
initially an attempt by some less hawkish American congressmen to
establish warm relations through continuous international scholarly
and artistic exchange—its brochures emphasize "mutual understanding"—between Americans and people from other countries,
including those toward which the U.S. government was politically
hostile. And it has been able to survive despite the end of that war
and the start of a new series of global conflicts, and this year even
expanded exchanges to Syria, one of the countries that the U.S. government currently considers to be harboring terrorists.

Intensive field research on the changing relations of fathers to
sons begins on the day of my arrival. The Souk al-Atarin is one site
for my encounters, and I choose it because of its reputation as a
traditional commercial center dominated by Sunni Muslims. I
quickly become an odd presence, part of the daily life of those who

work there: drinking excessive amounts of Arabic coffee in the morning and tea in the afternoon, listening to stories and jokes, sitting for extraordinarily long hours in shops as indecisive tourists and local customers occasionally buy something, or more often simply wander by. Whereas nearly all of the people who work in the souk have abandoned it as a living space, I decide—to the amazement of everyone I meet—to reside there and take part in its activities as well as its arrivals and departures.

My presence at the University of Aleppo, the second site of my research, where I am to teach a course on American secularism, is another matter altogether—contested, rumor-driven, and fraught with obstacles. Although my teaching is delayed for several months, I still visit the university and meet students informally once or twice a week. Founded in 1960, the university has a large, modern, and sprawling campus about two miles outside the city center, with over sixty thousand students (though some people estimate the number to be closer to eighty thousand). Study is tuition-free, but only in some fields is matriculation limited. There is a standard entrance exam, also used to screen students into majors, with medicine and engineering being the most coveted and restricted fields of study. The university is formally secular (dominated by the Ba'ath Party), most of the students are middle-class, and, in contrast to the Souk al-Medina, all of Syria's ethnic and religious groups are present.

In the cafeteria of the Arts and Humanities Building, I frequently meet for coffee with Abdella, a pious third-year student of English literature whom I encountered one night at Hammam Nahasin, and with a group of students, all male, all Muslim, all majoring in English, with whom he hangs out. Initially, I had suggested we exchange Arabic for English lessons, but these lessons never came to pass (once Abdella told me he felt quite guilty for dropping the ball on this). Still, we see each other weekly at the university; his friend Omar has a cell phone, enabling us to find each other after my appointments and lectures.

It is rare that a professor meets with students privately and socially, and each time in the cafeteria I sense that I am not merely the only professor present but the only person over thirty. At our first rendezvous, the students seat me at one end of the table, so everyone will have access to me, and Abdella then exchanges seats with another boy so he will be seated next to me, to my left. Abdella is ruggedly handsome, with a strong nose, brown hair, dark brown eyes, a shortly trimmed beard, and a quick, slightly nervous, smile. Omar, seated on my right, is darker than the others, and slightly pimpled, with startlingly deep, alert, black eyes and full lips. The other students around us—somewhere between one hundred and two hundred, males and females, watch curiously but without making much fuss; a few drop in now and then to listen. The big question they pose right at the beginning, almost with a sigh, as if dying to know but wanting to get this over: "Are you married?"

"No, divorced," I say.

"Divorced? Why?"

"We decided to lead different lives," I reply

"Are you getting married again?" they ask.

"No."

"Any children?"

"No."

And with this response, they are demonstrably frustrated. Such nonsensical answers! They follow up, "How old are you?"

Syrians everywhere pose this question to me, as they do to all foreigners, men and women alike, and regardless of how I answer, their most common retort is, "Just what I thought you were." Sometimes, I joke about my age and say, "I will turn thirty-nine this year, just like I did last year; it's good to stick with an age for a few years." This time, I answer directly, "Fifty-two."

"I thought thirty-five," says one.

"I look young for my age, while you look mature for yours," I say. "It depends on what kind of life you lead."

All of my responses border on the unimaginable for them, as does my grey hair (men with grey hair tend to dye theirs black), and I increasingly risk their disapproval but also pique their interest, especially regarding marriage and children.

"Why aren't you married?" they return to the point. "You need a wife to cook for you, to take care of you."

Figure 7. Wedding Dresses

The follow-up question allows me to evade the first one, "But I am an excellent cook. A wife would make me fat."

"Then we know why you don't need to marry," says one student half-heartedly, trying to be nice. They are obviously anxious to know who fulfills the other "wifely duties" for me but are either too polite or too apprehensive to go there.

Instead they settle on another topic, which they say they discuss all the time, "What do we have to do to be prepared to marry?"

I am unsure whether they want to talk about love, sex, and romance, or about the problems of the institution of marriage. Most Syrian men do not marry until they are thirty, which means these guys have nearly a decade to prepare. "First," I say, slipping into a safe anthropological mode—after all, it is my first encounter with students—"marriage is about property, and second it is not about you, really, it is about your families and the larger groups external to you." This academic reply proves very confusing to them, and not very satisfying, but I feel it is too early in my stay to respond more intimately or reflectively, with a personal answer about emotional and sexual preparation. For about twenty minutes, they keep asking for clarification.

I attempt a comparison of the pattern of serial marriage in America with Muslim multiple wives, or the Shi'a *mut'a*, a fixed-term temporary marriage, to make the point that there is no single monogamous marital pattern, even within Islam, and that whereas each marriage may be about pleasure (for at least one party in the relationship), it is also about social organization, an expression of a particular social opportunity. They seem puzzled, though what I say is at some level common knowledge. I remark that both before marriage and after divorce, arrangements with wives are frequently determined by property relations alone, and that sexual satisfaction (which surely is on their minds, though they never introduce the topic directly) is often not possible within a single marriage.

"As Sunnites," says one student (all in this group, as I am later told, are pious Muslims), "we abhor the *mut'a*." The others nod agreement. Syrian Sunnites assume, and in schools are apparently taught, that they are the only real Muslims; the other sects are all heretical. They express particular disdain for Shi'a (the dominant sect in Iran; a very small minority in Syria) and Alawites, who many assume are merely a Shi'a sect. Another student follows this with a question soliciting my agreement, also meant to understand whether I have moral character, "Don't you?"

"Yes, of course," I say, and offer my opinion, "It is not a moral institution; it exploits women for sex." I know the topic is controversial, but since one student introduced it, I take the opportunity to solicit their judgments of alternative Islamic practices closer to home, "But some Sunnites also have similar arrangements," I continue. "Look at all the Bulgarian and Ukrainian women imported to Aleppo to have sex. Who are their customers? Certainly large numbers of Saudi and Kuwaiti men."

"Not only them," admits a student seated to my right, "many local men here in Aleppo, too." The other students fidget some and are clearly uncomfortable with this critical turn in the discussion, yet they listen attentively and are supportive of others asking and answering questions.

I think some more about their questions, and my shifting role. Am I here simply to learn their cultural models of affinity and care, or am I to bring my own understandings to bear on our discussion, and make the students less naïve about the representations of any model of marriage, including their own and the romantic one that they watch in American films? I explain that marriage responds universally to insolvable problems; it is a human institution asked to do a number of impossible tasks: it must regulate relations between groups, childcare (by giving the child a name and descent), property relations, familial authority, and sexual practices. But it is never very successful in regulating sex, I add. A student on my left smiles and nods agreement.

Abdella concludes that he has to marry because he is unable to imagine not having a child to call him *baba*. That is something he really wants. Several students say that their parents will surely select their wives for them, or in any case they need their parents' approval. I tell them about a scientist who told me of a survey of Aleppians that found over 30 percent married first cousins, and over 50 percent married first or second cousins. This is perhaps why Aleppo appears more conservative than cities like Damascus or Latakia. I risk a provocation and encourage them to marry outside their groups, to foreigners if possible.

They do not respond to my statement, but instead return to the point, but less seriously, "Perhaps we'll convince you to marry again before you leave," says Abdella. "And to marry a Syrian," adds another. "Why would you want to stay alone?"

"Look at it this way," I explain, as simply as I can, "life has a certain meaning for us, as humans, that is different from animals who just repeat, instinctually, the same patterns all the time. We can, within our groups to a large degree, make up different meanings, which is why there are different cultures, and different marital systems, and different patterns of love, and these keep changing as people adjust and innovate. You can either decide to be exactly like your grandfather or you can ask, 'What opportunities are there for me now, in this year, 2004?' I, for example, can fly and come here, have new experiences, which I could not if I had a wife and children. I can meet you, talk to you, even learn from you."

"I would rather have children than fly," Abdella retorts.

"That is your choice," I say, and smile at his clever and wise response. "But the issue is not about moving around, really, but about being able to have other sorts of experiences, taste different cuisines, learn things one does not know. I am a professor of anthropology. I study others unlike myself. I see being unmarried as a particular set of opportunities."

"Earlier you had mentioned you get someplace with hard work," remarked one student, regarding an exchange about how I became a professor at Princeton even though my parents were both poor farmers with little education. I add, "Hard work and luck."

"Five percent luck," opines Omar.

"I think more than 5 percent," I respond, "but without luck you fail; hard work is not enough."

"Where does luck come from?" Omar asks.

"Good question." I had never thought about the origin of luck; they had me there. "I don't think it comes from anywhere," I say. "It just happens in the moment of doing something. It is accidental."

"It comes from God," he says with a broad smile, and the other students nod in agreement.

"Perhaps," I say, "but if you attribute everything to God, then God becomes an abstraction, and you cannot explain anything in particular."

My equally abstract response furrows their brows, reducing them to silence. Not what I intended. Perhaps they are not attributing everything to God, as I thought; perhaps they are using him only to explain accidents, circumstances that resist explanation. I think: how can I get out of this position of always explaining? But I am reluctant to question them further, to put them on the spot as they are doing to me. They know each other, and we are talking in public. To ask personal questions in front of each other might force them into denials.

"Yes," says Abdella, "one must ask what is the meaning of life, but I prefer the life of my grandfather."

"That may no longer be possible for you," I caution him, knowing that, as he told me in our first meeting in the hammam, he hopes to leave Syria as he has no job prospects at home. I mention that marriage is also an issue in the United States now, with a debate around same-sex marriage, *zawaj al-mithliyeen*. They know the concept, and all look down, as if ashamed or embarrassed. Abdella asks, hopefully, "Do you oppose this?"

"No," I say, to his dismay. "Everyone should get married at least once, regardless of who the partner is."

Nearly two hours had passed, and I notice they are tiring, of listening and speaking English, if nothing else, and I want to get back to the souk. We agree to meet again soon.

"Once you love deeply, you never forget"

Ali is forty-two and works in the souk with his brothers. He is an average-looking man of medium height, with dark curly hair and large round eyes, and a clever man, quick to joke, especially to comment on his taste for female tourists walking by, "Look, look! She is my cup of tea." Often, however, he looks miserable when he arrives in his shop in the morning. He persistently complains about his wife. "I don't fight with her," he says. "There is just no feeling. She is cold to me, cold"—he gives the word depth, a chill—"she is like a corpse to me." Once I bring an American tourist with me to his shop, and he complains to her about his wife. She scolds him, pointedly, "You only think of yourself. Maybe you don't make her happy. Why don't you think about how you are making her unhappy?" Ali undoubtedly thinks her out of line; he does not respond.

Other men are not so explicit to me in criticizing their wives. Every day when I greet Ali, with a peck on both cheeks, an extra one on the right, I take to asking about his wife and his children—he has six, five girls and one boy. He would say, "She is cold, cold. I devote myself to my children now. They need me."

I ask Ali's nephew why Ali is so unhappy, and he explains that Ali as well as another older uncle had tried to realize a very common dream: of having a second wife, one that they love. Muslim men are officially allowed to take up to four wives, though most in Syria are content with one, or, if unmarried, with the thought of one. However, since the first marriage tends to be arranged, at least for men of the over-thirty generation, many dream of marrying a second wife whom they would be able to choose themselves, on the basis of qualities that they value or on the basis of romantic love. All men I talk to distance themselves from the Gulf Muslims' practice of acquiring multiple wives, though they concede that if Syrians had as much money, they might, like the Saudis, accumulate more wives.

But neither Ali nor his brother are wealthy, and for this reason their other brothers eventually force them to end their relationships with foreign women. Since all the brothers work together, and will collectively inherit property from their father, who is still alive, an extra wife makes property issues very complicated. Moreover, sources of new wealth are scarce. Especially since the loss to Israel in the 1967 war, the government's financial investments in security and military hardware have meant less money for social infrastructure. Correspondingly, the economy has stagnated, unable to keep up with population growth. The one brother eventually ended his relationship with his Belgian girlfriend before marriage. Ali actually managed to marry a French nurse from Paris, and he stayed married to her for over two years. He even rented an extra house for them to share for the part of the year she stayed in Aleppo, and once he even visited her in Paris—"A magical month," he says.

"And your first wife," I ask, "how does she respond?"

"She wanted to kill me."

"With the kitchen knife?"

"No, not with knives. She wanted to use her hands, to strangle me, yes, or put poison in my coffee. One kilo poison!"

One problem was, he says, that the French authorities did not recognize his marriage to his French wife because he had to prove he was single. They do not recognize Islamic marriage, which is what he had with both wives in Syria. So, by French law, he had to divorce his first wife, his Syrian wife in Aleppo, before he could marry his French wife in France. But what most doomed his second marriage was that his French wife also began to demand that he comply with French law and divorce his first wife so he could join her in France.

" 'We agreed already,' I tell her. 'And what about my children?' I ask her. And she says, 'I will take care of them. I want to take care of them. Divorce your first wife and bring them with you to Paris.' But my family is against this. They do not want me to divorce my first wife. And I think, but that doesn't work: Who would take care of my kids in Paris? A French woman? French women like to travel, they want to go to the theater, to the cinema, to visit their friends. And I ask my children: They do not want to go either."

Because Ali speaks no French and his French wife speaks no Arabic, they conversed in English. But Ali's English is limited to simple, useful expressions. "It does not matter. We understood each other well; communication was not a problem," he insists.

"Do you still love her?" I ask.

"Once you love deeply, you never forget."

"My father says he saves for me"

Zuhayr is the oldest son of an oldest son, and today he is in a miserable mood. "I hate my father," he exclaims as he offers me a chair in his shop. His father had sent him a customer, and Zuhayr then sold him some engraved wooden boxes. But since the customer did not have sufficient cash on him, they agreed he would pay later. When Zuhayr informs his father of the delayed payment, his father is furious that Zuhayr agreed to this delay. "But he sent him to me!" Zuhayr protests. I try to comfort him, but he is inconsolable.

The next day Zuhayr is still stewing over his father's anger. "His shop is four times as large as mine," he explains about his father's shop, "yet I bring in four times as much money." His uncle, who has a shop across the aisle, agrees, joking that Zuhayr probably brings in five times as much as his father. "Also, he does not know how to sell," Zuhayr continues. "He comes to my shop, and in the middle of a sale, just like that, tells a customer of mine, 'You can have this for 50 lira,' when I had been trying to sell something for 100. And he complains all the time." Zuhayr's uncle again confirms this, adding that at home the father is even worse, representing the old way, more strict—as the oldest son usually is.

My own relations with Abu Zuhayr, the father of Zuhayr, as I and most others call him, are warm and friendly. He always goes out of his way to express concern for how I am doing. Once, after someone kidded Abu Zuhayr about not smiling, he approaches me and asks, "Have you ever seen me smile?"

I say, "Yes, just now."

Zuhayr, on the other hand, has an infectious smile, which he shows readily to the tourists, and he has memorized elaborate and often humorous greetings in flawless French, German, Italian, English, Japanese, Russian, Polish, and of course in Arabic, his mother tongue. He jokes with customers, badgers them into stopping, and then cheers them up with his smile; his raised eyebrows make his deep brown, wide-set eyes appear ever alert and intense. He says he learned everything about sales from his uncle, who says that his nephew now in turn teaches him things.

Zuhayr's shop is at a busy intersection, but it is one of the smallest on this street, with room for only one chair, and Zuhayr insists that size is everything. Customers feel more at ease in a big shop, he says; since they can take their time, he does not have to make a quick sale. Many shopkeepers with small shops put goods in the aisle in front of their shops, and Zuhayr shows me how he enlarges his shop by moving the table out near the edge, past where it is legal to do so, so he has a place to sit or stand inside. Inspectors do make unannounced visits to fine people for such infractions, though the rumor of their presence spreads so quickly that goods are removed from the street and shops shrunk back to legal size before the inspectors ever make it inside the souk.

Zuhayr explains his situation, "At sixteen I decided not to continue my studies, since I thought I would be working for my father later anyway. I work six days to have one day off. I earn 1,000 Syrian pounds; that is $20 a week, enough for cigarettes and one meal out, little more, the same as my other nephews, who are all younger. I cannot save anything with this salary. I cannot save to buy an airplane ticket to leave."

"Is there no way to schedule for you to get pay raises?"

"I don't ask for more because I know the answer. I have been earning the same for six years now, minus the two years' military service. Nothing will change until I marry, and I do not want to marry, not yet." In any event, Zuhayr needs a substantial financial raise from his father, most likely also the purchase of an apartment, in order to marry.

"But don't they have incentives for you to work harder, or be creative?"

"My father says he saves for me. They know if they pay me more I will save the money and leave, just take off. I am waiting for an opportunity, and if I get it I will leave."

"Would anything make you contented here?"

"The problem with this work, it is the same every day: get customers, sell to them even if they don't want to buy. I want to sell something people need, like bread."

"There is no money in bread; you should sell oil or water."

"I know I will be happy if I get a bigger shop. Then I will be satisfied, I can sell better; people will come in on their own."

The month of Ramadan presents a particular struggle for Zuhayr. Five times daily he does his prayers, which he usually neglects, and only once does he break his fast. On that occasion, his family is invited to his mother's parents for the late evening meal, but his father refuses to go. Zuhayr identifies with his mother and threatens to break his fast if they do not settle their argument. His father does not budge, however. So in the morning Zuhayr drinks a glass of water in front of them—meaning that sometime after Ramadan he will have to repeat a day of fasting. Afterward, he feels that his father is contrite, although no apology is offered. Moreover, the family had abruptly cancelled the visit to his maternal grandparents the previous evening, ruining his mother's plans.

During Ramadan, Zuhayr's unhappiness turns frequently to anger, either directed against himself for not selling more or against others for stealing his customers. "I am happy when I have a good day because my father is happy. I can see it even when he doesn't say anything. And when I don't sell anything, I see he is unhappy and I am unhappy, too." I am touched by how he maintains his identification with his father's happiness and sadness despite his struggles with the restrictions and authority imposed on him as the eldest son. The same might be said of his relation to Islam, which, though obviously more strained than that of his other male relatives and in fact of most of the men I meet in the souk, he nonetheless maintains it—it seems to me, more out of a principle of loyalty to his family and religious tradition than out of conviction or familial coercion. Nonetheless, Zuhayr's daily contact with foreigners in the souk reinforces his general pragmatism as well as a willingness to assert self-interest. He adds, "I've had enough of Ramadan. I hate it. I need a day off. I will take Saturday off even if they extend Ramadan until Sunday."

I explain how everybody had to work on the dairy farm where I grew up. My only brother, Bob, who is the oldest son in our family, and ten years older than me, abandoned the family at the age of sixteen to work for a neighbor. Bob wanted spending money to save for a car, in order to take girls out, but my father refused to pay him more. My mother, sisters, and father had to work much harder after he left, and I often sense my sisters are still resentful.

"Your brother was right," says Zuhayr.

"As long as she gets along with me, she will have no problems with my mother"

I never meet the mothers and sisters of the men and boys who work in the souk, because they never visit them there. But men do talk about their female relatives, the younger men most frequently about their mothers, with whom they have intimate and reverential relations. They say the worst insult one can pay to another man is to insult his mother, but, though they say this is common, I never did witness someone cuss another's mother. When parents are fighting with each other, many sons find themselves caught in between, but they uniformly tell me that if they are unable to stay neutral, they come down on the side of their mothers. Men who are married also say that if their wives and mothers fight, they tend to support their mothers over their wives. When I discuss this with women outside the souk, several take the opportunity to complain that their husbands never defend them against their mothers-in-law. This omnipresence and omnipotence of the son's mother, or the daughter's mother-in-law, is a common feature of Mediterranean families, irrespective of Muslim, Jewish, or Christian affiliation.

I ask one thirty-year-old man in the souk, whose father died a year ago and who intends on marrying in the next year or two, if he will continue living with his mother after marriage.

"I don't think I could financially afford another apartment," he says, and then adds, "my mother means everything to me. I couldn't leave her."

"What if she has conflicts with your wife, as often happens with mothers-in-law?"

"As long as she gets along with me," he says earnestly, "she will have no problems with my mother."

"What are you looking for in a wife?" I ask.

"Beautiful!" he exclaims, and laughs. "I want a woman who stays home, who I can talk with."

"Does that mean she should be educated?"

"Before my father died, I just thought about material things, things I want, but now I think I should have gone to the university. It is not all about money—though you'd never know," he lowers his voice to a whisper, "from the others in the souk. That's all they think about: money and gossip."

"Would you insist your wife veil in public?"

"Oh yes," he says without hesitation. "I do not want to share her beauty with others. She should have good morals."

In all our interactions, this young merchant is humorous, open and forward-looking. But when it comes to the idea of a wife, he resorts to a textbook version of traditionalism: a woman like his mother, whom he protects from the public and who remains largely hidden from view. From what other men tell me about their sisters, who are ambivalent about this traditionalist role, I am doubtful whether he will easily find or even be happy with such a woman for a wife. But for now, premarriage, that is his wish.

Everyone agrees that mothers are powerful. Even deceased mothers are powerful. Ali, who was pressured by his brothers to divorce his French wife, tells me that the reason he continues to work with his brothers, despite feeling quite stifled emotionally and economically, is his mother: "On her deathbed, my mother said it was important for all of us brothers to stay together."

In addition to reverence, sons grow up emotionally close to their mothers, who often treat them as the husband they had wished for, showering them with physical affection and promising unconditional love and loyalty. This relationship sets the horizon of expectation high for wives, who must learn early on in marriage, if not before, to cook their husband's favorite foods, to replicate the recipes of the mother-in-law. Many if not most fail this lesson. But when these women have children of their own, they replicate the same structure as their mothers-in-law; sons always prefer the cooking of their own mothers over that of the paternal grandmother. The wife's day will come, provided she has a son.

Some young men still living with their parents say their mothers cook to their tastes, pay attention to their moods and habits, cater to their favorite foods rather than those of the husband. Husbands and wives do not always share the same bed every evening, although this is often a matter of economic class, of whether there is enough money for separate rooms for the boys, girls, and parents. Men tell me that they were frequently able to climb into their mother's bed until the age of twelve, by which time, I assume, most young boys already have strong libidinal desires. The combination of intimacy and reverence for the mother makes the position of the new wife precarious and sets up a classical oedipal conflict between the father and son as well as dreams of mother-son incest.

"Do you desire your mother?"

The evolution of desire between mother and son is integral to shaping all other relationships, including between father and son and husband and wife. Incest is the form of its most radical intimacy, and because of the taboos surrounding this outer limit, few men will share with me personal stories of this desire. Third-person accounts are somewhat less threatening, and therefore more frequently offered. One journalist tells me the following story from his village:

A mother stops menstruating and notices her belly enlarging. But since she is divorced and lives alone with her son, she has no explanation. Eventually she goes to a doctor, who tells her she is pregnant. That is impossible, she says, I live only with my son. The doctor tells her he is certain she is with child, and asks her to explain anything suspicious or unusual about her daily routine: Where and when does she come in contact with men other than her son?

"With no one. Never," she says. "There is one thing, however. Every night when my son comes home, he first showers. Then we eat what I have cooked, and he makes a special tea for us before we go to sleep."

The doctor tells her they must bring in the police to investigate. The police arrive one night and observe through a window. They notice the son come home. He showers, he eats with his mother, and then he makes his special tea—putting a tablet in his mother's cup. The mother falls asleep, the son undresses her, the police arrest him. The son goes to prison. The mother gets an abortion.

I say to the journalist, "It is implausible that the mother would not have known about the sex. Even if she had been unaware of the sleeping tablets, the morning after she'd know she had sex."

"No," he insists, "the mother was naïve. The police observed the son's actions."

I want to ask him more questions of interpretation but sense I have reached the limits of acceptable prying. He had, as I requested, narrated a story of incest; an interpretation would perhaps risk revealing too much of his own fantasies. Yet I am curious about why he lets the mother off the hook totally, why in the story she would not be placed under the slightest suspicion. Surely the desire of the mother's son was not merely his own but the product of an interaction with his mother's desire, including her desire for him, sustained by her continuing devotion to him, and freed from certain restrictions by the death of her husband, of the boy's father. The death of the father, in other words, represents the beginning of freedom for both the mother and her son.

Once, discussing Freud with Ziyad, a bright student of English literature, he asks me about the difference in the study of literature in Syria and the United States. I reply that in the United States he'd be introduced to psychoanalytically informed readings.

"And you agree?" he asks.

"Yes."

He challenges me, "Then you believe that all sons desire their mothers?"

"Yes," I say, somewhat shocked by the bluntness of his question, "but that doesn't mean we are aware of the form this desire takes. It may not be sexual."

"Do you desire your mother?"

"You cannot take Freudian theory so literally," I say, and elaborate my understanding of infant development: all babies are first attached to the breast, and in most cultures a substitute, initially a pacifier of sorts, is introduced. But to wean the baby from the breast is difficult, met with tremendous resistance, because sucking the breast is not merely a physical habit but also represents an emotional attachment to the mother, and to wean the infant is to bring about a separation, a sense of primordial loss. This initial desire for the breast, and the mother, then, is normally interrupted, but it remains present as fantasy and loss, and then takes other, displaced forms as the child grows up. As the child becomes sexual, it takes the form of incestuous desire: fantasized, perhaps only in dreams not remembered, even though unthinkable.

"Then what about the Oedipus conflict? Do you want to kill your father?"

"He's already dead," I reply, "though I did want him dead many times. But, again, don't understand the father here as merely a physical person. He is also a source of authority, represents a force external to you, unlike the mother who was initially a part of you (actually, you a part of her). Hence there is ambivalence about submitting to this external authority, who, for most of us, interrupts, or takes the responsibility for, the separation from the mother." My intellectual clarification of psychic conflict meets with a shrug. Ziyad remains skeptical.

Traffic, or the Normal Order of Things

My usual route to exit the souk and go downtown is east in the direction of the Grand Umayyad Mosque. I turn left after I leave my apartment and pass, in the first fifty feet, in turn, stores for shoes, bedroom linens, blankets, baby clothes, umbrellas, buttons, and sundry odds and ends. Then I hit a small intersection. I have two options: If I go straight for the next hundred feet, I pass more baby clothes, textiles, fresh juice and cheese sandwiches, blankets; then I turn left for five hundred feet past raw cotton, ropes, silver, soap, and money changers. Or instead, I first turn left and then right, past two general stores with toilet paper, cleansers, sponges, brooms, and everything-for-cleaning kitchens and toilets; then butcher shops, a place I buy water that also sells soft drinks, yoghurt, milk, and halva, nut shops between a couple of bakeries, a few odd spice shops, several fresh vegetable and fruit stores, more butchers, another fruit store, more nuts; and then exit right through a one-person-at-a-time lane which opens onto umbrellas, canes, olive oil soaps, lavender soap, sponges. Either way, I end up at a second intersection in the open air, in front of the strategically placed money-changers—

one of whom always greets me and asks where I have been—followed by a row of more nuts, fresh and dried fruit, a restaurant, a public toilet whose strong urine smell, especially on hot days, forces me to hold my breath, and women's underwear, all across from the Grand Mosque.

The automobile and bus traffic begins at this final intersection, at the end of the Grand Mosque, with a view of the Citadel to my right. I cross the street where there are more linens, bedroom things, pajamas, bathrobes, leather, tailors, men's shirts and pants, women's underwear, industrial sewing machines, sewing machine parts. I cross another street, a very busy two-lane highway, with no intersection, hence no pedestrian crossing. I wait for the right moment and dart between speeding cars going one direction, then pause in the middle, standing as erect and thin as possible, and then I run between speeding cars going the other direction. This is Aleppo's worst street to cross. You have to just clench your teeth and go for it. On one side the traffic is four cars wide with five or six competing for the spots, on the other side two cars abreast in a lane for one.

So how do you cross with cars racing both directions? I often get stuck, not just between the two directions but between cars going the same direction. Never look back, I say to myself, only forward, and only in the direction from which the cars are coming. Since drivers pay no attention to lanes, they will simply route around you rather than slow down to let you cross. Sometimes, just before crossing, men will take my hand, or each other's, or women take each other's hand: some semblance of power in numbers. Because pedestrians are so concentrated on avoiding the cars, we often run into each other, or into the boys pushing dollies laden with goods.

The Russian market begins on the other side: mostly tailors, women's coats, lots of men's shirts, more sewing machines, Bazaar al-Shark, a fancy restaurant below ground on the right, an Armenian church on the left, a small mosque, bedroom things, leather jackets. I arrive, unscathed, at Bab al Farej, the clock tower next to the town library, epicenter of the old town.

Aleppians get used to this traffic, of course, so much so that they prefer walking on the dangerous street instead of the sidewalk, and they walk slowly, nonchalantly, as if they had the street to themselves. When I walk with people, I walk nervously, unsteadily, thinking I should go faster, and often I lock my arm in that of the man next to me and steer him back onto the sidewalk or we would always be walking on the street. I fear being sideswiped by the cars (actually it only happened once), but Aleppian pedestrians assume the cars or bicycles or donkeys will go around them, and true enough, they do.

It is also true that people throw garbage on the curbs, especially after work, and cats gather late at night to pick through it and fight; sometimes I see a person sorting through what's left, usually looking for plastic bottles. Such activity is dirty and unpleasant, something to be avoided; therefore, many people conclude, perhaps better to walk on the street, which is clean, washed by public trucks very late at night, occasionally even during the day; individual merchants and apartment dwellers are responsible for the sidewalks, which most try to keep clean, in fact sweeping them several times a day.

From late afternoon until early evening, the streets downtown are packed, mostly men and boys with sweaty bodies doing last-minute shopping for watches, jeans, perfumes, sweaters, shirts, electronic equipment, or simply loitering with friends after a day of work. They are skilled at passing each other without touching, just a slight turn of the body sideways at the last minute. If they touch, however, accidentally, nobody bats an eye. The smell of rose water on bodies, the preferred perfume, mixes with diesel from cars and trucks. I often walk another five minutes to the large public park, which is seductively lit at night, and where all visitors are greeted by the smell of jasmine trees so fragrant that I wonder why people do not plant them everywhere.

For longer distances from downtown, I take taxis, which are very cheap for a foreigner from the West: from seventy-five cents up to a couple of dollars. I strike up conversations with the drivers, who are mostly Kurds and therefore enthusiastically greet me as an American. "We are brothers," drivers frequently say to me; several

Figures 8a and 8b. Traffic

times they even resist payment. The assumption is, they inform me, that America will help establish an independent Kurdistan. "Bush good," they often exclaim. I learn to preempt this praise, not wanting to encourage the rather dangerous thought that the United States would actually support a Kurdish independence movement. In theory, perhaps; in practice, Kurds will be on their own, and the United States will be strategic about whom it supports and when. Early on in our conversations I agree that Americans and Kurds are brothers, but I give a thumbs-down and say, "Bush bad. War! Falluja!" I also meet Kurds who are not nationalists and who do not want to become part of a larger Kurdish state, but they are distinct minorities in their communities.

If I travel within Syria, I take the bus or train (which has railcars from the former socialist East Germany!). Men sit with men, women with women (unless they are a married couple), and seats are assigned. So I sit next to many strangers and meet all sorts of people, including a mullah who, after an intense conversation about colonialism and Iraq, offers me several CD recordings of his sermons. (My top experience with a mullah, however, is once after a long conversation about war and peace in a hammam, he takes off his ring and puts it on my finger, proclaiming, "We are friends," which makes me feel, for the first time in my life, as if I were a bride.) The intercity buses are usually on time and they are often full, but once we have a flat tire and wait for an hour for another bus to come and pick us up, and once we run out of gas a half hour after leaving the station.

Toward the end of Ramadan, the souk and the city itself become generally tense. The abstinence of the day seems to wear on people, so that by mid-afternoon I see a dramatic increase in the number of conflicts and physical fights. City traffic manifests this tension directly, and within Syria Aleppian drivers are infamous for their risk-taking habits. The end of Ramadan also marks the beginning of Eid al-Fitr, three work-free days of excessive eating, visiting all friends and both sides of the family, exchange of gifts, including the expenditure of a voluntary religious tax for the poor. In the days leading up to Eid, taxi drivers are unusually aggressive.

One day, I see two automobile accidents within the space of a twenty-minute ride from the souk to the university. The drivers jump out and are quickly in each other's faces, preparing to attack physically. A traffic policeman walks over and narrowly misses a blow from one of the men. I feel sorry for him; everyone seems to ignore traffic police. To be sure, some are known to stop cars and demand bribes. But their pay is minimal, and unlike in the West, nobody seems to respect their authority to give tickets. As they direct traffic at intersections, their effort seems to be merely to avoid an all-out traffic jam. Likewise, as in this case, most drivers simply circle around the occasional accident.

Returning from the university one day, my driver decides to pass every single car or truck on the road, and I literally fear for my life as he darts in and out of lines, inching forward at every stoplight to be positioned as the first to go once the light turns green. Twice I say that I am not in a hurry, but he ignores me. I dare not say more for fear of making him angry.

Another time, I am going from the souk to the airport in the late afternoon. I run into two friends, Ahmed and Rami, who work in a blanket shop near my apartment, and they offer to help me with my two very large bags. We walk to the intersection by the mosque where taxis pass. One stops and Rami negotiates for me. This driver insists on 500 Syrian pounds ($10), for a ride that usually costs 150. Another driver approaches and offers to go for 400. Rami says 300, and they repeat, in turn, "400! 300! 350! 300!" until the driver agrees, "300!" I put my bags in back and get in his car, in the front passenger seat.

The first driver gets out of his car and yells at the second for taking away his customer, even though there are other passengers waiting for a ride. He pounds the flat of his hand on the roof of our car. My driver gets out and holds his ground, arguing back, calling the first one names. He raises his right fist high as if to strike. The first driver is red in the face with anger, though, so he gets back in his car and drives at an angle in front of our car, blocking us from leaving. My driver then simply leaves me alone sitting in the car. I watch him enter the souk.

The car in which I sit is now blocking traffic. A policeman comes over and says something to me I do not understand. I shrug my shoulders, and say I do not know what is going on. My driver returns about ten minutes later with a small bag in his hand.

"Need to use the toilet?" I ask.

"No," he says, "I just bought olives for dinner."

I point to my watch, and say, "Airport, please." But instead my driver reengages with the angry one; they resume yelling at each other. We are still blocked from leaving, and the policeman, now seeing both drivers present, again approaches us. I place my hand on my driver's arm, hoping to calm him, and gesture for him to just drive on. He does, slowly, with his head stuck out the window, yelling all the while. When we arrive at the airport, he insists on 350 instead of the price we had agreed upon. I pay, angrily.

At stoplights, drivers avoid lining up behind others, but circle around the ones in front so that three cars fill two lanes, or four fill three, or five or six fill four. They position themselves like runners in a race so that at the last second, just before the light turns green one takes the initiative and inches, slightly askance, into the intersection ahead of the others. This move is rarely perfectly timed, since drivers usually must pause again for a few seconds for the cross traffic that continues even after the light turns green. Still, this last minute jockeying gives some driver the advantage of being the first to go, and that itself is usually the only, but also sufficient, reward for the clever maneuvering.

On the other hand, all this prepping for relative advantage for mobility and speed and desire to be number one is also counterbalanced by another behavior: as a friend puts it to me, "We Arabs like to sit." There is everywhere in Syria a readily observable attempt—in movement, in the slow caress of others, in speech, and in bureaucratic activities—to preserve a less hectic pace of thought and action, to slow things down and hold on to the moment.

Hanging out, not only sitting in the souk but also in cafés throughout the city, is a favorite activity. Mostly men, but also some women in some cafés and usually then only in late mornings or early afternoons, hang out: they sit, talk, smoke the narghile, and observe others walking by. At cafés, the only quick movement is that of the waiters, who tend to be very polite and efficient, and children, who play unobtrusively without much bothering their elders, and who tend not to have fixed bedtimes. Children move quickly from running to napping, however, simply slumping over in a chair or lying on someone's lap for a snooze. If they seek contact with elders, they are rarely turned away but handed gently and lovingly from one person to another.

As girls enter puberty, they quit running altogether and slow their walk much more than boys their age. In lectures at the university and in conversations with young women, I discuss with them not only how their bodies are shaped by lack of physical exercise but also its effects on their posture, self-confidence, sense of freedom, and ease of movement. Obesity is a major unacknowledged problem in Syria, and, due to inactivity, women become obese more frequently and earlier in life than men. In the souk, I see many middle-aged women so burdened by weight that they can at most shuffle. But men also have weight problems, and while this is certainly attributable to the quantities of food they eat, it is also a result of pleasure found in sitting. In the evenings many of the streets in Aleppo may be bustling, but only some young men tend to walk any distance to speak of, and then it is more at the pace of a meander. "Nightlife," then, does not exist in the racy, urban European sense, or in what one experiences in certain sectors of Beirut (with a hint at such a life for the upper classes in Damascus)—energetic dancing in nightclubs, loud music from bars, parties with strangers. Aleppians might instead simply talk about their life at night, which consists in homes of playing cards or backgammon, or watching television, or for men in public sitting occasionally in the hammam but more frequently and prominently in the café.

Another striking feature of the Aleppian café is the widespread use of fluorescent lighting. In all but the most posh public places and in most homes, long-tube fluorescent lights have replaced incandescent light bulbs (not to speak of the older, nonelectric period of candle use). People uniformly explain to me that their use of fluorescent tubes is an economic decision; they are cheaper and last

a

b

c   d

Figures 9a–9d. Children of Syria

longer (as well as being more energy efficient—an explanation not much offered). Occasionally people will add the desire to "be modern," or that now they are used to the glare. Never do they mention the aesthetic dimension of this decision, where it has its most dramatic effect. Regardless of intent, this kind of lighting has certain aesthetic effects that, when accompanied in public places by larger, clear-glass windows to the street, increase the transparency of interactions and visibility to outsiders.

Figures 10a and 10b. Shadow and Light

In pre-twentieth-century architectural styles, windows are not clear glass but latticework patterns cut into wood, which filter light into a room in various shapes and quantities. Ottoman-era tealight oil lamps and decorative hanging candle lamps made of brass and extra-fine glass illuminate not whole rooms but specific places. They cast shadows on objects, including people, with the double effect of revealing and concealing, accentuating a chin and mouth while obscuring an eye, lighting the page of a book while darkening the entire space of the room around its reader. Décor associated with the Ottoman period includes filtered lighting and partitioned rooms with few solid closed doors, both in homes and public places, which, much like the practice of veiling women, affords partial privacy but also arouses mystery.

Today this partial privacy is gone, unless one retires behind the closed door of a room in a home, in which case it would nonetheless be rare to find the older style of lighting. Ubiquitous are fluorescent lights, which in both homes and cafés embarrassingly reveal all blemishes on the face, every ball of dust in the corners of a room. Add to this the fact that in most private homes there are few pictures on the walls, and few of the exquisite Persian, Turkish, Kurdish, Bedouin, or Syrian carpets on the floors. The harshness and glare of fluorescent light opens all presence and activity to scrutiny, and, in the name of transparency and efficiency, eliminates the work of shadows. This style became dominant in the 1970s, and accompanied, fortuitously, the tightening of discipline and the building of the police state in the regime of Hafez el-Assad.

In these well-lit spaces, then, of homes, cafés, restaurants, stores, and shops, people bask in immobility, conversing for hours over a Turkish coffee or cup of tea, but this slowness is countered by the high speed not only of traffic, but also the speed at which people eat, and the quickness of the orgasm in sex—for men, that is. It is hardly in jest that many people confide in me that Syrian men lead the world in this respect, though in fact they share this quickness with many others.

Preparing to Teach

Although my field research in the Aleppo souk proceeds smoothly, my university teaching is delayed for three months. In the United States, I had studied Arabic intermittently for four years, and during the summer before I departed for Syria, I had learned the relevant Arabic terms for the topic I had been approved to teach—American secularism—though my linguistic skills were insufficient for teaching primarily in that language, which meant I would have to teach in English. During the previous academic year, an American Cultural Studies Program had been proposed at Aleppo University and was approved by the university president. The American Cultural Center (ACC) at the U.S. Embassy in Damascus had even made a ceremonial gift of fifty books for its library. Aware of this development, I thought a course on American secularism would be appropriately interdisciplinary and original for this program, and of general interest to the students, so I brought along novels, short stories, analytical essays, social theoretical texts, and films for teaching. The writers were as equally varied as the forms in which they wrote, and included Alexis de Tocqueville, Louis Hartz, Friedrich Tenbruck, Maurice Godelier, Flannery O'Connor, Frances FitzGerald, Richard Ford, and Barbara Ehrenreich, among others.

I had had some email correspondence about teaching with two professors in the English Department, whose head, Dr. Lababidi, would prove to play a decisive role in my appointment. On August 5, she emailed me a kind note, welcoming me to the university and stating that there were classes that used English texts in philosophy, sociology, geography, archaeology, and history. I might teach in any of them, but, she added a reservation reached after a meeting with several department heads and the dean of Arts and Sciences, "As for teaching in the English Dept, I'm afraid that your specialization—Anthropology and American Secularism—does not suit the course description of any of the courses taught at the English Dept. The Dean and I send you our best regards. You are most welcome to Aleppo University. If I can be of any further assistance, please do not hesitate to contact me."

This caveat confounded me because the whole point of the Fulbright Program is not simply to repeat the content of a course for which local professors are qualified but to share insights from other disciplines and perspectives with which this university's faculty may not be familiar. Later I was told that at the meeting about which Dr. Lababidi wrote in her first email, the discussion was abstract: my resume was never read, the range of my publications and teaching experience never discussed, even though my expertise has much in common with the field of literature and literary theory. But also I learned that it is common to argue that only courses already on the books be taught, and that all curriculum is geared toward final, comprehensive exams. Still, I sensed that the insistence I not teach in the English department was not about me or exam structure but about something else. But what? The other professor in English with whom I corresponded, who was also a vice dean at the time, assured me in an email that all would be worked out after I arrived, and that even the English Department would then welcome my presence. He encouraged me to be prepared, however, just in case, to teach an introductory philosophy course, or perhaps world literature, so I should bring appropriate materials along for these fields also. I then bought copies of Simon Blackburn's *Think*, Gunter Grass's *The Tin Drum*, and J. M. Coetzee's *Disgrace*, to supplement my already considerable range of reading materials.

Administrative Pleasantries

A week after my arrival, I visit the College of Arts and Sciences at the university, where I am introduced to its dean, two vice deans, and some of the teachers and department heads. The dean gives me a formal greeting, in Arabic, which translates into something like "You are welcome to the University of Aleppo. We look forward to your stay and will make every effort to make it pleasant. Should you have any problems, please ask," in between answering the telephone and putting his signature on the endless number of letters people brought him.

His office is decorated like all other large offices—formality is the word—just that everything is bigger. Drapes cover the windows to keep out the bright light and heat; a solid dark wooden desk rests at one end, opposite a large, rectangular wooden working table with chairs for eight; in the middle of the room, a glass-topped coffee table in between two rows of grandiose chairs fit for royalty with cushions upholstered in a rich textile (roomy enough for the most obese American to sit comfortably). What always strikes me about such rooms is how unsuitable they are for conversation. One must literally yell at times to speak to a person on the other side of the coffee table. The building that houses this faculty is new and still unfinished; the walls and doors had been recently painted and, until late September, there were neither names nor numbers on most of the doors. Still, there are few books on the bookshelves in any of the offices I visit, but students tell me that this is always the case— professors either keep their books at home or don't read much any- way. I do not linger as everybody seems busy in informal chats about the fleeting summer break or in meetings to plan the semester.

On my next visit, my purpose is to secure a letter from a depart- ment head stating interest in my employment. This letter would initiate the bureaucratic work necessary for my residency permit, which, I am told, can take more than three months for the Depart- ment of Immigration to process. I do obtain such a letter, from the head of Philosophy and Sociology, which is then forwarded to the dean and the university president for signatures, before working its way through the appropriate ministries.

On each trip to the university, I run into Abdella, the pious third- year student I had met at the Hammam Nahasin, along with several other students who tag along with him, all except one majoring in English, and all excited and inquisitive about a visiting American professor. They assure me that students would be most eager to visit my class, or classes, whatever they might be, even if in another department. With each visit, the number of students I meet grows, for upon hearing a conversation with a native English speaker, other students gather around, introduce themselves, and inquire about my plans for teaching. They tell me that nearly all their instruction in the English department is in Arabic, so they have little chance to speak English, even in the classroom, not to mention occasions to hear and talk with a native speaker.

Around the third week of September, I sense that there is some ill-defined but growing resistance to my teaching. For one, now the papers from the Fulbright Commission confirming my appointment, sent in early August, cannot be found, and recently faxed copies also have disappeared—so the ACC sends them a third time. For another, I am told that the proposal for the American Cultural Studies Program in which I am to teach is dead, killed over the summer while the person who initiated it was teaching abroad. Two acquaintances, independent of each other, tell me that Dr. Lababidi was instrumental in this miscarriage; she argued that the university had no need or was not ready for the program. In a meeting with the university president over the summer, the (new) American ambassador neither prioritized the proposal for the program nor offered additional support—quite regrettable given the urgent need for some kind of intellectual mediation of American culture and power in the Middle East.

As much as I am tempted to point to ineptitude—linguistic and cultural—on the part of State Department staff, the larger blame for the lack of carry-through and continuity on programs proposed has to do with the constant personnel changes in the U.S. State Department (appointments are generally only for two years!), with the concomitant lack of institutional memory. The old cultural affairs officer had just left and the new one arrived from service in Iraq, where she had been bunkered down, literally, for two years with no opportunity to interact with Iraqis outside the security zone. Also, of course, there is the coincidence of my presence in Syria during the huge shift of American resources to the military and Defense Department, a preoccupation within the U.S. Foreign Service generally with the occupation of Iraq (and, at the time, the fallout from the torture scandal at Abu Ghraib and the reinvasion of Falluja), and persistent underfunding of State Department cultural activities.

Whereas the European Union is building a very strong TEMPUS program of intellectual exchange as well as expanding economic and political relations with Syria, and the French are strengthening their cultural programs at Aleppo University and in the city, the only visible American presence here is its violent military occupation in Iraq, the neighboring country, seen every evening on television. In grappling with the American empire, people in the Middle East are left alone with fantasies formed through advertising, American movies (most of those shown are violent and deal with war—*Troy*, with Brad Pitt, played all fall), and television news, without much direct experience that might challenge prevailing simplifications and stereotypes. After 9/11, the George W. Bush administration made only one serious attempt to reach the "hearts and minds" of Arabs, and that was the infamous "Shared Values" campaign of Charlotte Beers, the former advertising executive turned propaganda chief for Muslim affairs, who resigned in March 2003. Several Syrians surprise me by mentioning this campaign. "Ineptitude," I confess feebly, appropriately embarrassed. Beers's official title was Undersecretary of State for Public Diplomacy, but her expertise was neither diplomacy nor cultural translation but advertising to American audiences. She spent a great deal of money on target ads showing patriotic American Muslims mouthing pro-American slogans—and nobody in the Middle East believed them.

What the propagandists do not take seriously is that Syria has its own cultural dynamic, which manifests itself in local institutions, all only peripherally and only in some spheres open to influence by an American policy that itself is relatively incoherent. Less than a month after my arrival, I am startled by the release from a vice deanship of the instructor who had been most personally helpful and had assured me things would work out, and by the release from his duties of the head of the Philosophy and Sociology Department, who had written the letter for my residency permit. Other faculty members less direct and forthright in style replace both this vice dean and the head of the above-named department.

On my very first visit to the university, I accidentally met one of the incoming "vice deans," as they call them (there are two, and the irony of the title does not escape me), a congenial man trained in France who teaches in the French Department. I am soon introduced to the new head of Philosophy and Sociology, so I continue to hope things will progress and I will still be assigned a class. In fact, merely to bring this process to an end, I reluctantly agree to teach two half-classes, one in sociology, one in philosophy, without seeing the reading lists or expected content for either of them. The other half of each class is an Arabic-English translation component, which I am obviously unqualified to teach. The idea is that I divide up the reading list, once it appears, with another instructor teaching the translation in his or her half, while I would teach content in my half. Several people then tell me that classes will not likely start before the first or even second week of October anyway—six weeks after my arrival! So I should be patient, there is still time to work things out.

But I begin to fret about this chaos, and therefore schedule a meeting with the president of the university. A medical doctor by training, he is sympathetic and to the point. He appears enthusiastic about my proposal to teach a course on American secularism, and not simply to fill in for standard courses already on the books. The university is eager to take advantage of my expertise, he says, and I leave our meeting with the impression that the deans would follow through on his wishes.

Before arriving in Syria I had spent ten days in Beirut, during which time I gave interviews with the newspapers *An-Nahar* and the *Daily Star* on *The Case of Ariel Sharon and the Fate of Universal Jurisdiction*, a book I had edited that was soon to be released, about the impact on human rights of the attempt to use the concept of "universal jurisdiction" to seek redress in the courts of Belgium for the Sabra and Shatila massacre. I had hoped these interviews would be read by people in Syria, on the Internet, of course—*An-Nahar* is altogether unavailable in print in Syria, the *Daily Star* only in Damascus—and facilitate intellectual contacts once I arrived. I download copies of the interview in an Internet café and have glossy copies made. In my meeting with the university president, I give him copies, as I subsequently do to a few other interested people.

These newspaper interviews do have an effect, and come back to haunt me in unexpected ways. Initially, they did indeed turn out to be helpful, as Dr. George Jabbour, a Member of Parliament from the district of Safita and former adviser to now-deceased President Hafez el-Assad, had read the *Daily Star* interview on the Internet. He contacts me—though the American embassy initially was confused about my whereabouts in Syria! We meet in Aleppo and, as he had contemplated studying anthropology before moving into international law and politics, he is interested in alternative approaches to comparison and international relations. He had completed a pioneering work in 1970, *Settler Colonialism in Southern Africa and the Middle East*, that took up comparatively the issues of Palestinian and refugee rights. I give him a copy of my book on the fate of universal jurisdiction, whereupon he offers to send me his best student, Basil, who lives in a village near Homs, to translate some of my work into Arabic.

So while I am presented with this unexpected prospect of reaching an Arabic reading public, the more informative ethnographic opportunity to teach at the University of Aleppo is somehow being blocked. With each passing day the teaching part of my Fulbright task seems more like a mirage. Clarity arrives on October 3, when I am informed, at the direction of the dean of the College of Literature and Human Sciences, that the deans have collectively submitted a letter to the president saying basically what Dr. Lababidi had said in her initial email: they regret that there are no courses on the books in the entire college for which I am qualified to teach, as my specialization—anthropology—does not fit their course needs. I am devastated. I want to teach not primarily because I am convinced the knowledge I might impart will change much of anything, but to learn from students and professors about how Syrians of the educated strata, the class of people outside the souk where I am spending most of my time, experience paternal authority. It dawns on me that this state of limbo can easily persist until my visa runs out. I call the ACC in Damascus and inform them of the problems; they say they will think about what might be done.

Ten days later, the embassy people are still thinking, and the letter from the deans supposedly submitted to the president still has not turned up on his desk, so they say, or, more likely, his office never acknowledges receiving it. I am advised to make believe it does not exist: it has only been allegedly submitted. After all, only a few people had actually seen it, and my own knowledge was merely word-of-mouth. That same week my security clearance from the Mukhabar-rat, the state security, arrives at the Ba'ath Party headquarters, and is then forwarded to the university office that deals with foreign guests. My residency permit is still being processed based on the conditions outlined in the very first letter submitted by the president.

While talking with a group of students from the French and English Departments a few days later, I run into the other new vice dean, a sympathetic woman whom I had met several weeks prior, at which time I had complained to her about the lack of hospitality and the general fog surrounding my status at the university. At that time, she had promised to look into this, and reiterated her opinion that the university needed visitors such as myself. I should be giving a seminar not just to the students, she said, but to the faculty also. This time, however, she seems in a rush to avoid me, but with the students present I take the initiative and confront her. I force one of my visiting cards into her hand (she already had one from our previous chance encounter), and I insist—in English, then French, and then Arabic, to avoid possible misunderstanding—that she promise to call me and tell me what the problem is. She promises.

Another week passes in which nothing happens, so I resolve to travel to Damascus and set up appointments with the American Cultural Center and the U.S. ambassador and the Ministry of Education. Once in Damascus, I set out to meet other academics at Damascus University purely for intellectual exchange. I have a lovely meeting with the head of the English Department, who encourages me to begin teaching a course on semantics in his department the very next day, if I like, without prior approval from the Ministry. That afternoon, since the officer in charge of Fulbright Program at the ACC was on vacation in the United States, I instead meet with the indispensable and extremely competent Syrian employee who does much of the work for the staff, and with a Foreign Service Officer in charge of public relations. I repeat to them the story I had already told several times to the officer in charge of the Fulbright

Program (now on vacation). They then call the man in charge of International Relations at the Ministry of Education, who agrees to make some calls himself, including to Dr. Lababidi and the president of Aleppo University. To escape this impasse, and to avoid forcing the president to confront his own recalcitrant faculty, or whoever else is blocking my appointment, I propose no longer to do a course but instead to give a series of four lectures on anthropology and American culture, plus show a series of four American films after which I would lead a discussion. Meanwhile, the Fulbright officer on vacation returns, and after talking with the deans at Tishreen University in Latakia, obtains confirmation that they would be most eager to host as guest a Fulbright Professor with a Ph.D. from Harvard who teaches at Princeton; I am told I may go and teach there—a three-to-six-hour train ride from Aleppo—immediately.

Two days later, a trusted friend in Aleppo, who is a medical doctor and poet, offers to get to the bottom of the delay in my appointment by setting up a meeting with an important friend of a friend of his at the University of Aleppo. We enter the office of this friend of a friend, who turns out to be none other than the head of the French Department who had recently been promoted to one of the vice dean positions, and whom I had already met several times. He merely reiterates what we already know, in a kind and soft-spoken voice, and pleads general ignorance. I suggest that he call the president while we are sitting there, since I know discussions are taking place with the Ministry of Education at that very moment—I even have the phone number! He responds that he is merely a professor of French literature and only trying to help. He asks if we instead want to see the other vice dean next door. I reluctantly agree, and after we enter her office I realize it is none other than the sympathetic and ever-friendly but evasive woman on whom I had recently forced a second visiting card.

She must have felt a bit sheepish for not having contacted me as she had promised, but if so she never lets on. Thoroughly pleasant and commiserative, as usual, she acknowledges for the first time that she knew of my problems, and she acknowledges openly that Dr. Lababidi does not want me to teach in the English Department, a fact, she reveals, that was reiterated the day before in a meeting with others present, including the head of the History Department. She does not explain why this meeting took place or why I was a point of discussion, but I suspect it took place at the insistence of the Ministry of Education. At the meeting, she explains, she and the head of History had both argued that anthropology included literature and language and economy and had much to offer students and faculty. "I know anthropology," she tells me, "I have even read some Malinowski."

"He's very important," I replied, "the founding father of modern fieldwork."

But, says the vice dean, Dr. Lababidi remains unconvinced and adamant about her point-of-view.

I mention that both in Damascus and Latakia people are eager to have me teach, and immediately. I do not understand, I say, the reason for the resistance and delays in Aleppo. How could one woman, who herself is ignorant of my own qualifications and of the discipline I teach, block directives of the university president and the Ministry of Education?

This dean, like the other one, is unwilling to go there, which I suspect would probably have been to a discussion of the role of the Ba'ath Party in university politics. She replies that people in Latakia are more open than in Aleppo, and actually I'd be happier there. I should take them up on their offer. Perhaps that is true, I say, but I have an apartment here, my residency permit is through Aleppo University, and the Fulbright agreement with the Ministry of Education is to teach here.

"We begin with the base here, and the base is the department, which controls what is taught," she explains.

"But the base is different than policy," says my friend, suddenly agitated and impatient with this drivel, "and certainly she must follow general policy, as set forth by the Ministry of Education." The vice dean merely shrugs her shoulders, helplessly. I tell her of my alternative plan, to go outside the departments and give public lectures at the university. I ask, "If the president gives an order that I give some lectures, who would follow up on it? Is there any way people here, like the deans, might actually execute his orders, set up a room, do publicity?"

"I would be personally happy to do so," she replies, "to set things up, if he asks us to. We all have something to gain from this."

Two days later, the trusted Syrian employee at the ACC calls the president, who had been in meetings with the Ministry of Education the previous few days. The president verbally reaffirms his commitment to my presence at the University of Aleppo; I should not go and teach elsewhere in Syria. He agrees to my proposal for public lectures and film showings. But he requests a letter from the ACC at the U.S. Embassy outlining these lectures and says it will take a week for him to respond. He also specifies two people, the vice dean who had been removed from his duties and a linguist, to be given the assignment to organize the lectures through the Program in International Relations, which had been put to sleep the previous year but apparently could now be revived. All correspondence is completed within a week, and I receive a note, in Arabic, that the university is eager to have me teach in practically any department of my choice—"Faculty of Arts and Humanities, Department of English Language, Philosophy and Archaeology . . . Faculty of Architecture."

My initial thought is to take a copy of this letter to every department head in the Faculty of Arts and Humanities who might have consented in the earlier attempt to prevent me from teaching in Aleppo, but to act as if each one personally had actually supported me, and to thank them profusely for their support. A friend advises me to wait.

"But we are homophobic!"

Three months after my arrival in Aleppo, I give the first of four lectures at the university. Students approach me after each, and invariably invite me to their homes for dinner with their parents. One night, Aref, a quiet, waiflike twenty-two-year-old student, organizes a dinner. We had met not at the university but through other students who invited him to join us one evening at a hammam. By coincidence, several hours before we rendezvous, Basil, the advanced student who is translating some of my essays and stays with me when he visits Aleppo, calls to say he will be arriving shortly. I quickly call Aref to ask if I can bring Basil along. "Of course," he says. This is convenient, I think, because I can ask Basil to translate some of the conversation this evening.

Aref and several friends meet us in the city center, and we take a taxi to Aref's home, a large apartment in a new middle-class housing complex about ten kilometers from the city center. The taxi driver is angry because we squeeze, sardinelike, six into a car that legally carries only four, and he complains the whole trip. We unpack and get out of the car, and give the driver a large tip. The complex looks barren and desolate, as the landscape around Aleppo is flat and rocky with few trees. It is still a construction site, with many partially completed buildings, and piles of stone and pieces of plasterboard lying around. This is, the students tell me, one of the new suburbs around Aleppo that are built with new money repatriated from family members who work in the Gulf. Alongside these upscale neighborhoods are illegal squatter communities of incredibly poor people who live in shacks. A few of them manage to send their children to the tuition-free public universities. Free access to education is one of the services the Ba'athist regime still provides, despite an increasingly dire federal budget, in accordance with its official socialist ideology of egalitarianism.

Aref's father greets us at the door, and several other classmates arrive shortly. He seats us in the parlor, a square-shaped room with throne-size chairs and two sofas situated along the walls. The room is lit by fluorescent lights, effectively removing the shadows and softness of surfaces, framing us all in an unflattering glare. The students ask me many questions about study in the United States: curriculum demands, general problems, costs, how to fit in as Muslims, places where they can pray, what they can discuss with other students without getting into trouble, if they can express critical opinions.

"Who should we make friends with?" they ask.

"Anyone you like or find friendly," I say.

"Are there Muslims in American colleges?"

"Yes, of course, many, but religion in college is only as important as you want to make it."

"What about food?" they ask, and it dawns on me that in some small towns Islamic dietary prescriptions—specifically the eating of halal meat—will not be that easy to hold to. But I don't want to alarm them, so I simply explain that there are choices in most places and they can find or eat whatever kind of food they like.

"How can we make sure we don't eat pork?" another chimes in.

"Americans generally do not eat that much pork," I say, "and no one will try to deceive you."

"Maybe we should hang out with Jews; at least we can eat the same things as they do," one student concludes. The others seem to agree with this conclusion and do not follow it up, as if satisfied. I am amused by their pragmatism, since it is unlikely that any of these students has ever met a Jew (the last group left Aleppo in 1994), and Syrian government propaganda is relentlessly anti-Israel. Members of Aleppo's modern Jewish community—once considered the crown jewel of the Sephardic world—were mostly refugees from the Spanish Inquisition, part of the wave that fled Spain in 1492, and renowned for their skills in commerce, banking, and crafts. The Great Synagogue dating from the fifteenth century still stands, under the protection of the Department of Antiquities, three blocks from the Souk al-Medina, its floor about ten feet below ground, a reminder of how cities grow by building on top of ruins. Though closed to the public, it has a sign on its door stating it should be respected as "historical property"—there is no mention of religion, though people in the neighborhood know what it is, of course, and many men use one of the outside corners as a urinal, precisely what the sign forbids. When President Assad recently received a Jewish delegation (which also visited Aleppo), the media described the visitors not as *Jehudi* but as "followers of Moses" (Moses is also worshipped by Muslims). The founding of the state of Israel in 1948 produced the first wave of Jewish emigration out of Syria, as well as the first large flow of Palestinian refugees into Syria. Since then, the Syrian government has often taken the lead among Arab states in criticizing Israel, but this message has obviously not had the effect of demonizing Jews among this group of students. They have no problem imagining hanging out with Jews in another setting; they do not appear to hold any deeply felt anti-Jewish sentiments.

"What about lesbians and homosexuals?" one asks.

"What about them?"

"How do we avoid them?"

"They are everywhere, you know, in every institution." I say, "You have to get used to it."

"But it is an abomination, a sin," says another.

"They are humans just like you. As with Christians, you'll like some and not like others. And if you do not want to have sex with someone, just say no. People will accept that."

"But we are homophobic!" exclaims another, undoubtedly exasperated by my unwillingness to yield to their prejudice.

I am stunned that he even knows this English word: "homophobic." Perhaps it comes from an awareness of the recent debates in the United States on gay marriage, a topic about which I hope to lecture. But I have not yet lectured anyone on anything, and since these students do not read newspapers, they most likely heard the term on American cable television. So he thinks he is homophobic even though he does not behave that way! This is completely at odds with American or European homophobia, where the concept originates and is widely disseminated. By contrast, many Americans behave homophobically but do not think of themselves as acting that way.

At any rate, I do not take him seriously. He is not who he says he is. I smile, and say, "Get over it. You'll have to leave your phobias in Syria. Learn to accept people for what they do, for how they relate to you. As long as someone is not injuring you, how they live is not your concern."

"But it is wrong," says another student, adamantly rejecting my ethical relativism. "It is against nature."

The tenacity of their questioning surprises me, and I am thinking: Why are they asking ME? I resist my inclination to respond reflexively. Some of my Syrian acquaintances who have a lot of sex with men (they are also invariably married, and most have sex with their wives also) have told me that if anyone asks them about homosexuality, they have learned to just deny everything—and then have sex. In other words, they do what I might consider "having sex" but do not call it that. The worst thing to do, what ends all communication, is to say one is interested in sex. To speak the word, "sex," this Western word, changes the way people think about what they do. So there is, at least unconsciously, a kind of high-wire act going on here, where the students, who clearly want some kind of friendship with me, are also pressing for an utterance that would foreclose that possibility. In the United States or in Europe, I would not have much patience with the assertion "we are homophobic," but here I sense that the students are genuinely curious but awkward in their language use. They are uttering words, strongly evocative words, without being emotionally invested in their meanings, rehearsing arguments without being much concerned about the outcome. At least I notice no emotional stress, no avoidance of looks, no raising of the voice; they give no sign of being disturbed by the issues.

I move into the professorial mode again, reluctant to question them in front of each other about their own knowledge. I explain that homosexual behavior is present in all species; most ducks cannot even tell the male from female. I stop myself. I dislike using these analogies from other animals or even other primates. Ultimately, human behavior cannot be explained or justified with reference to that of other species.

"Should we date?" another student switches the topic.

"Yes, of course. As much as you want," I say.

"Can we marry an American?"

"Why not? Marry several times," I say, "so you know what it is like. But if you don't marry, you should definitely have sex anyway."

"We cannot do that; it is not allowed."

"Then you will not likely be able to find an American or European to marry," I say, "because most women your age in the U.S., women who will be open and friendly with you, will want to have sex first, I suspect, to know what you are like."

They tell me about a special American Fulbright program for Syrian students to complete their bachelor's degree at U.S. colleges, called Partnerships for Learning Undergraduate Studies (PLUS). Several of them have applied. Last year, they say, the Americans selected six girls, no boys. There are about ten students in this room with me; three of them made the short list and were invited to Damascus for an interview.

I ask why they think no boys were accepted last year.

"Girls have higher grades," one explains, "because they do not work and have more time to study."

"In my experience," I say, "what matters is how time is structured and not the amount of free time. Anyway, isn't cleaning and cooking work?"

They insist that housework is not comparable to the kind of work they do. I ask a boy wearing a baseball cap if he had come to any of my lectures.

"No," he says, "I couldn't come because I am working for my father."

I ask the others where they work. Six answer this question, and five of them work for their father, four (including Aref) full-time.

Aref's father and brother then enter, and Aref points to his brother and says, "Can you believe that we are brothers?" His brother stands about 5 feet 10 inches and weighs well over 200 pounds, Aref is about 5 feet 5 inches and weighs perhaps 110. In addition to being small and skinny, what stands out about Aref—his Arabic name means "I know"—are his ears, bat ears that attach at a nearly 90-degree angle to his head.

I do not mention the ears, but say, "Yes, it is possible, with computer imaging, you add a few pounds to yourself, take a few from your brother. Perhaps then."

We move to the dining room, which also serves as an Ottoman-style living room except for the fluorescent glare of the lights. We are seated on pillows around a rug, spread out in the middle, on which huge amounts of food are placed. Instead of utensils, everyone is given pita bread to tear into pieces and use to dip up the usual diverse assortment of treats: hummus, baba ghanoush, tabbouleh, french fries, lamb kabobs, garlic cream, grilled chicken chunks, baked kibbeh with pistachio nuts, *muhammara*. Eating this way is an awkward and dangerous practice for me, as I invariably tend to dribble the juice from something, regardless of how careful I am, on the front of my shirt or pants. Tonight it is even more difficult as I cannot sit comfortably on the floor. The week before I had badly sprained an ankle falling, with my suitcase, down a flight of stairs in Damascus. I cannot fold one leg under me, so I keep adjusting my position. While eating the focused discussion breaks down into many small conversations.

We wash our hands and return to the parlor for tea and coffee and continue discussion, this time including Aref's father, brother, and uncle.

The conversation turns to religion. One student begins by asserting that Islam is the only true and complete religion, that Allah is the all-knowing and the Koran the perfect book—unlike the Bible, which was compiled by different authors and revised. He asks if I agree with this, and I say no, I do not think there is such a thing as a complete religion. Students then rapidly fire a series of big questions:

Where do you think we come from? (We do not know for sure, but I hold to the big bang theory.)

Do you believe in an afterlife? (I don't know and have no way of knowing.)

Predestination? (That's a hard one for me to be agnostic about; there is no evidence whatsoever. "Without that, we're lost," says Ziyad, with a worried laugh, "We need it." I realize from his response that he is listening closely and taking seriously the consequences of acknowledging any truth in what I say.)

What is the meaning of life without God? (It is what we make it to be. I keep emphasizing that science cannot answer these questions either; it can only address certain things. Belief begins where facts are insufficient or inadequate to explain. The question is, when facts are insufficient, what do I do for explanation? I do not then resort to belief, but I remain in doubt. I do not believe in certain things because I do not need to; I do not need this security of knowing everything that is unknowable. What need do I have to believe in predestination? I explain that as a child I desired to believe in predestination, to explain how I was born into a family unlike me, a family that did not take thought that seriously, that did not aspire to be artists or intellectuals. But today I do not need to believe that; I have other explanations for my difference.)

Aref's father asks, "In your opinion, what do you think of Muslims and Arabs?"

This is a difficult question to answer. He wants to know, I suspect, not just what I think but what the West thinks, what America thinks, and why Americans are anti-Islam, and why there seems to be no economic or political progress in Arab countries. It is a question Americans would never pose, certainly not in this form, not from this location of vulnerability. He searches not for a compliment but for an explanation of a negative representation that he has internalized. Those present begin a series of rapid-fire questions in Arabic. I ask Basil to translate, and again I slip into the professor mode. What else can I do? I try to give as clear and succinct and honest an answer as possible. I am not an expert on Islam or the Arabs, I say, so this is only my opinion. First, all world religions—Judaism, Islam, Christianity, Buddhism, for example—are similar. Most came about in an "Axial Age," a turn away from mythical explanations to intense reflection on the meaning and nature of life, and, as they organize and become institutions, they become forms of politics, too. So, first, religions are not simply systems of explanation, ways of expressing spiritual needs or addressing God but ways of exercising power. That is the status of some Christian sects, especially the "evangelicals" in the United States today who are, in my opinion, more concerned with exercising power than with spiritual questions.

Second, I say, what makes Arabs singular is not the same as what makes Islam peculiar. Arabs are unusual today, in my opinion, in that you are all ruled by dictatorial states that prevent political and cultural development, and then there is the oil wealth in the Gulf— one single external factor—that has a distorting effect on the social systems and religion of all Arabs. As for Islam, I think the religion is in a crisis, that what it lacks as a religion is a reformation, or if there have been reformations, the most influential mullahs do not recognize them. What reformation does for Christianity is build into the religion a sense of critique of itself, of renewal, of the search for alternatives. There is, to my knowledge, no similar process within Islam today, at least not that I observe in Syria.

The students do not agree with these claims, and several vehemently dispute them. There is a tradition of reformation within Islam also, they protest. I ask for an example, but nobody responds. I explain that Sufism could be understood as one possible source of renewal, but that in Aleppo all the Sunnis I know dismiss Sufism as heretical, outside Islamic religion. They do not consider Sufism as internal to Islam because, they say, it is not in the Koran. This insistence that everything is already in the Koran, I reply, prevents active thinking about the need for reform.

The students react aggressively but politely. What they are hearing is heresy. If I were a Muslim, they would condemn me as an apostate, but then again, I would not be here; they would not have invited me. They say that I am overgeneralizing, based on a Christian understanding of Muslims, without having read the Koran. "Have you ever read the Koran?" they ask, several times.

"No," I admit, "but why would reading the Koran necessarily lead me to believe its content? Belief is about something else, about the inability to maintain doubt, the need for answers without proof." They insist I would find the Koran perfect and complete if I read it. My understanding of religion, I reply, is not Christian but scientific—science applied to the practice of religion, or in this instance, applied to the use of holy books. I am fully conscious while speaking that in the American or European context I would never attribute to science this kind of explanatory power, or situate myself unequivocally as a scientist. Anthropological understandings, like those in the humanities and social sciences generally, are at best highly probable bets, established with more-or-less rigor and subject to certain forms of verification. But they are historical understandings, the best available at specific times, and cannot claim conclusive proof, nor should they be asked to. I risk replacing a religious dogma with a scientific one. But here I sense that these students have no real understanding of the reach and power of science and its historical relation to belief. I simplify.

"Science does not answer certain questions because it cannot answer them, given its methods of discovery, rules of evidence and proof. But many religions claim to have answers to these questions. Science is simply agnostic on these questions. And I myself have no answers to them." But, I add, since many of the students present study literature, they might think of themselves as literary critics, and they might read the Koran with the same skills they use to read other texts, which means that the text is not complete without a reader, that the reader must interpret the text, and that readers come to different understandings of what it means because they ask different questions, questions that are a product of their specific experiences and histories.

Basil is doing a fantastic job of translating my responses into Arabic, even elaborating certain things about which I am cryptic, and he clearly enjoys this moment, as he is the one usually introducing skepticism to others. Here he talks but is not responsible for my words. After a period of silence, I return to the issue of language and speech, and explain that a word is not the same thing as it describes, that this difference—a problem of semiotics, of symbolism and interpretation—is what makes us humans, a species unlike others. If words symbolize, then they mean different things in different contexts. Water, for instance, means many things to humans, but it means only one thing for animals. Among humans we symbolize water differently—"H_2O," for instance—or we make a distinction between holy water and drinking water. These symbols must be interpreted. The Koran is not complete itself, but is completed by readers, as are all holy books. Therefore, we have experts—mullahs, priests, rabbis—who are very human, very fallible, not perfect, who disagree about the meaning of holy books. Within Catholicism, for example, the Pope now claims infallibility—he speaks directly to and for God—but popes disagree with each other, even reverse each other over time. So, I conclude, knowing that I have given them a potted version of religious theory, but wanting, at the same time, to use this as an opportunity to understand how they might respond to this kind of questioning, "God may be perfect but we understand his word imperfectly."

I guess we cannot go any further, concludes Ziyad, and the students seem resigned without being convinced. There is too much at stake for them to be convinced; they would have to give up too much. This is all too much; the exchange is too new for them to accept what I say as true. I am perversely satisfied at having brought them to this place of philosophical discomfort, which is, I admit, comfortable for me. They now doubt me—the truth of what I say—without necessarily rejecting me, and therefore are positioned as agnostics, a term that is alien to their religious teachings. Anyhow, I think of my role not as convincing them beyond a doubt but as introducing doubts into their understandings, questions that they may later, in my absence, entertain. I tell them that reaching points where you cannot go further is good in that impasses are necessary to understand the limits of one's own thought; where communication fails is where understanding might begin. Progress in thought is impossible with agreement alone. Before I leave, one student takes me aside and says, yes, he agrees; Arabs, he says, have no concept of reformation because they insist everything must be traced back to the Koran, which they assume to be complete. It is unlikely that he is the only student who concurs, and I sense that in some cases students are trying to get me to express opinions or doubts that they themselves wish to utter but are unable to. Moreover, such settings as this are known for several levels of surveillance (not just spies, but also spies spying on spies) and, as I was to learn later, someone present did report our conversation to the Mukhabarrat.

"So, what do you think of Muslims?"

When I arrive in Aleppo, the owner of my apartment in the souk tells me that I should use the public bath—el Hammam Nahasin—across the street, "You can get a scrub. They are very good and cheap and open all night." The shower in my apartment is a simple stone stall directly next to the toilet bowl, functional but not very aesthetic, whereas the hammam is an elaborate maze of semiprivate and fully public rooms, with sauna, swimming pool, and a large slightly cooler entrance room with a marble fountain in the middle, and niches of various sizes where you undress and dress and recover from the heat of the bath, and can also order tea or coffee or even enjoy a meal. So on my third evening in the city, a half hour before midnight, I arrive by taxi—fifty cents for a short ride from the old city center—at the entrance to the Citadel, and from there walk through the dark, empty, and cavernous-appearing souk to the door to my khan. I get my keys out but turn around, tempted to look inside the hammam, a gesture I subsequently repeat nightly, and hesitate: the two men in charge motion for me to come in. The hammam is below street level, from another era, much like the Great Synagogue, on top of which the present-day souk rests. The hammam tenders sit below, smile, beckon as if they know me, and in all likelihood they do; by now all the workers on my street know me, or know of me.

They had undoubtedly seen me fumbling with my keys the last two nights. Entering my khan after everyone has left the souk is an ordeal: first I open the small padlock on the small three-foot iron door inside the huge eighteen-foot iron door, crawl through, then open the huge padlock on the huge iron door, then muscle the door open a crack to go back outside to lock the small padlock, return inside and muscle the huge door shut, relock it, and then wander upstairs in the dark, feeling my way around if there is no moonlight, to open a gate on the first floor, and finally open the human-friendly door to the apartment.

I usually tell people that I live near the Citadel, across from the Hammam Nahasin in the Souk al-Medina—three local landmarks. There are two signs outside; one reads "HAMAM ALNOHSIM," the other "HAMMAM EL NAHASIN (NAHASIN BATH) 13th A.D.-C.7th H." Transliteration of Arabic into English is notoriously arbitrary. Places seem to take poetic license with their own names, not because people cannot decide how to spell a name in English but because they play with the sound. In emails to me people have even spelled it "Nahasine," or "Nahosine." And if I were to spell it in English by sounding out the written Arabic letters phonetically, it would read "hammAm a-na-hAseen"—but that is a rule more to the taste of the Englishman or German than to the Arab.

Tonight appears to be family night, and unlike in the center of cosmopolitan Damascus, most hammam visits in Aleppo are family

Figure 11. Entrance to Khan al-Nahasin

affairs, gatherings of male relatives for an evening out. Aleppian hammams are certainly not like the bathhouses and saunas in European cities, which tend to function both as places for relaxation after sport and sexual pickup joints. At Hammam Nahasin boys of all ages run around in packs, screeching, jousting, joking, eating, picking on the errant stranger. Adult men sit among themselves, talking, drinking tea, taking turns sitting in the steam room, just outside it against the large marble stone at the center, or in a side room getting massaged. Or they retire back to the entrance room itself, to one of the niches that surround the central marble fountain, to change clothes, drink, rest, sleep, talk, play backgammon, or watch television.

Upon entering, you are offered a short wrap-around bath towel and wooden clogs. The youngest boys are all naked, but many men have brought their own bath attire. Some wear a kind of cotton pajama pants, a few bathing suits—speedos or standard swim trunks. One man wears what looks like tight-fitting underwear, which clings to the crevice in his buttocks when wet and is much more revealing than if he had worn the traditional towel wrap. Men share much physical contact with other men, as do men with boys, and boys with boys, sitting side-by-side, arms around the shoulder, leaning on or against each other, stroking arms, legs, backs, holding hands.

The atmosphere in this hammam—and they are not all the same—is sensual, even erotic, but the sexual overtones are very discreet if not fully subliminal. Fathers and sons (those older than six or seven) assert a dominant presence, and men caress their sons when the boys are not running wildly. Fathers hold sons between their legs, sit them on their knees. I think of the American scandal around the coerced nudity at the Abu Ghraib prison in Iraq, which men in Aleppo sometimes invoke as a joke about maltreatment that is beyond the limits of acceptable. "My wife punished me for being late last night . . . but not like Abu Ghraib." Or "My father . . . but not like Abu Ghraib." For these men at the hammam, nudity presents no problem; it is the content and the coercion, especially at the hands of an occupying force from the West, that they regard as humiliating. For American soldiers and the American media, on the other hand, flesh, the public showing of flesh, was itself central to their image of how to humiliate Arab men.

In one of the relatively open basined bathing corners, I use a finely decorated brass bowl to pour water over myself, and I wash thoroughly with the olive oil soap that I purchased on entering. After some time in the steam room, I wash again in cold water in adjoining rooms. In a connecting passage just outside the major steam and bath area where men cool off, two long marble benches face each other, with four or five boys and young men on each, and as I look for a seat, the boys on one bench squeeze together to make room for me. I take the opportunity to practice my Arabic. They ask who I am, and guess: French, German, Swedish, Danish, Dutch, English. And finally, American? That was unexpected.

I am particularly tired from trying to speak in Arabic only the whole day. People understand me—"He speaks *foos-ha*" (classical Arabic), men politely tell their children, puzzled at the way I speak their language, my accent, my diction, my choice of words—but I strain with limited success to speak and to understand them. Boys aged ten to twenty-five fill the other spaces on my bench, and on the one across from me.

A young man with luscious lips, crooked teeth, and a most exquisitely sculpted chest comes over to my bench, directing the boy on my right to change places with him. He introduces himself as Abdella; he speaks English well and is an English major in at the university. Even though he took it upon himself to approach me, he seems shy. His eyes are quiet and inactive, his soft brown hair has curled from the heat of the sauna and reveals a prominent forehead. He asks if I am married. No, I say, and then talk about myself, making it a point to emphasize that I will be teaching at Aleppo University this fall. Abdella's eyes light up. He introduces his uncle, only a few years older, sitting across from us, and his cousin, who is studying theology in Dubai because, he says, the libraries there are better.

"Better than Damascus?" I ask.

"Oh yes, better," he replies.

We go down the line of boys and young men sitting on the benches: age, relation, interests—all family, a family reunion. It is Abdella's very first time in this sauna, he says. Some of the boys are living in Damascus, some in Dubai, some in Saudi Arabia. One cousin, the oldest in the group, asks, "So what do you think of Muslims?"—a question I have already come to expect.

"I think they are no different than other people; they just practice another religion," I say.

He responds, "Then why do we have the problems we do now with the rest of the world?"

No equivocation here, but his response suggests that he is seriously puzzled at how his own self-perception can be so at odds with the "rest of the world." I try to be equally direct: "The problems within Islam today have something to do with Saudi money and the influence of this money on Islamic movements," I explain. "There would be the same problems within Christianity today if American Christian fundamentalists took over European Christianity. They would radicalize the religion." They listen attentively; the older boys nod as if in agreement. It reassures them to hear, from me, that they are not the problem.

"Another problem with Islam today," I add, "is that nearly all political regimes in which Islam is practiced do not allow people like you to matter, to have a voice, and that encourages radical resistance."

Another cousin asks, "Why does America hate Islam so much?"

"This is a different question, and needs another kind of answer. Perhaps you would first like to tell me what you think."

The two cousins then offer different explanations, one having to do with control over oil, the other with Israeli dominance in American affairs. I find this group of young men genuinely curious, refreshingly undogmatic. The older cousin asks if I am a scientist, and when I say yes, he defines science as forms of explanation that eliminate emotional bias.

"That's wishful thinking," I say, and smile at his spirit of generosity. "Science has more to do with rigor of thought, and an experimental method that questions common assumptions. Science may strive for objectivity, but it does not eliminate emotion."

It is getting late, it is hot, and I am tiring, so I thank them for the exchange and excuse myself. The cousin studying in Dubai says, "My house is yours, please visit me anytime in Dubai." Abdella reaffirms that he definitely wants to take my class, whatever it is, at the university, and he expresses the wish that I teach in the English Department so he can get credit for it. We arrange to exchange language lessons, and he promises to call me soon.

"My friends will be very impressed that I met you," he says. He accompanies me out, and I give him two calling cards. "Will you remember me when I call?" he asks.

"Of course," I say, "don't worry, I will be waiting."

"I'd like to be the next president"

I ask the men in Khan Nahasin below my apartment if there is a laundromat somewhere in the souk. They look puzzled, as they expect all apartments to come with washing machines. The next day Rami, an economics student who holds three jobs and speaks excellent English, comes to solve my problem. The business he works for in my khan has sent him. He is a well-groomed young man with a symmetrical, round face, a finely trimmed beard and mustache, black hair, small fine hands, and alert black eyes that wait and respond thoughtfully. His clean image makes him look pious to me, but that's merely an inference. He smiles pleasantly and asks why there is no washing machine in the apartment (there in fact is—I just cannot find it), since custom has it that the owner supplies one; he offers to take my laundry home with him. Two days later, I go to the shop where he works and pay him; my clothes are now clean and pressed. I ask if he knows someone who might want to exchange English for Arabic lessons. Rami says he is too busy, but his assistant, Ahmed, pipes up that he would like to, and from then on Ahmed appears daily at my door, an hour before work, four or five times a week. Our half-hour English, half-hour Arabic lessons soon turn into mostly English discussions, and I become friends with Ahmed, who studies economics one day a week in Latakia. Soon he also begins doing research for me on property inheritance in the souk.

He likes visiting me in part, I assume, because of my unusual apartment, in a building constructed in its present form in 1599. In fact, although people do not understand why I might want to live in the souk, everyone loves visiting me. It is rare for a man to have an apartment alone, and if he does, it would probably be used only for sex. The few people who stay single tend to live with their parents,

Figure 12. American Consulate

regardless of age. When Western intellectuals visit me, they especially love the books on all the bookshelves; in my work room the books I brought for teaching and reading, old *New Yorker* magazines, cameras and a tape recorder, notebooks pocket-size and large; and in the sitting room maps, world gazettes, and nineteenth-century French and Italian gazettes and journals with summaries of political and cultural events in Europe written explicitly for the expatriate or to nurse a European-identification from abroad. The woman who owns this apartment, Jenny, traces her lineage back to the early Austrian and Italian consulate families and the caravan trade.

When I visit Aleppo's Christian cemeteries, I find it hard to orient myself among the large but clearly demarcated number of sects: Maronites, Latins, Greek Catholics, Greek Orthodox, Armenian Catholics, Armenian Orthodox, Syrian Catholics, Syrian Orthodox, Chaldaen Catholics, Nestorians, and Protestants. In the Latin (or Roman Catholic) section, I run into the big tombstone that marks

Figure 13. Christian Cemetery

the grave of Jenny's family. Most Friday mornings, when the Muslims are praying and the souk is empty, she visits the apartment across from mine, the former Belgian consulate, where she was raised, and conducts private tours of the residence. Her grandfather was a doctor of medicine and a great humanist, who had studied with Freud in Vienna, invented the first antimalaria vaccine, written a novel, and gathered together a magnificent collection of Roman mosaics, Arabic pottery, Chinese ceramics, Hittite statuary, Palmyra bas reliefs, and Persian carpets—a testament to the cosmopolitanism of Aleppo's history.

Several months into my stay, Jenny confides, "When I initially considered renting the apartment to you, I thought twice, because you are an American. Maybe I don't want this responsibility, but, I thought, you are at the university, it is not my responsibility, they will take care of any problems." I tell her about my work with people in the souk, and my problems at the university. "Don't ask," she says, "people will be suspicious; just let them tell you." Shortly before I leave Aleppo, she says, "I actually think you are very brave for coming here, not knowing anyone and living in the souk alone."

I, however, think of my stay in her apartment in the souk as more fortunate than brave. It's how I meet Ahmed, who, unlike the Western tourists, takes little interest in these nineteenth-century artifacts. He is more curious about the technologies I brought with me, but even that interest is limited, partly by politeness. He himself has a computer and an Internet connection at home, as do many of the young men I meet in the souk. My machinery is not that new to him. What interests him more is how I put it to use, how I use machines to learn. I give Ahmed a *New Yorker* "Talk of the Town" article on economic crisis, and suggest we discuss it the next session. It proves way too difficult—it took him several hours to work through ten lines—so instead I decide to narrate in English and to read brief passages in short stories about America and then discuss what he understands in Arabic.

I begin with "A Good Man Is Hard to Find," the brilliant short story by Flannery O'Connor that I brought along to teach. Ahmed seems to follow events until we get to the end, where the Misfit, who had escaped from the Federal Pen, murders (or has his accomplices murder) a whole family—the father Bailey, his wife, their two children John Wesley and June Star, the baby, and finally the grandmother. Why, I ask Ahmed, does he think the Misfit, after having all the other family members killed, ultimately himself shoots the grandmother three times in the chest? Ahmed speculates that the grandmother perhaps had a knife and intended on killing him. I ask him if perhaps the grandmother provoked in the Misfit another kind of fear, a fear of memory of his own misdeeds and the cruelty of his family that the grandmother, in her incessant talking about good and evil, had brought to the surface. But Ahmed wants to believe in the goodness of all, and he cannot help but think that the murder is a response to an actual threat; the Misfit could not have murdered for "fun" or due to an unconscious psychological reaction.

On September 11, Ahmed shows up with Rami, who wants to take part in the English lesson also. I ask them about the anniversary of 9/11. Rami says, "I have a very strange feeling watching the pictures. How could they have been so unprepared for three planes? Where was the National Guard?"

The event coincides with an Islamic religious holiday, says Ahmed, and in his mosque the imam did mention it, briefly, and expressed sympathy for the victims. "This kind of act, he says, "is against Islam." I question the two of them on whether Islamic ideas of martyrdom cannot also be used to support such attacks. They say, and repeat vehemently, "It is wrong for a Muslim to kill innocent people."

"What would happen if they did this on Christmas?" Ahmed speculates. I state my opinion that bin Laden picked neither religious nor national symbols or holidays, such as Christmas or Independence Day, but something that symbolized American economic power and international ties—the World Trade Towers.

We discuss Michael Moore's film *Fahrenheit 9/11*, which showed for a month in Damascus before making it to Aleppo. I go several times myself, in both cities, to get a sense of the audience reaction. Each time the public is lively and engaged, laughing in spots, respectfully hushed in others. A friend who went to one of the first showings in Damascus, in a cinema next door to a hotel frequented by Saudis, says the audience sat stunned throughout, quietly absorbing the different personal stories, alternately laughing and crying. Rami and Ahmed say they were moved and shocked by the scenes of the planes ramming through the tall towers and exploding.

Ahmed personally is fond of the episode where Bush gazes emptily into space during the reading of the "My Pet Goat" story. When I go, the theaters are close to sold out. The audience is genuinely touched by the story of the woman who lost her son in the war; some women in the audience wail along with her when she cries.

In October, Ahmed and I discuss elections. The Kerry-Bush American presidential campaigns are in full swing, and widely reported in the Arabic media. Ahmed says the key question posed by most people here is whether Kerry has a different policy regarding Palestine, or the Arabs and Israel, than Bush. The difference is difficult to articulate, I say, because the proposed policies are, in fact, indistinguishable, though I suspect that in practice Kerry might not be so one-sided in his support of Ariel Sharon. But I can cite no public statements to support my opinion. Ahmed concludes that if he could vote he would support whoever was good for him and Syria; he would not consider the issue of Palestine above all others. Some other men in the souk tell me that they would support Bush because they know what he stands for; they do not know what Kerry would do. Several friends insist that they should be allowed to vote for the American President, as U.S. policies also affect Syrians, perhaps even more dramatically than most Americans. They argue for a form of world participation in American elections.

During the festival of Eid, Ahmed gains about ten pounds, and for several months he has jowls and a slight belly and begins to look chubby. He reveals to me that he is depressed, and says that because I am his friend he wants my advice. He is depressed about his future. "What future?" he asks. The threat of military service hangs over his head. He would like to leave and work in the Gulf to escape military service, but does not have the contacts for that. English is a struggle for him; he senses no progress. He does not have a girl-friend, and has never had one. Women do not take to him, he says, and he doesn't really know them, know how to respond to them, to make conversation, or enjoy them. He has friends—male, he means—but he is not close to them. He does not earn enough on his current job to support himself; he relies on his parents for food and lives with them. He says that he joined the Ba'ath Party when he was sixteen, and attended their youth camp once, but he joined not for ideology—he does not carry the membership card with him—only for the networks, perhaps to get an economic advantage in the future. His father had joined as a young man also, but was expelled; then he rejoined five years ago. Nobody else in the family is a member. Thus far, he has experienced no benefits from membership, and the Party does not even contact him.

I try to put his problems in perspective: he is young, needs experience, and must complete his education before opportunities will arise. I say that I have confidence in him; he must have patience. I ask what he would really like to be. "I'd like to be the next president," he jokes, "failing that, economics minister, since that is what I am studying, or secretary of state."

By spring of 2005, Rami and Ahmed had both made some decisive changes. Rami quit two of his jobs, and now works only for his uncle, managing the crew at his factory. He will return to the university, to get a doctorate in economics, perhaps specializing in design and advertising. He thinks he must do something to change the image of Islam in the West, perhaps through advertising. Ahmed has two more years at the university to obtain his degree. He applied for a job as manager of a large shop that sells blankets, in another souk in one of Aleppo's suburbs, and got it, based on the interview and recommendations alone. It means even longer hours but also a big pay increase. After several months, he writes, "i am a little fat. i weigh 80 kg. i have problems in my life. i don't like anything (my family—my job—my cousin—my friend—my college—everything). my salory increased but it is not enough. it's a bad time in my life, but the good thing now, i see a girl in the road every time when i return to my home and i love her but i never talk with her."

"The religious people see this and hate it, but they cannot turn it off"

I visit Hammam Nahasin again in late October, this time with Basil, whom I am increasingly fond of for his self-deprecating and wry humor. He arrives in Aleppo in the late afternoon. I want to introduce him to an art gallery owner who had expressed interest in publishing a collection of my essays. The meeting is awkward, as Basil is polite and deferential, and does not want to assert himself. I cannot understand the gallery owner's vague responses. Is it my Arabic, or is he being noncommittal? He says I need not concern myself with the topic of my essays, as long as they are not critical of Syria; the censor will approve whatever he submits to publish. He wants to translate one of my books already published in English, but I explain that they are written about Germany and Europe for Western audiences. I would prefer to translate more recent essays on accountability that are more specifically relevant to people in Syria. I leave the meeting thinking he is flexible and wants me to submit for publication whatever I like, but I am still uncertain about the terms of his support.

Someone in the souk had told me there was an evening concert of classic music (I assumed Arabic) at the Citadel, so Basil and I trek up to the top, only to hear an Austrian choral group singing folk songs! Their performance confronts the limits of my cultural and historical horizons. It takes place in a Roman-like amphitheatre built in the middle of a castle, a one-of-a-kind fortress that was never conquered by the Crusaders (though later by the Ottomans). A senior Syrian archaeologist had earlier given me a private tour of the Citadel, and he explained that this amphitheatre existed only because a local politician thought it a good idea, but he himself, and the Department of Antiquities, had opposed building this "Roman monstrosity," inspired by first-century European architecture, in the middle of a thirteenth-century Arab ruin. Then, the Viennese choir! I have visited Vienna many times, and just outside Vienna is a monument to a Christian force (of German and Polish soldiers) that defeated a Turkish siege of the city in 1638, an event that for Austrians signifies an early and decisive defense of Christian Europe against Islam. I might have found the concert enjoyable if any attention were paid to these historical discontinuities, but there was merely a juxtaposition of unexplained ruins: early Austrian folk music, Roman amphitheatre, Arab castle. All traditions clinging to their origins, colliding out of place and time.

I can not put myself in the mood to listen, nor can Basil, so we decide to eat instead. We pick up some chicken and hummus at a nearby stand and take it back to my apartment. The evening is still young by Aleppo standards and after eating, Basil, who is a chain smoker, suddenly becomes aware that he has forgotten to buy enough cigarettes to last the night. He says he can buy some at Hammam Nahasin. I say, great, let's go to the hammam. Once inside, Basil grudgingly takes off his jeans and puts on one of the wraps they give us, but he refuses to remove his T-shirt. "I hate these kind of collective baths," he says, and adds, with a giggle, "I hate traditional things." He wants only cigarettes.

My efforts at convincing him to join me for a bath fail. "Okay," I finally say, "then you smoke out here"—I, in fact, detest smoking— "and I'll go in for a quick massage and loofah, a soapy scrub with a sponge made of rough hemp fibers. (Later Basil tells me that he envisioned merely drinking tea with me in the large outer room, without ever entering the bath part, but I had no idea that you could use the hammam without also using the bath. Miscommunication. In any case, I cannot resist the opportunity to interact with the public.)

I already have my bath towel wrapped around me, so I enter the steam area, and within minutes an attendant ushers me out again and directs me to an open space on the marble floor for my massage. I am disappointed I have no opportunity to enjoy the steam room first. Men and boys stand around, wandering in and out, noticing everything but going about their own business without much ado. The attendant hurriedly washes the floor and, in front of everybody, directs me to remove my bath towel and lie facedown. He proceeds businesslike with a massage and scrub, both far too quick and cursory for my tastes. Often the attendants—and certainly this one— have no feel for the body, and no sense that there might be pleasure in this for the customer. Nonetheless, after I am asked to lie on my back, I do enjoy looking up at the domed ceiling with its concentric circles of star-holes from which tiny trajectories of light beam into the room. These rooms always strike me as a mix between planetarium, health spa, café, and erotic bath.

When the attendant is done, he motions (for me to get up with a simple turn of his hand) and gives me a clean bath towel. I enter the next set of rooms, the steam room area, where a large group of about fifteen young men and boys are talking loudly, a smaller group of about six appear to be taking turns in the small steam room itself. All of the rooms radiate from central courtyards, of which there are two, and none of them have doors. Everything can be watched; even the sauna room opens directly onto a central courtyard, this one with a large marble stone in the middle for resting. It is the hottest part of the hammam. If someone wants privacy in one of the niche rooms with basined bathing corners, they, or an attendant, hang a towel or sheet in front of the entrance.

The steam room is empty when I enter. I sit for about ten minutes, and then retire to one of the long benches facing each other in the outer, cooler room. I say hello to the assembled youths, and a scene similar to my previous visit unfolds. A young man who reminds me of Omar Sharif smiles kindly and says hello. The boys on the bench across from him make room for me, and several others quickly join us, jostling each other for a space on the benches; a few stand.

"Where you from?" one asks.

"Ana Amreekee, " I say, meaning "I am American."

"Ameerkee," several repeat in unison, and I am confused whether I am identifying my own nationality correctly. Am-REE-kee or Am-EER-kee? Later, I ask a friend, who says, "Amreekee? Ameerkee? Same thing."

As the boys compete for positions, the one sitting next to me, upon hearing that I am American, stands up, and with great fanfare runs to the bench facing us. His enlarged eyes suggest to me parody, so I play along: I get up also, take his hand in mine, and pull him back to my side. He mocks resistance but ultimately submits. I put my around his shoulders, and assert that I am a friend of the Arabs and that we are friends, whereupon the tallest of them, an unattractive, chubby boy of about sixteen, jerks the young man next to me off the bench, plops himself down in his place, and cuddles up to me like a purring cat. He softly rests his head on my shoulder and tenderly caresses my hand. Just as abruptly, he points to another boy on the other bench. "That boy likes to get fucked," he proclaims, loudly, then leans back and lifts and spreads his legs. The other boys laugh. I wonder what I have gotten into.

There is a lot going on here, I think, some not-so-subliminal desire. But the lewdness suggests aggression, and I sense it might be good to de-escalate the situation. I practice my Arabic and begin talking about quotidian things, asking them where they live and go to school, telling them where I live (across the street), that I am a professor who will be teaching at the university. This does not much dissipate the tension. The boys are largely quiet except for bursts of shouting until several begin questioning me about how much I had paid for the sauna that night. As I had not yet paid, I initially do not understand the question. But then it occurs to me: they are trying to protect me from overpaying. They insist I pay a maximum of four dollars, for the massage and baksheesh, inclusive. I agree, though later I pay what the attendants ask me, ten dollars, including baksheesh.

All along, the young man who resembles Omar Sharif keeps smiling. He now stands up, asks me if I swim, and says there is a swimming pool in this hammam, which I had not seen on my first visit. He reaches for my hand and leads me through several corridors, the other boys close behind. His name is Khaled, and he lives in a suburb north of the souk. I melt as I look into his dark, attentive eyes and at his finely chiseled face. He is only about five foot six, with a perfectly proportioned body that initially makes me think he is a boy; most adult men are larger and carry a bit of fat. But his end-of-day beard stubble and hairy chest suggest a more distant puberty, perhaps even a man in his late twenties.

The boys become very loud again; they chant and sing, their sounds reverberating off the marble walls, floors, and ceilings; they jokingly slap each other. One attendant approaches and tells them to be quiet. Another asks me if they are giving me trouble. They answer for me, "He is okay. We are doing nothing wrong. Ask him. Ask him." I assure them all, I am fine.

The steam from the baths makes it hard to see clearly, and I don't have my glasses on—nearsightedness haunts me in hammams, but Khaled holds my hand tightly as he leads me to the pool. It is small, enough for perhaps three people abroad, two breaststrokes to the end. Three men are already in the pool, at the far end. I would love to swim nude, but that does not appear to be an option. Everyone is wearing trunks of some sort, while I have only a large long towel wrapped around me, and I fear it will come off in the water. The boys are adamant I swim and begin a chorus chanting, in Arabic, swim, swim, swim. Khaled finds a bath towel somebody left behind and rolls it into a belt that will prevent mine from coming undone. He carefully reaches around and ties the rolled bath towel around me.

Khaled and I jump in, followed by the guy who earlier made the lewd joke, who seems driven by an aggressive erotic mania, unwilling to declare me either friend or enemy. The other boys now stand and observe quietly. I swim the single stroke it takes to get to Khaled, who surprises me by putting his arms around me and pulling me to the pool's edge. I feel his breathing, and I feel his breath. My God, in front of the others, and they are definitely watching! Khaled lets go of me, I swim the length of the pool twice. The water is cold and does not seem that clean. We climb out together. The other boys are still watching. I tell them, now it is their turn, they must jump in also. Khaled himself jumps in again, dives, actually, and the others follow him.

I sit down on a bench in the back of the room. Khaled then joins me, sitting so close that our arms and legs rub against each other, even though there is plenty of room for him to create distance, if he liked. He tells me about himself: he lives with his parents, is not married, is not a student but works in a store. He repeats his name several times, I tell him where I live, again. He smiles. I think of poor Basil, waiting for me outside, and ask to be excused. I stand up. Khaled takes me by the hand again and leads me back out, where an attendant is eager to take over, baksheesh written all over his face. Khaled literally hands me to him, and we say goodbye. While sitting outside with Basil, I notice Khaled peek around the corner once to see if I am still there.

Basil is whiling away his time, drinking tea, watching television, bored, I am sure, but not much bothered by that, and he still has not smoked though he now has cigarettes. He reiterates his dislike for Syrian tradition. On the television is one of the ubiquitous Arab MTV-like stations, which is playing an Arab rock video that Basil says is the first import from the new Iraq. The lead dancer is a tall, leggy blonde (dyed hair, of course), and the camera darts back and forth from her legs to her long golden hair. When it pauses in the middle, she shimmies her ample breasts. The scenes of the video are cut to a quick tempo, and they become most frenzied in the whirr of her hair, which she aggressively and wildly flings around like the spin cycle of a washing machine. Nearly all such videos focus on a romantic encounter of man and woman. In this one, the leggy blonde is there to be seduced by the lead singer, a man, of course, who is older than her, fat, and remains fully clothed except for the few top buttons of his shirt that reveal a hairy chest. She—this modern, fully made-over figure—is the point of identification for the audience; she is the audience to be seduced by the singer and his love ballad. In other words, Tradition is to seduce the Modern.

"This is the new Iraq," declares Basil, with an ironic chuckle. "The religious people see this and hate it, but they cannot turn it off. They like to watch it, but it makes them angry. That is our problem. There is no in-between. Either this, or tradition. I hate Syrian tradition, especially the traditions that divide the sexes."

Basil is speaking from the heart, as yesterday, he explains, his girlfriend broke off their engagement. His studies require that he spend three days a week in Aleppo, and, he adds, his parents refuse to let him marry her because she is not educated enough, and she does not intend to study further. I ask if both parents agree on this.

"They disagree on almost everything but not on this," he chuckles.

So who is actually terminating the engagement, I wonder, his parents or his girlfriend?

"She called twice last night," he explains. "Once to say she'd call back, the second time she said nothing."

Basil is understandably saddened by this, perhaps depressed. Only last week he was riding a cloud, and confided in me that he had the most wonderful girlfriend in the world, that he was very happy with her. Now, he is forced to call it quits at what seems like the moment of falling-in-love. But he does not blame it on his parents, who offer him the kind of emotional and financial support no girlfriend could replace. And they think he can do better. He still loves the girl, he says, and will keep talking to her. "I owe her that," he says. His most bitter criticism is reserved for the social tradition that prevents young men and women from sharing in activities. Only after marriage will he be able to interact daily with any woman outside his mother and sisters, and then perhaps not with a woman he knows and likes. "We have total separation," he says, "and we cannot do anything without our parents' approval. Fathers here have power over you until death."

A month later, I take a bus to Homs, and Basil picks me up at the bus station. We walk across the street to the waiting taxi of a friend, who takes us to a collection of minibuses, where we catch one to his Alawite village. His father is a retired agricultural inspector and now supports himself as a small farmer growing olives, grapes, and pomegranates on very rocky soil bordering the Syrian Desert. I am amazed anything grows here; there is no rain, but they can tap into local springs underground. He employs the poor, mostly Bedouins, in the area to plant and harvest the crops; they get half the profits. Basil and I raid the pomegranate trees, and I immediately stain the front of my white shirt with red pomegranate juice. (The women in the family just as quickly wash it and return it to me, dry and pressed, the next morning.) His father sold some very lush land in other parts of the country to put his children through school, and Basil, who first studied law and now international relations, feels acutely indebted to him. One never sells land. One of the reasons Basil stays in school is to escape military service; he feels the drills and general disciplinary climate would kill him. But how long can he hold out?

The family greets me warmly, and that afternoon, his mother and sisters present us—me, Basil, his father, and younger brother—with a meal fit to feed an army, with beer and coke for drinks. The younger brother is a beauty; similar features to Basil but everything came out perfectly proportioned. "I bet the women love him," I say.

"Yes, says Basil, "they all want to marry him. That's why he doesn't take his studies seriously and doesn't want to leave the village." He pauses for a moment, then chuckles, "He sleeps well at night." The women in the family—all unveiled, all who shake my hand—float in and out, serving food, checking in on the conversation and making sure we are satisfied. Whenever there is a lull in the conversation, they turn to Sara, a darling light-brown-haired, blue-eyed, two-year-old girl on the verge of speaking, and command expectantly, "Say, 'Mr. John.'" She readily agrees to their requests, and mumbles something they recognize as "Mr. John"—I don't. Her father had worked in Germany as a *Gastarbeiter* and they insist Sara now looks like a German to everyone.

That evening, first his father and two brothers-in-law (one a general in the army, the other an agricultural economist), and later younger male cousins and friends, visit us at Basil's private quarters, a small two-room cement structure on the farmland about a half mile from the family house. Basil takes a scooter back and forth. We drink tea (they prefer a bitter Argentinean tea drunk through a metal straw) and they elaborate for me on the recent history of Syria, openly and critically. Basil's father was a member of the "revolutionary generation" and served the Party until 1980, by which time, he thought, it had become too security oriented and uninterested in its initial secular goals. For leaving the Party he was punished for ten days, he laughs, and then he returned to local-level agricultural work in the village. I ask them what legitimacy Bashar el-Assad has, other than being Alawite and the son of his father, now that nobody believes in the old Ba'ath ideology. They respond calmly that he is a "good guy," and they see no alternative. I ask them if Syria is still "the heart of the Arabs," and whether that includes the Arabs in the Gulf. They say yes, it does include them, but Arabia ends before Pakistan. They add they are skeptical of Muslims from other parts of the world who cannot read Arabic.

The next day we travel to Palmyra, Syria's greatest tourist site, initially written about in the second millennium BCE, then part of Alexander the Great's Macedonian Greek Empire, and finally, part of the Roman Empire, whose ruins mark it today. We rent a minibus (I have to fight with Basil, as always, to let me pay for it) and pick up Basil's younger brother, two younger sisters, and three male cousins. Some are dressed in loose sweatpants and shirt, others (including the two young women) in supertight jeans; one man wears a baseball cap. Only one person had already been to Palmyra, and we rely on my *Lonely Planet* guidebook for orientation. They ask quite penetrating questions about my research: whether agents of state security—American or Syrian—do not object to it, what I mean by "death of the father," what anthropology is. And when I refer to any psychological or social insight, they usually cite back to me an Arab or Islamic poem or saying that expresses the same wisdom, only more elegantly. We encounter some young Italian tourists who refuse to talk to me and reproach my Syrian hosts for cavorting with me, an American.

Palmyra is stunning only in part because of its magnificent ruins, evidence of a large, imperial capital now in the middle of nowhere. It is also an oasis in the desert; small plots with palm trees, date and olive orchards, and hot and cold springs ring most of the central ruins. We wander into one of the gardens, and then visit Palmyra's two museums—the folklore museum that displays native Bedouin and local tribal costumes from the nineteenth century and the museum of Palmyran history (necklaces, clothes, tools, shards, busts)—but the best artifacts have been stolen or sold and are now in other museums or people's private homes. The Syrians with me are more enthused about the joy of the collective trip—drinking beer and coke, eating nuts, sandwiches, talking—than seeing the ruins, which mean much more to academic specialists, history buffs, and the tourist industry.

That night at Basil's, his best friend, who inherited a bookstore from his recently deceased father, stops by, very depressed because his ex-girlfriend of five years just got married to someone else. Basil spends some time comforting him, and we pointlessly watch, or listen to, Syrian films on DVDs and some television. The TV is always on when people are around. I ask about how they deal with the incredible choice—up to four hundred stations from their satellite dish. They say that pornography is a problem, and that some parents try to block it, ultimately unsuccessfully. This new global choice is effacing the distinction between city and country, at least image-wise, and perhaps it contributes to explaining why young men who, despite an often desperate interest in contact with women, are frequently dissatisfied with the choice of brides presented to them and therefore want increasingly to delay marriage.

"God will tell us when we have to do something"

The assumption of the infallibility of the Koran comes up often in conversations with students about knowledge. After a film screening at the university, Aref and Ziyad and several other students accompany me to the beautifully renovated Hammam Yalbugha al-Nasri across from the Citadel. People say they renovated it for the tourists, but whenever I visit, most of the customers are still Aleppian. We arrive early, around 9:00 p.m.; it is nearly empty, and begins to fill only as we prepare to leave two hours later.

It is the very first hammam experience for Aref and Ziyad, and both appear anxious about the massage and loofah, the harsh full-body scrub. The more experienced students reassure them, and explain where to put one's money, watches, clothes, shoes. I invite along Jihad, a friend from the city who works as a tour guide and also had attended the film screening. The students are suspicious of him and keep their distance. Several take me aside and ask if I am sure he does not work for the Mukhabarrat. He asks too many questions, they say. When I tell them I trust him, and even if he does work for the secret police, I do not see how he could do us any harm, they remain skeptical but are more polite. Still, they tell me not to trust him. The attendant, a solid, hairy-chested, slightly paunchy man of about forty, treats each of us, in turn, to a massage with olive oil soap, working from front to back and bottom to top, from toe tips to finger tips, and then the loofah.

Like most of the Syrian masseurs I have experienced, he is rough and not attuned to our bodies. The work is neither a sensual experience for him, nor really for us. He is careful to stay away from the erotic zones, wary of brushing the hemp fibers against the genitals, and unlike attendants at other hammams, including at Hammam Nahasin, he shuns massaging the buttocks. On the other hand, when he gets to the underarms, he vigorously rubs the soapy hemp fibers against the delicate skin. I close my eyes tightly and wince. When Aref is done with his loofah, I notice that the attendant has scrubbed so hard that he has bloodied one whole shoulder and arm of Aref's thin body.

We alternate between the steam room and one of the side niche rooms, where we use brass bowls to pour cold water over ourselves. Earlier in the day, we had passed an SUV (sports utility vehicle) with a New Jersey license plate parked near the university. I say, "They're a crime. The owner should be arrested." My remark startles them. Surely, they say, I must also want an SUV, don't I? I explain the concept of "gas guzzling," that this truck masquerading as a car symbolizes ostentatious consumption and the unfair distribution of world energy. It is also an unnecessary expenditure of energy, and makes the United States dependent on Saudi oil, which is one reason the United States is fighting the war in Iraq and why Americans support repressive Arab governments: we need their oil. They listen quietly to my diatribe; they obviously have other concerns.

Environmental consciousness is hard to find in Syria, and it is clear the students are unused to conversations on the topic. I ask if they know about "greenhouse gases" and the cancer that results from the hole in the ozone layer, and they say no. I warn them about the danger of ultraviolet rays, and assert that we have a moral responsibility to keep the planet healthy for future generations, which means we stop excessive polluting. "But," says a student, finally protesting, "God created the planet. If he wants us to do something, he will tell us."

"God has no explanation for the ozone layer," I snap. "WE have created this pollution, we know how we have created it, and we now know how to stop it. It is only science that can tell us what to do about it."

"No," they say, confidently, "the Koran predicted this," and they offer examples of things that have come to pass which were mentioned in the Koran. I do not want to lecture them, not now, not in the hammam, but I am more than usually disturbed by their philosophical passivity, especially their refusal to acknowledge any human responsibility for environmental pollution. Other scholars may think of their response as merely another expression of "textual authority," the tradition of citing formal Muslim scholarship—codified writing, primarily from the shari'a, or Islamic jurisprudence—as legitimation or rationale for all action. But at this moment, all I can think of is who among their friends and acquaintances encourages such disrespectful attitudes toward their own environment?

Once a tourist convinced me to take a taxi with her to an isolated Syrian beach, an idea that the taxi driver found incomprehensible. Why not go to commercial beaches, those already set up for visitors? It takes us several hours of travel along winding, unmarked roads, littered by trash of all sorts strewn on both sides of the road, from abandoned cars to washing machines to tin cans, plastic bottles, and rotting vegetables, before we discover a most beautiful alcove, a high cliff on one side, the water warm and perfectly clear. We notice two guns perched on top of the cliff to guard against intruders, and there are signs of an army unit nearby. The beach is not sandy, so we have to crawl over slippery rocks, resulting in small cuts on our knees and hands. As we swim, soldiers on top of the cliff wave at us (though we cannot hear what they are saying, probably to get out) and drop large bags of garbage over the edge, landing halfway down. This is not neglect but willed abuse!

Remembering this sight, I tell the students that the Koran is an historical document and, however insightful, it does not envision such things as industrial pollution, oil-burning cars, plastic bags, and a host of illnesses, like lung cancer, and we should not think less of the Koran for not imagining the future.

"No," they insist, "we do not need science to explain this to us. God will tell us when we have to do something."

I decide to try a different approach and offer some examples of ways in which science is not necessarily opposed to Islam. In the back of my mind, perhaps in my unconscious, I am rehearsing arguments I could be having in my own country, with fundamentalist Christians and leaders in the Bush administration, who also dismiss scientific understandings of the environment when inconvenient. I point to the complementarity of Arab science with Islam, that Muslim scholars made original discoveries in math, astronomy, and medicine, and that Western science, people largely trained by the Christian church, translated these great works from Arabic and built European science upon them.

"But I am sure these scholars were pious," says one student.

I pause, amused by his clever retort; the student is being consistent, at least and, perhaps, goading me on. "No, not necessarily," I say. "There was Arab-Islamic patronage, much as there was later Christian patronage, but many of the scholars who worked for Arab rulers were not pious, not even Arab." I then admonish them, "You selectively appropriate your own traditions, which are more diverse and contradictory than you are aware. You should read more and become aware of the early history of Arabs and Islam."

One student replies, perhaps in jest, "I am uninterested in Islamic history. That is why I am majoring in English literature." Syrian students compete for spots in the most desirable degree programs, and because English is not the most desirable or competitive (it ranks somewhere in the middle) of programs, it allows a certain measure of freedom from social constraints that many other programs do not.

To be sure, I am out of control in this discussion, and I know it. Am I not in a bathhouse? What am I doing lecturing as if in a classroom? While talking, I become aware that with these students I slip into a Socratic mode, as I try to get them to engage with their own tradition and with me in a critical way. But they seem more accustomed to the professor-as-lecturer than the teacher, to someone just delivering a monologue they can either accept or reject. Though both professor and teacher roles position me as a source of authority and therefore as structurally analogous to their fathers, teacher and father are not identical, and I struggle to find the appropriate balance in interaction. My usual mode in the field, the one I more frequently take in the souk, and the one I had in earlier fieldwork in Germany and Europe, is what I consider more typically ethnographic: listening more than explaining, engaging in more of an exchange, where I draw out people's explanations of their worlds. It requires little authority. Here I cannot easily or consistently separate the professor from the teacher, the teacher from the ethnographer, the ethnographer from the father. I stop.

Suddenly Ziyad says he has to leave the room. "I am sorry, sorry," he says, and begins to fall to his knees. He is fainting. Another student helps to lift him up and puts his arm around Ziyad's shoulders.

Ziyad leans on him for support, and they walk slowly into the cooler waiting room. "I am sorry myself, Ziyad, we should have exited earlier," I say, "it is hot in there."

"Kiss Daddy! Kiss Daddy!"

For several weeks Ziyad is adamant about a visit to his home, but I delay. Another visit to another family, I think. On display the whole night! Again! I know that a good ethnographer never turns down an invitation. But every night my final two weeks in Aleppo I have committed myself to activities, including several lectures outside Aleppo. I have already met Ziyad several times at other student homes, where the women in the family had cooked for us, or someone purchased take-out food from a local restaurant. In these Muslim households, we eat and have discussions only with the other men and boys. Ziyad plays on my guilty conscience about delaying a visit to his family and begins to ask personal questions, "Who are you seeing today?" "Why are you unable to come?" I cannot say "no" forever. He has actively sought my friendship; I agree to the Saturday evening before my departure.

Figure 14. Kiss Daddy

Ziyad is in his final year of completing a bachelor's degree in English literature. As a pious Muslim, five times daily he is bound to perform a fixed ritual of prayer, called the *Salat*. So if we spend more than a few hours together, he routinely asks me, "Can I go pray now?" or "Is there some place to pray here?" I invariably find the question, and his politeness, charming. But why ask me? In the souk, men pray regularly in front of me: they roll out a rug, fall to their knees, mutter their prayers, stand up, roll up the rug, and go on with business.

"Go. I'll wait," I say. If we are with other students, they take turns going to pray, leaving someone with me at all times. With so many mosques in Aleppo, and with prayer rooms in most university buildings, there is bound to be a place to pray around some corner, so it is relatively easy to perform the required prayers. But why am I in a position to tell Ziyad whether or not to pray? It is none of my business, I think; it is his obligation, his duty, his choice. But he thinks otherwise and solicits my agreement before disappearing—for about fifteen minutes each time.

Once, after I voice some criticism of the university, Ziyad says, "It is a curse to ever have been born in this country." I am taken aback by the intensity and generality of his complaint. This kind of sentiment is the opposite of the pan-Arab solidarity the Ba'athist regime tries to produce. Ziyad thinks of himself as a social outsider, and he harbors a sense of deep cultural alienation, much deeper than he is capable of expressing, perhaps deeper than he himself is aware of. He wants desperately to avoid being identified as Syrian. American would be best.

"Who would Americans think I am?" he asks. I tell him Syrians are very diverse so it is hard to characterize them since they fit no physical stereotype, and, anyway, Americans have no clear image of what Syrians look like. He is immensely pleased when I tell him that neither in pronunciation nor looks would Americans think he is Syrian—he has light, innocuous brown hair but very dark and bushy eyebrows, clear brown eyes, medium-muscular build, hairy chest and legs (a friend who saw his photo called him "a cute bear"). "They might think you are from anywhere," I say, "Spain, England, even southern Germany."

"Really?" he asks skeptically, and repeats this question frequently.

When I first meet Ziyad, he guesses that I am from "near Canada." "Close," I say, "northern Wisconsin; it is the vowels." He declares his major interest to be "dialectology," and asks if I would be interested in giving a lecture on this topic.

"Tell me what it is first," I reply, "I have no idea." When I use words Ziyad has never heard spoken, he repeats them several times, carefully, precisely, and then gives me one or even several dictionary definitions he has read.

He asks questions like, " 'had to go'—do you pronounce that 'hada go,' 'hadda go,' or 'haD To go?' "

I say, "Enunciate the 'D' and 'T', keep them separate. Don't slur or people will think you are lower class."

But Ziyad does not care about class; he is interested only in being recognized as American. Even without ever having visited the United States, he is able to detect and reproduce exactly several American dialects—culled from American movies and National Public Radio, which he listens to daily. I tell him not to mimic American actors, most of whom have bad diction, but to pay attention to NPR or BBC.

"I don't want to learn British English," he says. "I want to learn American." He sometimes reads for me in English, and asks me to correct his pronunciation. But I tell him he is fluent. He speaks better English than most members of my family.

"How is that possible?" he asks.

"Your vocabulary is larger," I explain; "your understanding of grammar and control of syntax are better. Most Americans do not speak good English."

"How can that be?" he asks. "It is their language."

Often boys ask me what I like about them. When Ziyad and his friends who study English literature ask, I say, "Your curiosity."

"What do you mean?" they ask.

"For example, for language, you are curious about learning languages," I say.

"What do you dislike about us?" they ask. "What are our faults?"

"Your faults are not for me to tell you but for you to discover," I reply. "But I would encourage you not to focus on language because of its technical qualities alone. You already speak well enough. Appreciate the poetic qualities of language; appreciate tone, what can be done in writing and talking. You should now aim for cultural competency." Cultural competency! They had never heard this term before, so I throw out some names of contemporary authors: Andy Warhol, J. M. Coetzee, John Updike, Doris Lessing, Joan Didion, Toni Morrison, Tony Kushner. All unknown. I encourage them to enjoy reading, not to memorize or read for class alone but to read as a form of pleasure, like eating. They do not react to my exhortation. Their relation to the activity of reading appears limited to memorizing and reciting the Koran, which certainly involves poetic appreciation. But that kind of reading has little to do with the pleasure of critical reading and interpretation about which I speak. Later, I give Ziyad about ten old *New Yorker* magazines I had brought with me. "Read these," I say, "and you'll have cultural competency."

On the night I am to eat with his family—father, mother, brother, sister—there is a constant drizzle and chilly wind. We meet downtown and walk about two miles to his parents' apartment. He shows me a paper, taped to the refrigerator, with a list of English euphemisms for going to the toilet. "You want a copy?" he asks. I decline the offer. I recognize perhaps half of them. "Take a leak?" "Water the horses?"—yes. "Going for the Jimmy Riddle?" "Syphon the python?"—not a clue.

"I downloaded them from the Internet," he says, proudly and mischievously. I go through and point out the ones he can safely use in public without offending anyone.

His mother, who works as a high school French teacher, has cooked for several days. She serves all the traditional Arabic dishes— hot Kurdish cheese pastries, baba ghanoush, falafel, hummus, *mouttabel*, *muhammara*, fresh lettuce, bell peppers, and onions, along with a main dish of chopped lamb baked with tomato slices on top—and a sautéed chicken salad, a more modern concoction which his father had prepared. As usual, the table is laden with dishes, each overflowing to the point that taking the serving spoon out is impossible without making a mess on the table. There is hardly room for our plates, and my own is precariously balanced, half off, half on my corner of the table. I eat way too much as everything is truly superb, and I thank them profusely throughout.

Ziyad and his father sit on chairs across from me, while I sit alone on a small sofa. The father, who teaches agriculture at a secondary school, and does odd plumbing jobs, often with Ziyad's assistance, is tall, slender but muscular, partly bald, a very handsome man about ten years younger than me. He sits quietly, smiling but never fully relaxed, saying very little and perhaps not understanding much of what we say. As Ziyad and his brother are English majors, most of our conversation is in English. They all speak other foreign languages: the mother only French, the father Romanian and French, the two sons only English. Ziyad occasionally translates into Arabic. His younger brother looks much like him, except he has no beard, and his hair is long, shiny black, and his eyebrows frame raccoonlike eyes. He is, in other words, a stunning beauty. He wears a sweatshirt, sweatpants, and a stocking cap pulled tightly over his head. Not intending a rap look, he dresses this way just for comfort. For most of the evening, he squats next to the father, stroking his arm and holding his hand, but every time he gets up to carry dishes back and forth to the kitchen he has a spring in his step, almost as if dancing. The mother and daughter stay in a separate room off the kitchen, and they either shut the door or switch off the light the several times I walk past to wash my hands or use the toilet.

The fact that the women serve us and yet remain out of sight, though a common family arrangement in Syria as well as in many parts of the world, nonetheless makes me uncomfortable. I also feel awkward because I want to speak Arabic, just to be inclusive of the father, but the boys want to practice their English. I relent, perhaps out of relief more than deference to their wishes. Once Ziyad's brother comes over and sits next to me, and asks, "Do you really hate your father?" Ziyad must have told him something of our conversations about psychoanalysis.

"No, just some disagreements."

"Why do you conflict with your father?" he persists.

"I love my father. He is dead now," I say, "but having conflict does not mean I did not love him."

Their father sits passively through this exchange, smiling now and then. This conversation is about him, of course, and there is something queer in talking about him, the father, my host, in his presence.

After we finish the meal and just before dessert, the daughter, who is still in high school, comes out of the bedroom and joins us. She sits on the other sofa, along the far wall, and listens, saying nothing. Perhaps they have brought her out to interest me in marriage.

Indeed, Ziyad's brother asks why I am not married, and why I have no children.

I say, "Different opportunities. If I had a wife and child, I most probably would not be here with you."

"Why don't you want to remarry?" he asks

"Once is enough," I say.

Ziyad confides in me, almost as an aside but with a nervous giggle, that the whole family would like to leave Syria, that they had planned to emigrate. His father is underemployed and has no better prospects in Syria. He received his doctorate in Romania, and he financed it on his own, by alternating years between working in Syria and studying in Romania. But the best jobs only go to those with good contacts, either educated in Syria or sent by the government to study abroad, and he lost those opportunities by going to Romania without governmental support.

He tells me of an embarrassing episode of family history. Four years ago, they paid $3,500 to a company in London to immigrate to Canada, but they have heard nothing back.

"That is a lot of money," I say. Perhaps two years of both his parents' salaries! "Did you contact them about the status of your application?"

"Yes, once. They said, 'Don't contact us, we'll contact you.'"

"What makes you think they are honest?" I ask.

"We know another family that was successful. They are in Canada now."

"I would write a letter, and send a new letter every month until they answer."

"I guess we've lost it," he scoffs. "There must be a curse on this family."

Around 10:30, I stand and suggest I might leave, but Ziyad's brother pleads, "Oh, but we're enjoying you so much. Don't go."

I sit back down. The mother, who has remained hidden the entire time, finally comes out, after hearing I am ready to leave. She sits on the other sofa by her daughter, and orders her raccoon-eyed son to get a box of chocolates they keep in a special place. I say, "No, no, I am full." But the family collectively insists I take a couple. Then the mother fetches a large key ring from the next room, and insists I take it, and then two prayer beads.

"Which one do you want?" asks Ziyad.

"No more, no more!" I insist, "I don't have room in my luggage," and I accept what seems to be the least expensive of the two.

"Why don't you take the other one?" Ziyad asks.

"No, please, I like this one," I lie.

It was raining heavily and the rain had just let up. It is 11:00, I stand up, again. "I really have to go, pack to leave and all; it was all wonderful, the food the best I have had in Aleppo, really superb."

They all stand, reluctantly but perhaps also relieved to let me go. I take the hand of Ziyad's brother in mine and kiss him on the cheek, thrice, the elaborate three-peat, and I take hold of his father's hand, intending to shake it, when Ziyad says, in English, "Kiss Daddy! Kiss Daddy!" The whole family giggles, and I am standing there, holding his father's hand, looking into his eyes, hesitating. Time seems to slow down.

The younger brother chimes in, "Kiss Daddy! Kiss Daddy!" So I reach over and kiss Daddy, and he cradles my head in his free hand and kisses me, the three-peat.

I put my shoes on and leave, with Ziyad. We ignore the moment just passed, the triangular dynamic of desire, the boys wanting to see me in an embrace with their father, the father passive, excited, expectant. What of that embrace? They want me, from America, from the West, to kiss Daddy, to comfort Daddy, to console him in his distress at failing the family, at being underemployed, at having squandered their futures by investing years of savings in a hapless British swindle.

And the voice of the West? The family hears nothing, despite the siren calls and their large monetary investment. Silence. Not even a reply! No, they are not going to the West, not as a family.

Or, perhaps there is a possibility. I appear. There is hope for you, Daddy. He is not with the Mukhabarrat. Don't leave, stay a little longer, whatever it takes.

Ziyad walks me to a side street nearby, we wait a few minutes for a taxi, I give him a peck on the cheek, just one, and return to my apartment.

a

b

c

d

e

f

Figures 15a–15f. Faces of the Souk

⚊ Chapter II ⚊

The Souk

"Come into my shop and let me take you"

On my sixth day in Aleppo, he calls out, dazzling me into smiling, "Merry Christmas! Don't you remember how to say hello?" It is only September! I crack up and, though I am in a hurry, turn around and introduce myself. Majid is thirty-two years old and works with seven brothers in the souk, each with his own shop. When he was twenty-one, a travel writer who passed through described him as a "moon child." Majid eagerly shows me the passage. "Now I am just the moon," he says.

"Then I am the sun," I reply.

"And I am the star," says one of his nephews who happens to be in the shop. We all laugh. I tell them I am not a tourist, actually, but living around the corner from the shop, and planning to teach at the university. Majid says he hates tourists, "They are so hard to deal with. I'd rather be a drag queen somewhere," and he takes one of the pashmina shawls he sells off the shelf, plants his feet squarely, rocks his shoulders side to side, and the shawl miraculously wraps itself around him. He stands facing a mirror, dignified, imperial, as if he had just triumphed over some silly foe. Outrageous! I dub it "The Wrap." I have to leave and, as I walk away, he shouts, loudly, brashly, in a voice that all the other merchants are sure to hear, "Adorable!"

Majid does not single me out for this special treatment, but almost as a conscious counterpoint to the other, more staid merchants, he yells after customers, or heralds the beauty or uniqueness of someone, anyone, who walks by. "Bette Midler!" he shouts, when a ten-year-old nephew who has her exact hair and cheeks walks by. "Sally Field!" he shouts, when a twenty-year-old nephew who has her exact seductive, underaged Gidgit-like smile walks by. "Julia Roberts!" he shouts, when a twenty-four-year-old nephew who has her exact fleshy lips and oceanic smile walks by.

Majid is one of the merchants I visit daily. He has worked in the souk his entire life, except for the five years he spent in Australia, where he lived with his boyfriend, now ex-, and eventually obtained citizenship. He loves Australia, and dreams of some day returning to start an alternative café. But he also loves his large family, and these brothers, sisters, nephews, and his father, he says, are why he returned to Syria. Within days after we meet his voice cracks as he says, "My mother died last spring, after a long illness. That was very hard." And throughout the fall season, when other customers ask how he is doing, he qualifies his naïve and shocking presentation with a reference to the heart-rending loss of his mother.

As for Syria, he jokes, "We need a tidal wave to wash all this dirt into the sea." Meanwhile, he arranged for his closest brother, two years older than him, to follow him to Australia. He will also stay there, with his wife and children, as long as it takes to acquire citizenship. While Majid was in Australia, his brother took care of the shop where they both had worked, protecting his interests in the family textile business and sending him money. Now he is reciprocating.

Majid has a unique talent for sales. His brothers call it "Majid's Show," and I meet many tourists who return to Aleppo's souk just to have an experience in his shop. When Majid shared a shop with his brother, the one now in Australia, they used to put on The Show together, a tag-team presentation where one played off the sensibilities of the other. Some tourists think The Show is gay, but they confuse, I suspect, a sensibility for an identity, for The Show perfects the gay thing called camp, what Susan Sontag so famously defined

a

b

c

d

Figures 16a–16d. The Wrap

as "unmistakably modern . . . a variant of sophistication . . . that converts the serious into the frivolous."

Other shopkeepers occasionally copy the style of The Show, but there is always something wrong in their performance—too slow, too timid, too clumsy, too literal, too corrupt—not enough.

"Come into my shop and let me take you," says Majid to two young English men. They look baffled. "No," Majid corrects himself, "make you." Pause. "No, let me sell you something." Majid grins ever so slightly, and the tourists move quickly from tense caution to relaxed agreement, as if to say, "Aha, we understand each other."

Majid says to a Dutch couple pondering whether to buy one or two shawls, "They say, when the sun shines, make gay." Pause. "No, make hay." They are unsettled, perhaps a bit offended, ultimately relieved. "Only one letter, small difference," he concludes. And then, if they are still undecided, he takes a silk scarf and squares himself, rocks back and forth so that the scarf wraps itself around him. I can tell from their puzzled expressions: the woman thinks, how beautiful and funny; the man, how strange, but as I'm on vacation, I'll play along.

Or, if the customer cannot decide what to buy, Majid finds a scarf appropriate to the person and says, "This, for women, men, or in-between"—and he does The Wrap.

"Do you have a brother?"

I take two ex-Princeton students who are traveling in Syria to Majid's shop. One is tall with blue eyes, red hair, and freckles—an exotic look for Syrians, very un-Syrian. She is tense, and Majid's humor is not working. He asks her, in an innocent, singsong voice, "Do you have a brother?" I can see she is suspicious: Why is he asking me this? And she wants to answer "no," but the truth is "yes." So she hesitates, shakes her head yes and says, "No." But then corrects herself, and says, "Yes."

Majid asks, "Does he look like you?"

Figure 17. Italian Soccer and Oscar Wilde

Again, she is puzzled: Why does he want to know what my brother looks like? This is Syria, a police state, an enemy of the United States!

"Does he have your eyes?" he asks.

"Yes," she says, confident at last.

"Tell him," Majid concludes, "I am waiting for him." And he does The Wrap; her stern look gives way to a big smile.

Tourists do not always react guardedly to this confusion and camp humor. Some eagerly engage, though there are national differences, with exceptions, of course. The Germans tend to be the most stiff, the Americans the most uncomprehending, the Italians the most oblivious, the French the most confident, the Spanish the most chaotically fluid, the Lebanese the most imperial, the Turks the most savvy, the Kuwaitis the most demanding. Majid calibrates his reactions to the degree of registered shock, counting on the fact that most tourists who visit Syria have at least a subliminal desire to experience surprise.

Some groups enter the shop uninvited and aggressively tear everything apart, as if in a bargain-basement sale in a large department store. Within minutes the shop looks like a hurricane went through it: silk and cotton scarves, shawls, patterned tablecloths, napkins, and bedspreads scattered everywhere. It takes up to a half hour to put the goods back on the shelves. Others are very timid and must be seduced into entering.

A group of Spanish tourists comes by, three women and two men, with ages of about forty-five to fifty-five. One woman has very short hair, Annie Lennox at her most butch, and some stray hairs are streaked in different colors. Majid says, "*Adoro su pelo*" (I love your hair). She keeps a stone face. He adds, "*Puedo lo tocarlo?*" (Can I touch it?).

"No," she says sternly.

"Artificial?" he asks, in English, as if he is asking Marge Simpson who does her hair.

"No," she says, "I do it myself."

He is relentless and raises the ante, unwilling to be serious, "Just the color artificial or the hair artificial?"

The woman's face is unmoved. She either does not get it or does not want to.

"You have a brother?" he tries another approach.

"*No te entiendo*" (I don't understand), she says. Another woman in the group repeats the question in Spanish ("*Usted tiene un hermano?*").

"No," she answers.

"Seyches," Majid says, and the tension deflates like a balloon in a collective gasp of recognition: Seyches has become well known as a gay tourist resort off the coast of Barcelona, and Majid knows that the mere mention of the place will either strike a chord of tolerance or of horror in a Spanish tourist. The woman who had translated raises her hand in horror, as if to shield herself from a klieg light, and she shakes her head vigorously "No, no, no." The group moves on. "If you say 'Seyches,'" says Majid, "that ends everything. I got tired of them."

Majid's favorite call to customers as they pass by is indeed, "Merry Christmas!" With most tourists, this at least results in a smile, though many are too embarrassed to stop. Some will take it seriously, however, and stop to correct him. One German man stops and frowns, "Do you know what that means?"

"Yes," says Majid, "but we want to celebrate early in case we miss it."

The man forces a smile, "No, it is too early in the year." The desire to correct is, for some, irresistible and compulsive. It also provides the opportunity for strangers to assert themselves in a situation of general insecurity. Majid asks me, "What will I do when Christmas comes? I'll have to think of something else."

"Ossi oder NorMAL?"

Among the foreign customers, there are very few Americans in Aleppo this season. Crowds of Turks come on particular weekends, and there are frequent strays from Lebanon, Kuwait, Iraq, Singapore, Hong Kong, Malaysia, and Japan. From Europe, I see mostly British, French, German, Polish, and Belgian tourists. Some French are regulars, people who live in Aleppo and teach in the local French schools or work in the Catholic Church. The Germans are heavily involved in archaeological digs, so they also have a semipermanent group of residents. In the shops I know well, I engage more intensely with Germans than others, since I can converse fluently and make them feel comfortable.

As German-looking tourists pass nervously, afraid of contact yet wanting it, Majid or one of his nephews will yell, "Ossi? Sind Sie Ossi?" (Easterner? Are you Easterner?). The East Germans are, of course, stunned that someone here might recognize in them this difference between East and West and know about the déclassé sense of coming from the former socialist zone; the West Germans often smile and issue a quick denial.

Two men in their early twenties enter the shop speaking German. Majid asks, "Ossi oder NorMAL?" They are thrown off-guard. If they are Ossis, they might say "yes." If not, they either grin, accompanied by a vehement denial, or stare blank-faced. Majid tells them to take a seat and orders Turkish coffee or tea from a young man who comes by every fifteen minutes with a tray. He informs them that I speak German, and to the non-European customers sometimes even introduces me over my ready protests—to protect me, he says—as German.

"Gorgeous," he exclaims about the smaller one with a shaved head, who later identifies himself as Kristian from Köpenick in (the former East) Berlin. "Are you vegetarian?" asks Majid, having exhausted his German and moving on to more confident ground. "*Vegetarier?*" they ask each other. Kristian shrugs his shoulders, "I don't know vat you mean." But being a good sport, he shrugs his shoulders and answers the question literally, "No."

"*Was meint er?*" Kristian asks me. I am in stitches and cannot respond. He has no idea what is going on and keeps shrugging his shoulders, a blush slowly overtakes him. Majid fixes his eyes intently on Kristian, then points to him with a nod of his head and says to me, emphatically, "Butch!" Kristian lets out a forced smile and looks to his friend for help.

Three Germans in their early thirties enter the shop. One tall blonde woman and two nondescript men. The woman wants to look at scarves. Majid first shows her the cotton ones, then the silk. He does the fire test—silk doesn't burn—also proof of his honesty. "Here is a brown one," he says, and follows quickly with, "Blue." "Red." "Yellow." "You want a homosexual color?" he asks. The woman says, "We don't need zat."

"Maybe you have a friend who is homosexual," he says, and takes a yellow scarf and whips it around his neck. The Wrap. The woman and one of the men smile; the other remains cool. "Not zat," she says.

Four Germans, presumably two married couples in their forties, pause in front of the shop. "*Bitte*, come in," says Majid. "Cheaper than Aldi!" (Aldi is this cheap German chain.) They relax and laugh, "*Wie kann er das wissen?*" (How can he know that?) "*Sind Sie Ossi?*" he asks in a naïve-sounding voice.

"No," they assert defiantly, "*aus München.*"

"Then you are NorMAL," he says, putting the accent on the last syllable. This doesn't really please them either—most Germans would rather be cool or blend in, and as *Wessis*, they do not like to think of themselves as pathologizing their Eastern compatriots. Majid does The Wrap. They smile at each other and buy several tablecloths.

An innocent-looking couple in their early twenties enter the shop. They stand out: he is a big, raw-boned blond, she a thin, reddish-blonde with freckles. "From Poland?" Majid guesses.

"No Slovenia," she says.

"Lesbiana?" asks Majid, his big blue eyes opening wide.

"No, Ljubljana," she corrects him, with a straight face.

"Lesbiana." Majid repeats calmly.

"No, Ljubljana," she says quietly.

"Lesbiana?" Majid asks plaintively, again.

"NO, LJUB-LJANA," she says, irritated at his stubborn insistence on mispronunciation.

The young man is studying ethnology at Karl's University in Prague. We discuss our common interests. His study, he says, is a mix of the old Chicago urban studies and Manchester school of cultural studies. Majid is crazy about him, and his girlfriend understands this right away. "Butch!" Majid declares adamantly. They tell us they met last year through the Internet, while she was traveling in Africa.

"Do you have a brother?" Majid asks the boy.

"No, just a sister," he says.

"What a pity," Majid says with resignation. "Do you?" he asks the girl.

"Yes," she says, glad to be part of the conversation again.

"Is he like him?" asks Majid, pointing to her boyfriend.

"No, opposite type, thin and not that tall," she explains. They have tea and leave the shop. "Gorgeous! Gorgeous!" exclaims Majid loudly.

Four Germans—two boys, two girls—are in Majid's shop one day when I arrive. Majid says, "You can speak German with them. He"—pointing to a tall, thin brown-haired boy—"is vegetarian." The girls try on scarves while the boys sit on stools chatting. One asks the other, *"Was meint er? Ich bin Vegetarier?"* (What does he mean, I am vegetarian?). *"Ich weiss nicht."* (I don't know), says the other. *"Es muss ein Code sein*" (It must be a code). Majid gazes intently at himself in the small mirror in the middle of his shop and busies himself with The Wrap. The boys look away, the girls just look dumbfounded. He asks the blonder of the two girls if she has a brother.

"Yes," she says.

"Does he look like you?"

"Yes," she says.

"Is he available?" he asks. The group then breaks into a discussion among themselves, in German. The "vegetarian" boy says, "What does that mean? Available?" The other boy shrugs his shoulders. The girls are silent. I pipe up, "It means *zu verfügen stehen*?" The vegetarian boy and two girls smile and laugh softly, but the other boy shrugs his shoulders again, as if he still does not understand. I ask the two boys, in German, why only the girls buy things, "Why don't you also shop?"

The vegetarian says he already bought something, two scarves. The other boy doesn't answer. I repeat my question to him, specifically, adding, "Why are you the exception?" He says he does not know what fits people. I say, "But buy for the future, to have a gift ready when you need it. "Yes," he says, "but I don't know for which person."

"Then you can give it to a third person," I say.

"That makes no sense," he scoffs, obviously irritated.

I don't' let up; I know I am being a bastard. "But it is very human, to exchange," I say. "You give something to someone and they give it to someone else." He is silent, no smile, no nothing. Majid's nephew asks me to translate. After they leave, he concludes, "I hate Germans. Ten years ago, they used to be the best customers, but today, they are worse than the Poles. Eighty percent think they are better than others, and they don't buy anymore."

Majid also claims to have problems with German tourists, though he has a German boyfriend who works as a tour guide and in that capacity visits him at least a couple times a year. "I often don't bother with the Germans," he explains, "it takes hours to sell them anything. The first thing a German tourist says is, 'I don't have any money.' As if I were begging from them!"

Toward the end of one day, a German husband and wife, about sixty, walk by slowly, obviously tired from a day of tourist activities. They peek into the shop but are not eager to enter. Majid engages them in conversation, assuring them they need not buy anything, and before they know it, they are sitting in the shop, drinking coffee. Majid unfolds some tablecloths. The man says, "But I don't need anything."

I intervene, in German, "But your need is not the point of buying. You buy for other reasons, because you are on vacation, or because something pleases you."

"But my home is already full."

"Then buy some more and give something away to your friends in Germany."

"Our suitcase is already full."

Majid asks me to translate. I say I was just giving them a hard time. Sometimes, I, too, do things just to combat the boredom of sitting.

Majid tends to let Europeans off the hook and reserves his dislike for Arab customers, specifically Syrians and Lebanese, who ask that he sell at cost, without making a profit, or who just want to see what he has or compare prices without intending to buy anything. To these people, when they ask for a price, Majid points them to shops in another part of the souk and says about his own goods, "They are too expensive for you."

The Souk's Logic of Exchange

My daily rhythms and concerns are very much influenced by the rationalizing, maximizing logic of the capitalism of America, my home, even though I am living in the souk of Aleppo, where merchants live by a different economic logic. My routines are dictated by intellectual and academic interests—curiosity about paternal authority and the changing legitimation of a non-Western secularism, sabbatical-year time release from teaching at Princeton, lecturing in Syria as part of an international exchange. But theirs, by contrast,

Figure 18. The Rhythm of the Souk

are dictated more by a local way of life and an ethos that is decidedly not capitalist. Clifford Geertz, in a masterful essay on a Moroccan souk, has characterized this "bazaar economy" as "a distinctive system of social relations." It is, he maintains, "a cultural form, a social institution, and an economic type."

The merchants in the Souk al-Medina do manage time but they do not engage in time rationalization. Most arrive in the morning at nine or ten, and leave at six or seven or eight, depending on the expectations of customers, on seasonal or weekly intensity, on rumors of tourist groups, or if they feel well or not on a particular day. They do employ people, including themselves, and they do pursue profit—two of the characteristics of capitalist exchange—but there is no formally free wage labor (children work for free; sons for the promise of future support; cousins and nephews for a monthly stipend). And profit is not pursued above all else, impersonally, or for its own sake, but is imbedded in the way of life of Aleppo and the souk, which is decidedly personal, unsystematic, and oriented above all to the reproduction of exchange activities in their broadest sense.

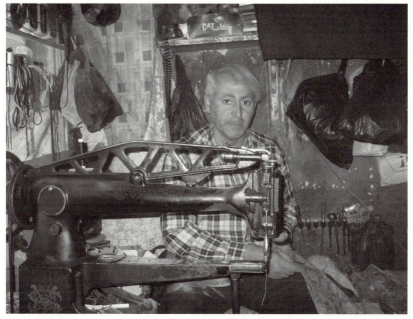

Figure 19. Shoe Repairman

The provision of almost all goods and services involves intermediaries, sometimes intricate networks of intermediaries, from close kin to unseen local producers and transporters who live outside the city, and one of the preoccupations of merchants is to learn about these networks and enter into them, or prevent others from entering. I hear of few plans for business expansion either to expand trade spatially with relatives in diaspora, as, say Chinese merchants are skilled at doing, to create franchises in other cities in Syria, or to consolidate or monopolize the production and sale of a particular thing. Expansion, to the extent it exists, tends to be within the souk and limited to immediate kin. Hence, for those with fewer sons and smaller families (and the general trend is a radical reduction in family size), opportunities for expansion are severely limited. An unwillingness to employ daughters (partly, I assume, because it would include assuming responsibility for their husbands, should they marry) makes this problem intractable, unless merchants shift logic altogether to a capitalist one: an impersonal, rationalized system of economic exchange.

Aleppian merchants emphasize that Damascus has a more stable, year-round clientele, making selling there more relaxed. Damascus is the capital and serves a huge hub of cities, and every tourist who visits Syria stops at least in the Souk Al-Hamidiye in Damascus. But in Aleppo, the low and high seasons are radically different, the best being summer to fall and certain holidays: the Muslim Eid al-Fitr and the Christian Easter, and three months of intense weddings in late winter. Sellers fear each customer might be the last for a while; they must make sales now or never. Since all prices in the souk are negotiable, they vary from shop to shop and customer to customer. Western tourists find pricing particularly confusing, as they seek to ascertain a market price or an exact monetary value of an object before purchasing. Many tourists I meet complain bitterly that a merchant around the corner told them he would have sold them the same carpet, figs, jewelry, or scarf for half the price. Some then seek to return the merchandise, which at times works, as merchants also take pride in their knowledge and integrity, and those I know well resent the accusation of deception or exploitation. What such tourists ignore is the hospitality and care extended to them in the process of selling, the time taken and skill displayed in commercial exchange, not simply in the serving of drinks and small talk and jokes but in the attempt to provide a service, to elicit tastes and give customers some equivalent of what they what. There are, of course, always exceptions to this behavior, especially some younger men, who tend to have poor relations with their fathers or lack relatives to employ them, and who use their charm to milk naïve foreign customers as much as possible.

Merchants also themselves engage in periodic price wars, which, since shops of similar goods tend to cluster in one row, is easy to do and can quickly become vicious and personal. They tell customers that they overpaid and suggest they return goods already purchased elsewhere and buy instead from them, or, in the extreme, just to get back at a disliked competitor, they offer goods to customers below cost. Most of these wars seem to be triggered not by a calculated strategy of profit but out of resentment at the success of a particular seller.

Periodically during the day merchants count their cash—openly, without attempting to hide what they are doing. Most keep books to register cash received, though these figures are never exact. The accounting system is very relaxed, and once in a while fights about irregularities break out among employees (who are usually also close relatives) about people not making good sales (offering too good of a deal to the customer); unfairly undercutting the price of the competitor; not repaying money lent; stealing business; or repeating negative gossip, rudeness, or abuse. Fighting tends to be among younger men, who might punch others with their fists but rarely strike at the face; it is not unknown to flash knives. But the ethos of the souk also demands that hospitality be extended to relatives, other merchants, and customers (especially tourists) alike—shared water, coffee, tea, occasionally food. Hence, crowds almost always intervene to stop fighting.

Taxes are assessed largely on the basis of size of the stall, amount of goods on hand, and precedent (how much tax was assessed the previous year), with hardly any attention to income from sales. Taxes are higher in the Souk al-Medina than in other souks, largely because more Western tourist money is taken in there than elsewhere. In most shops, credit cards are accepted, though this means going to a third party to do the paperwork and make the transaction—an extra 7 percent tax, minimally. As accounting books are irregular and unreliable, and as no receipts are kept, tax collectors raise taxes on the modernist assumption of economic progress; they assume sales have increased. Most expect small bribes, but the amount is minimal, and nearly all merchants whom I asked do not think of the bribe as extortion. If a merchant refuses to pay, however, the collectors come with policemen, nail the shop shut, and post a sign declaring that it is officially closed. These shops usually reopen within a few days, police return again after several months, and this pattern is repeated until some fishy and ultimately ambiguous settlement is reached. Merchants tell me that it costs more to resist the tax collectors than to simply pay the minimal amount they ask for.

State inspectors also visit for safety, health, and other kinds of violations. Sometimes they come to find someone who owes back taxes, but more frequently to assess fines for violations that they discover during surprise visits. Upon the spotting of an inspector, a rumor spreads so fast that merchants nearly always have an opportunity to hide the potential violation. One of the most common violations is to extend a shop into the street or aisle. Upon the rumor of an inspector's coming, merchants quickly shrink their stalls back to their legal size. For example, upon the rumor of an inspector in the area, a large burlap bag of mint leaves, another with pumpkin seeds, and two others filled with spices are moved into a neighbor's textile shop, which effectively blocks part of his door but frees the street. Several hours later, after much grumbling, the neighbor dumps the burlap bags back in the front of their owner's shop. Not a word is exchanged; this helping behavior is assumed.

Fathers, Sons, Brothers, and Inheritance

For most men, emotional dependence on the parents is too great to risk a break by questioning their authority or trying to establish much personal autonomy. In addition, they have compelling reasons to accommodate the wishes of their brothers and uncles, on whom they are also dependent. Intricate ties of shared employment, shared real estate, shared investments, and promised inheritance force brothers, as well as uncles and nephews, to cooperate with and support each other. Sometimes these fraternal ties are further reinforced through marriage—for example, two brothers wed two sisters or they marry cousins. With the death of the father, however, new authority relations must be established, and this often results in explicit anger directed at siblings and relatives, after which it is assumed all will return to relations with each other, newly balanced, as if nothing had happened.

The cost of separating from a brother, especially from a joint inheritance, can be immense, emotionally and financially. In the souk in Aleppo where I live, all the brothers I know fight but ultimately settle their disputes. In my visits to Damascus, however, I find myself in the middle of an unsettled dispute between two brothers. Hosam and Abdul, who are approximately my age and look rather alike, had, upon their father's death eight years ago, inherited two shops in a wonderful handicraft souk. Located in an old villa, it is small and quaint but has a large, open courtyard in the middle. Of the two shops they inherited, one is small but is squeezed in the middle of a row of shops; the other is large but at the very end corner of the souk. I met both brothers for the first time in 1999 and had bought two carpets from Hosam in the fall of 2004. On each subsequent trip to Damascus, I visit them, and they recognize me immediately, but I am always concentrated on their merchandise and do not pay much attention to which brother I am with. In spring 2005, I return with the express purpose of buying several carpets for gifts. I enter the first shop I come to, and as a returning customer I trust them, perhaps foolishly, and immediately fall for three rugs. From the asking price of $350.00 for the three, the brother lowers it to $280.00. I pay and leave to visit the other brother.

When I enter the second shop, and the brother there sees me carrying a bag of three rugs, he flushes with anger and asks if he can look at them. Then I realize that this is Hosam, the brother from whom I had bought rugs the last time. He is adamant that two of the rugs are flawed and I should return them, or I should insist on paying half price. I am reluctant to do this, especially on the blue Persian kilim, which I like most. He maintains the dye will not hold. The flaws seem minor to me, but I return, dutifully, to the other brother, Abdul, and complain about the price and the flaws. Initially he refuses to deal, then agrees to lower the price, but only 10 percent. After some embarrassed negotiating, I return one carpet (with the thought I will buy an alternative in Hosam's shop) and negotiate a reduction on a second.

I return to Hosam, still red-faced, and he asks me to spell out what I did. To be caught in such explicit fighting between brothers is unusual—and makes me very uncomfortable. I explain, and Hosam still insists I was overcharged; I should return again to his brother and demand a greater reduction. I say that I am satisfied with the price and ask him instead to show me some rugs, and I purchase one.

Later, I ask a neighboring merchant if he knows what is going on. The two brothers, he explains, had an argument and split the business into two after sharing it since their father's death. Since the two shops offer different advantages, they could not agree on how to separate, so they initially moved back and forth, alternating shops monthly. For eight years, then, on the first of each month, Hosam would take all his goods and move into Abdul's shop; Abdul would take all his goods and move into Hosam's shop. Now, they are sabotaging each other's businesses, while still forced to switch shops monthly.

Such fights between brothers following the death of the father surely take place in Aleppo also, but I do not witness any during my stay. I make it a point, however, to follow two other cases of inheritance after a father's death. In one case, Fadil is a single son who, at the age of twenty-nine, inherits three small shops from his father. In order to run the shops, he must employ distant cousins, and he constantly complains to me that they do not know how to sell. Therefore, he runs back and forth between the shops, which are located near each other, to either assume responsibility for sales or to monitor the activity of his employees. Sometimes he even closes one of the shops rather than bother with the hassle of controlling sales there. Once, while he was in another shop monitoring his employee, a customer stole his expensive cell phone. Other merchants had seen the boy run, but nobody seemed to recognize him. For a month, Fadil was beside himself. His goal is to sell his three shops and assume ownership of a larger one, in a more prominent place, which he can then manage on his own, or to sell them all and find another business. On my last visit, Fadil was proud that he had saved enough to buy himself a small Japanese truck—ten years old—and he had set up a television in one shop. The next step will be to install a satellite on the roof.

The other case involves a young man who declared his independence from his father, though the father is still alive, by buying his own shop. He is the object of much gossip, and rumors swirl around him, especially about how he acquired this wealth, either by selling himself to Western tourists, or by working for the Mukhabarrat. Through unparalleled network skills, he knows literally everyone in the souk and can direct customers to fulfill their needs, for both goods and services. His shop stands slightly outside the Souk al-Medina, and therefore he has been able to buy a neighboring space and expand it some, with a secret back room and two floors. He has hired a brother to work for him, along with several friends. The police keep a close eye on him, and, aware of his success, periodically extort money from him. Once they even imprisoned him for tax evasion, a charge perhaps real enough but used usually for political purposes and also simply to extort money from the vulnerable.

Dream Collector

Majid calls me a dream collector because I make a point of asking people about their dreams. Freud famously defined dreams as the "fulfillment of a wish," and I see them as windows into complex motivations, how people envision their world, and what they generally want from it. Dreams are especially important for recording wishes that people are most reluctant to express openly to themselves or to others. Most people I ask say they cannot remember their dreams. Majid's nephew, Mahmood, who assists him in the shop, says he remembers only the dreams that repeat. In one, he is licking a woman, sometimes even her feet. His uncle overhears him and says, "He asked for dreams, not nightmares!"

The next day when I ask Mahmood again, he says, "I dreamt of having a knife and using it on my uncle Majid."

Mahmood also thinks by "dream" I mean simply what he wants, and whom he desires—whom among the customers that walk by he consciously desires. From his shop he yells after them: "Miss!" "Señora!" "Fraülein!" "Mademoiselle!" "Señorita!" "Madame!" Invariably the women he singles out are the older ones in the group, the grandmothers, who cannot believe this hunky, broad-shouldered twenty-year-old has his bright eyes on them, and then, as they walk away, he closes his eyes tightly and says wistfully, "My cup of tea."

I try to explain to Mahmood that I want not daydreams but dreams from his unconscious, from his sleeping hours, and he must remember or write these down as soon as he wakes.

Majid dismisses my wish, "Mahmood only dreams during the day."

One late afternoon, as I prepare to leave his shop, Mahmood says, "I will dream for you tonight, perhaps not of women but of boys."

I reply, "Let yourself go in your dream, Mahmood, perhaps dream of goats or sheep. I don't care."

"But I want to have a dream for you," he says.

"Don't," I reply.

The next day, Mahmood greets me with a dream, "I was swimming naked. There were lots of people: boys, girls, women, men. And the water tasted like blood. What do you think?"

"I don't really know, Mahmood," I say, "but perhaps you fear nudity, or the mixing of naked men and women, that it will result in violence."

Another time, I was at the home of a friend from the souk, who had also invited Aleppo's French Catholic priest, who rarely says anything in these settings. My friend's brother joins us later in the evening to smoke the *narghile*, the local water pipe. I never smoke with them, and I am perhaps the only person they do not offer a toke to when smoking. "I am Stalinist on this issue," I say, and encourage them minimally not to puff deeply, and to smoke later as opposed to earlier in the day. Sometimes, if the business in the souk is very slow, people begin smoking shortly after lunch. Even more than cigarettes, smoking the *narghile*—the tobacco comes in many flavors—appears to have an anesthetizing effect and induces dreamlike states, states of reverie where people can quit thinking without discomfort, where they can enjoy being in a group but no speech is required. I experience the most prolonged silences when others are smoking the *narghile*. Of course, it is selfish of me to want people to be thinking, elaborating, explaining all the time, so for the most part I try not to be a pest and just let everyone continue their normal routines. At the same time, I tell them, especially young men and women, "I want you to live; that is why I don't want you to smoke." Alternately, in my less selfish moods, I think: let them smoke. Who am I to tell them how to lead their lives?

My friend's brother also knows I am interested in dreams, and, smiling, he says out of the blue to me and the Catholic priest, "Last night I dreamed of Jesus. I saw him, and we actually shook hands.

It was very nice." The priest does little to acknowledge this generous sharing of a dream, perhaps a wish for religious connection, or reconciliation—but that is the priest's way: quiet and nonexpressive, toking away on his water pipe, smiling, rocking back and forth, nodding his head.

I say to the brother, "That is a beautiful wish." How wonderful, I think, for this adult man, a father of three sons, a Muslim, to be reaching out to two Christians. Even though Muslims consider Jesus a prophet, and therefore the connection he was making was nothing extraordinary, Christians seem to have no way of appreciating his dream of greeting their God.

I rarely remember my own dreams, but the urge to collect them stirs some kind of odd memory work on my part. I dream about Spot, my dog, a whippet, who is staying with a friend in Ithaca, New York, while I am in Syria. It is summer, I am on a farm, and it is the harvest season of cutting grass and baling hay. When the hay mower goes through the fresh grass, it cuts indiscriminately. But that grass is filled with small animals, especially nests of newborn mice and rats, which the farm cats enjoy hunting, even during the harvest season. I remember as a child discovering chopped mice and rats in bales of hay; sometimes our cats, too, would return home chopped up, and sometimes they simply returned home injured, missing a leg or part of their tails, or cut badly. In my dream Spot had had an accident with the hay mower. There was also a party going on, in the house of a well-to-do friend. My partner was there, downstairs, and he just got up and left without telling me.

I am disturbed by my own dream. Dreams of the anxiety of separation never end. So I buy a big tub of yoghurt, some bananas, and nuts, and I stay home that night, also to nurse along some stomach problems I had been having.

Dream of the Mistress

When I ask people about their dreams, they also think I am asking them about their aspirations. Amir, a vendor in the souk who lived in Germany (his father was a *Gastarbeiter* in the 1980s in Bavaria) between the ages of twelve and thirteen, is both an employee and employer. He is employed selling jewelry in a medium-sized shop, and he also employs a man to run his own smaller jewelry shop down the street. In both businesses, his relations are not with kin but impersonal, based purely on shared monetary interests. I am impressed that Amir converses in five European languages—English, German, French, Italian, and Spanish—with a grammatical precision that betrays a disciplined intelligence. He admits that he has a great ear for sound, and for the ability to reproduce it, but also explains, humbly, he is competent because in the souk he repeats constantly the same content in conversations in these languages. He is married but also has a Spanish lover who visits several times a year, or he occasionally travels to meet her in Spain or Turkey. His wife is very jealous of this relationship, he says, especially about the trips he takes.

Most men say no when I initially ask if they would like to take a second wife. But as I get to know them better, the desire for a second wife is often close to the surface. Whether this desire becomes explicit seems to depend most on whether men can afford it monetarily, and very few men today can. Many wives accept a second wife only under certain conditions—they must be lower in status, less educated, and willing to accommodate themselves to (and even work for) the first wife. As in the story of the forty-two-year-old Mohammed who had married (and divorced) a French woman, the longterm success of such an arrangements requires both money and the cooperation of the first wife. Foreign women as second wives present peculiar problems to a native first wife, as they are usually better educated, of higher status, and financially autonomous.

Amir appears to balance a traditional Muslim marriage with his Arab wife and a mistress arrangement with his Spanish lover. The fact that many European women are willing to share love and sex without marriage creates the novel opportunity for Amir to live a set of relations that are half–European, half–Middle Eastern. He recently bought a small villa in the souk, and is fixing it up in his spare time. A French family offered to rent it for three years, at $600 a month, which is a lot of money in the Syrian economy, but he says he is not interested in the money. He could have rented it to someone last year also, if he had wanted to. The house is his dream, and it is just for him, he says, "I like to go there and just sit sometimes." But, though the house seems to symbolize autonomy, something just his own and not embedded in his social obligations, I suspect that he sits in it also dreaming of his mistress, and her occasional presence is part of the dream of the house.

"How great is my disappointment when I see my dreams breaking down"

Within days of Basil's agreement to translate some of my essays, I meet the owner of the gallery Kalimat, who expresses interest in publishing them. He says he likes the way I think, even though he has hardly heard enough Arabic from me to make any more than an intuitive judgment about the quality of my thought. He wants to branch out into publishing interesting new writing, he says, in addition to art books. I suggest he contact a friend in Beirut who also had been engaged in select publishing for small audiences. All of a sudden, with no planning and little effort on my part, I have a translator and a publisher in the Arab world, though still no teaching assignment.

Instead of giving Basil an already published book to translate, I give him a few recently published essays that had stimulated much debate within the field of anthropology, and some talks that I had not yet published—all on the general topic of national and international accountability. These essays, I reason, would be more interesting and socially challenging for an Arab audience than my previous work dealing primarily with Germany during the Cold War or in its immediate transformations after, or with Europe more generally. We meet frequently to discuss problems in translations—concepts for which Arabic offers many more possibilities than English, such as gift, exchange, dominance, legitimation, international order, and sex.

After several months, the gallery owner's enthusiasm for publishing wanes, so through a friend in Beirut I submit the manuscript to An Nahar, one of the leading publishers in the Arab world. Three months later, the editors at An Nahar send me an email—our correspondence is in French—rejecting the manuscript, not because of the quality of thought (which they praise) but because of problems in the translation from English to Arabic that might make it difficult for an Arabic-speaking audience to understand some of the essays. I cannot judge the accuracy of the translation myself, but I suspect that the topic—an anthropology of accountability—is simply too unfamiliar to make much sense. My prior conversations with the publisher led me to conclude that his own understanding of anthropological topics stopped with the work on the structural study of myth of Claude Lévi-Strauss, which may be related theoretically to my own work but is far removed topically. Additionally, the publishing house and its editors are suddenly preoccupied with leading the Lebanese protests to end Syrian occupation (more frequently called hegemony), which result in massive, peaceful street demonstrations in Beirut, a withdrawal of Syrian troops from Lebanon, and ultimately in the tragic assassination of Gibran Tueni, the publisher himself.

Then a friend introduces me to a couple of publishers in Damascus. One agrees to publish my manuscript immediately, but demands I pay $2,000 up front for the first edition. Since I am not used to paying to have my work published (I usually get an advance!), I decide instead to submit it to Ammar Abdulhamid, a civil rights activist and founder of DarEmar, a new press in Damascus. Ammar is the coordinator of the Tharwa Project, an NGO that promotes initiatives on minorities, diversity, gender, nonviolence, and civil society. Most important, for my purposes, he has built up a team to translate classical liberal political and social theory into Arabic. Whenever I hear the name of his project—*tharwa* is the Arabic word for wealth, I instead think of *thawra*, which means revolution, and of the *jeel al-thawra*, the revolutionary generation of Ba'ath Party members who took control of the Syrian state in the 1960s. Once I ask an Allepian friend who is a dentist about his experiences with this generation; he tells me a funny story from the 1980s: A professor who was their best teacher in dentistry used humor to make concepts understandable. In making everything into a joke, he could mitigate the threat of his critique, which was that dentistry in Syria had to change its methods, all of them, totally; hence Syrians needed *thawra fi tibb al-asnan*, "a revolution in dentistry." In every lecture, he would repeat and elongate the word—*thawwwwwwra* in dentistry, *thawwwwwra* in dentistry. Eventually the university did not renew his contract, officially, they said, because they wanted to give the younger generation a chance to teach.

I had heard that Ammar's hair was waist length, and that he was a radical, and I had read about the controversy surrounding his one published novel. So at our first meeting, in his office, I say, "I have heard of your book *Masturbation*."

"*Menstruation*," he corrects me and smiles.

"Freudian slip!"

Ammar's hair is now short and tidy. He speaks American-accented English, which he learned while completing a bachelor's degree at the University of Wisconsin, Stevens Point, and he says he owes his interest in liberal theory to that period of his life. I grew up not all that far from Stevens Point and have a hard time imagining how such a Wisconsin experience—in my days, Stevens Point was known only for its powerful high school football team—could have radicalized anybody, much less produced an interest in political theory. Ammar also publishes a blog, which he calls a "heretic's blog" (http://amarji.blogspot.com/), with entries such as:

> It is because I was so filled with fear yesterday that I am so rebellious today, and will continue to be.
>
> The regime reaps what the regime sows I guess. Their foolhardiness begets and feeds mine. That's the irony of it all.
>
> My demons rape me. I spit acid in my demons' face. My demons rape me again, and so again I spit acid, until we are all eventually vanquished. There are no winners in this game. Nor will there ever be.—So be it, for now.
>
> If my demons want me dead, mine will be a public crucifixion—this I promise. If my demons keep me alive, theirs will be a public trial—

constant, nagging, merciless. If my demons get me by the throat, I'll get them by the balls. If they get me by the hand, I'll get them by their hooves. And if they hang me by my legs, I'll piss in their face, and perhaps even mine . . . who cares?

I might just be their last straw, you know. I might just be that little tiny hair that will soon break their backs.

I can imagine how this blog written as a literal allegory with a raplike rhythm offends Syrian governmental authorities, to whom it is obviously addressed. Unlike most American rap, the text is remarkably lucid and unambiguous in its message; its grammatically correct English seeks to clarify and offend simultaneously.

Ammar's team of translators check my manuscript, and express enthusiasm for publishing it. But a couple of weeks later, Ammar sends me an email with some disappointing news:

Dear John,

Sorry for the delay. . . . [D]espite the need for some serious revisions in certain parts, the translation of the book is, nonetheless, good and we actually want to go ahead with it, as per our agreement. The problem is that this whole thing is rather academic now. My family and I are planning to leave the country soon. We have just received a clear cut threat from a certain General. Life is no longer safe for us here. So, at this stage, I cannot commit any resources for this endeavor. I am really sorry, but I have to make sure that my donors get their funds back or that I pass them along to our representatives in Lebanon. Having said this, let me say that I have really enjoyed your work, and I look forward to staying in touch with you in the future, the States being our most likely destination at this stage.

Sincerely,

Ammar

I notify Basil, my translator, who is beside himself about the bad turn of events. Additionally, he reports that he is unable to complete his exams and applications for graduate study in the States—his father needs extra money to pay the Bedouins who harvest his crops. Basil must work overtime as an accountant to make up this difference. He writes, "Surrounded by many obstacles, you cannot imagine how much I suffer and how great is my disappointment when I see my dreams breaking down." I then submit the manuscript to a German publisher of Arabic texts in Cologne, through a contact with my Egyptian-born Arabic tutor in Princeton. The Arab-German publisher, unfortunately, speaks no English, so I have Basil send samples from the Arabic translation, and I correspond with him in German. He responds that his press is too small.

"Every woman thinks I only want to sleep with her"

Zuhayr is one of the most attractive young men in the souk, and I notice that he likes to be told that he looks good. Three young Italian women stop in front of his shop. At first they appear fearful and try to walk past quickly. But Zuhayr yells after them, "Excuse me! Excuse me!" And something about the innocence of his voice or his smile or refined looks charms them into turning around. They obviously find him very attractive, and linger, looking at the boxes and shawls he is selling, but they do not buy anything. One asks him if he has ever visited Italy.

"No," he says.

"You should come, you'll have no problem with women there," she says. He looks at me after they leave, raises his eyebrows and scoffs at this compliment, wanting to believe but not trusting himself to. Other than traveling within Syria during his army service, he has only been to Damascus a few times and never been outside the country.

"What do they mean?" he asks me.

"They mean that women in Italy will stick to you like flies to honey," I say and, after a pause, add, "Today you look like a movie star." He is wearing a white, half-sleeve shirt and jeans, and radiates a kind of soft, masculine beauty.

"Really?" he asks, enthusiastically. He smiles widely, and confides, "I dream of being in the movies. I would be the tragic type and play the hero."

"Which heroic actor do you like best?" I ask.

"Sylvester Stallone."

"He's not my type. What do you like about him?"

"I like the way he smokes, without emotion, and how he throws his cigarettes away—Zuhayr mimics Stallone, tossing a butt into the middle of the aisle, and then, like Stallone in his Vietnam films, he mimes spraying bullets all over.

The Italian girls spend several hours in Zuhayr's shop over the next several days. The evening before they depart, they set up a rendezvous in a café. Zuhayr invites me along, and brings two cousins. At some point in the café, the girls begin to cry. Two days ago they were ready to go home; now they want to stay. They are very taken by Zuhayr's attention. He makes them promise to come back to the souk the next day, and he will give them a gift. This makes them even more emotional, as they never even bought anything from him after spending hours drinking tea and coffee in his shop, and here he is offering them a gift. The rest of the evening, each in turn flirts with him, looking searchingly into his eyes, touching him, stroking his hand, engaging him to talk about himself.

To me, it seems obvious they want to sneak him into their hotel room. But Zuhayr does not take them up on this implicit offer, and later he explains why, "They were so distrustful at first, and now they want to stay, but cannot; their flight is tomorrow. I like that."

Another time in the souk, toward the end of the day, an American woman, also quite taken with Zuhayr, is sitting in his shop. It is very hot and humid, and we are all sweating. He stands up, picks up an aerosol underarm deodorant, and sprays himself all over. "You are asphyxiating me," she objects, coughing, and tries to wave the mist away with her hands.

"I'm sorry," he says, not comprehending her environmental objection. "I'm done. You don't like the smell?"

"No, you smell good now." she says, "If I were a mosquito, I'm sure I'd have eaten you up by now."

After she leaves, he asks me to translate. "Beaten me up? She means beat, they would beat me? Why?"

"No," I say, she means, "Mosquitoes bite. Not 'beat' but 'bite.'" And now I am confused and explaining the wrong thing, "What she was saying is not 'beaten' but 'eaten.' She mumbles. It's a compliment; she wants to eat you like a mosquito would."

Nearly daily in the afternoons in late summer, I see a French girl in Zuhayr's shop. Caroline is about ten years older than him. She lives in Aleppo and has a three-year contract to teach at the French school. The French Catholic priest had brought her to the souk one day and introduced her to Zuhayr. They communicate mostly in English, but Caroline also works with Zuhayr on his French, and she gives him French music cassettes. He plays the songs constantly, memorizes some of the lyrics, and then asks me what they mean. He speaks much better French than I do, but I have a larger vocabulary and can read better.

"Why don't you make a date with her?" I ask.

"I don't want her."

"What do you want?"

"Every woman thinks I only want to sleep with her. When I was young, they ignored me. Now, I like it that they want me, and then I say, 'no,' so they know I want more. Now, I wait; when I find the right woman, I will be loyal."

After about three months of visits, Caroline makes a scene in the shop and says Zuhayr is ignoring her; he knows what she wants. She will come back one more day, and then he must leave with her or she will never return. Zuhayr describes the scene to me and asks me what to do. Do what you want, I say.

The next day, Zuhayr goes to her apartment after work. It was his second sexual experience (the first was the year before, with a prostitute).

"How was it?" I ask.

She told me how her opinion of me changed; that in the beginning, when we first met, she had the opposite opinion of me than she has now. Then she thought I was just a flirt, just interested in using her for sex.

"She didn't want to let me go," he says. "Every time I get to the door, she starts kissing me again, and we go back at it."

"Will you do it again?" I ask.

"If I am really horny, yes, again."

Indeed, it turns into regular sex, which has a calming effect on Zuhayr; he seems to me more relaxed and contented, less moody. He explains that he realizes he cannot please her; she always wants more of everything. She wants him to spend nights. "But I cannot. My parents! I have to work the next day," he excuses himself. He visits her several times a week, and she comes to the souk daily. In high school, he explains, before he served time in the army, he used to go to the homes of friends every night, to talk, listen to music, smoke the narghile, play cards. So his parents are used to him coming home very late, after they have already gone to bed, but they expect that he will sleep in his own bed and be there when they wake up.

Despite the nocturnal visits, Zuhayr remains noncommittal. "She called twice today," he says; "I never call her, she calls me."

"Why not?" I ask.

"Better to play hard to catch," he smiles; "I'll wait for her to make the move again."

"Why, if you like her?" I ask.

"Because I am unsure," he says.

Caroline sends Zuhayr text messages on a cousin's mobile phone, or email messages to his Hotmail account. She writes in French, and Zuhayr asks me to translate. Love messages, sweet, poetic, expressing the joy of newly discovered, or rediscovered, pleasures. Once she wrote him a message on the Internet just before they had sex. He had to wait until he went home to retrieve it, and then he printed it to show me. She wrote that Zuhayr was sad, and she detested his sadness. She wanted to give him all the things he deserved, and she hoped to do that tonight.

They take a trip together with some of his cousins and the Catholic priest who brought them together. Zuhayr dotes on Caroline the entire day, ignoring the priest, who then stays away from the souk for a whole week, as if punishing Zuhayr. Several times in the next few days Zuhayr calls him to persuade him to return. Even though the priest had initially set up the contact, I suspect that he secretly wanted Zuhayr for himself, at least emotionally, and is ultimately disappointed at the lack of attention. Zuhayr explains to me that he feels bad about the priest's absence, that in the future he will pay him more attention when they are together.

The dynamic of the relationship with Caroline changes quickly, and Zuhayr reluctantly draws closer. Soon the tables are reversed:

he says he is demanding sex from her when she is tired and not in the mood. "Four times yesterday," he says proudly. "She didn't want to, but I forced her."

Caroline proposes to marry him. They can live in another country. She suggests former French colonies—Algeria, Morocco—or elsewhere in Europe—Greece or Spain. She does not want to return to France but would reconsider if he so desired.

"And what of your parents, do they know what is going on?" I ask.

"My father senses something but says nothing. My mother doesn't know."

"But surely she senses a change in your mood, at least," I say.

"They know what I'd do if they said something," he confesses. "They'd lose me. I'd go work for someone else in Aleppo, if necessary, in any shop. They know that."

"Why not marry her?" I ask.

"Do you think I should marry her?" he asks in return.

"It is an opportunity. It depends on what you want. I think you should do what is best for you."

"I cannot," he says. "My mother. It would kill her."

The souk is a place of rumor, and Caroline's presence becomes a source of gossip. Zuhayr tells her not to come daily anymore.

"It's a scandal," he says. "Everyone talks about it. Even men in neighboring shops, and way down there"—he points far in the distance—"they stop by and ask me about her. They want to know everything."

"Don't your cousins who work in the souk talk about it?"

"Not much, at least not in public."

Cell Phone, Cassettes, String Underwear

Toward the end of the year, I tell friends in the souk that I have to take a trip to the States for a week, and they begin to make up shopping lists of what they want from America. They all promise to reimburse me for whatever the items cost.

One friend is going to do his military service soon; he wants a tiny used cell phone that he can tuck secretly into his boot. I tell him that he can buy these in Beirut, and cheaper than in the States. But, he insists, the Americans must have more choices. He distrusts the Lebanese.

Zuhayr wants a new cassette player to use at work during the day. I say, you can buy this downtown in Aleppo. But, he insists, the brands they have are cheap and break right away; Syria does not get good quality imports.

Majid wants three pairs of string underwear: red, black, and white. "Majid," I say, "you cannot get these at most shopping centers in the States, I have to go to a specialty store in a big city." He protests, "But we do not have them here at all. Try, if you can, to find them."

"That is fieldwork!"

I am sitting in a shop in the souk. A fairly tall, slender man of about forty wearing loose pants and a kind of cowboy shirt walks by and catches my eye. He shifts his eyes quickly from me to the opposite direction: a signal I should follow him. I stand up and excuse myself. The aisles are crowded. He paces himself to stay about nine feet in front of me, turns several corners, and walks into a large toilet next to a mosque. A middle-aged man sits at the entrance, presumably to take coins for its use. We walk past him to the urinals, and stand side by side: I take the opportunity to pee. We check each other out. The toilet is busy, and his eyes keep shifting to the door; he seems to anticipate some intervention by the man there. He motions, again only with darting eyes, that we should leave.

Outside we exchange names. Mohammed works in an area south of the souk. I tell him to meet me in front of Khan Nahasin in a couple of hours. But when I return home he is not there. The next day he finds me in the souk and catches my eye again, and I follow him down the aisle. He says he came yesterday and waited for me, but an hour earlier than I thought we had arranged. He begins walking, I do not know where, but I follow, obeying the dictate of a good ethnographer. I always hope to be put into situations, unusual situations, not of my own construction.

Outside the souk we arrive at his small Toyota truck. "Not my apartment?" I ask.

"No, too many Mukhabarrat," he says, referring to the supposed omnipresence of the secret police in the souk. Instead, he will take me to his home, just outside Aleppo.

"But where is your family?" I ask.

He has a wife and four children, but he says they will not be there this time of day. We drive, and drive, and drive.

Ten minutes go by. I ask, "How far is it?"

"I want your shirt," he says. I am wearing a rough linen Barney's short-sleeve shirt. The color is an unusually dark green. When I say no, he smiles and suggests we trade shirts.

"But I have only four shirts with me, and I need them all for lectures at the university," I explain, though of course this is merely an excuse. Of all the clothes I brought with me, I like this green shirt too much to part with now, and I would never wear the Wild West patterned one he has on.

He explains that he had been sick last year and had a heart transplant operation, and pulls up his shirt to show me the scar running the length of his chest. "Still recovering," he says.

We end up driving half an hour, about fifteen kilometers outside the city. We do not go to his house—why did I even think we would?—but pass by his village, and many fields of pistachio trees, and turn onto a dirt lane. We drive through several very flat fields, a rather sad landscape with a few stalks of wheat sprouting out of an unrelentingly drab, brown earth. We arrive at an olive orchard.

Mohammed is horny as hell. He gets out of the truck, unbuckles his belt, unzips his pants, and pulls his organ out of his underwear. He barely looks at or touches me. What is his vision: dueling cocks? This is not my idea of sex, but I give him credit for being direct about what he wants. The field is rocky, the ground dry and dusty and soft, my sandals sink into it. There is no place to lie down. No matter, that is not his intent. It takes about ten seconds: he comes, with a kind of pained look on his face—pain, release, pleasure—and takes a Kleenex out of his pocket to wipe himself clean.

On the way back, he again expresses desire for my shirt. Why don't I just give it to him?

Instead I keep saying, "I am the gift. Aren't you happy with me?"

"Oh yes," he says, and looks pleased, though I think he is just being nice. He asks about how much I earn, how much a house in the United States costs, how much a car, how much food. I am annoyed that so much of his curiosity is focused on money but, then again, why not? He explains that tomorrow is the beginning of Ramadan, a month of fasting and abstinence when Muslims are to concentrate on their faith, and he can have no more sex until after Ramadan.

"But that is only during the day," I say.

He interprets what I say to mean I want him to spend a night with me. "No," he says, "I am married, the fourth time. And you?" The question is usually the first one asked; he has waited a long time.

"No," I say, "divorced."

He has five children, three sons from his present marriage, and one child, also a son, from one of the other marriages.

I express admiration for all of his sons, but I ask why he divorced so often. He simply shrugs his shoulders: not happy.

I tell Majid about this experience, not of the usual desire deferred but where someone seemed to have found his object. He laughs, "That is fieldwork!"

"A father, perhaps a brother"

Between the souk and my apartment, at the foot of the hill leading to the old Christian quarter of Jdaideh, I discover a row of candy stores where I can buy chocolate. I ask a young clerk which are the best. He doesn't know, but agrees to let me taste them. I try about four, offering him the first bite of each half—as an Arab, he cannot refuse—and then I taste the other half myself. His lips do not so much as wrap around the candy as kiss it, along with my fingers. I introduce myself as an American.

Mustafa is twenty-one, about six feet tall and still a bit pimply, with bright and mischievous eyes, wavy dark brown hair, shapely lips, front teeth with a small gap between, and big hands that betray a workingman's touch. He wears a t-shirt and tightly fitted, stone-

washed jeans, and describes himself, jokingly, as "rough and tough."
He came to Aleppo four months ago, after failing his secondary
school exams, and now does remedial study in the morning, then
begins work at noon, or, on those days when he skips school, he
works ten until four in the afternoon, or perhaps until eight or nine.
"I can stay up a whole day and get by with very little sleep," he
explains.

The next time I drop by, he puts his arm around me and proclaims
to a clerk next door, "We are friends," and simultaneously lets out
an innocent, infectious laugh. I take his hand, as men do here when
they are creating intimacy or confidence, but he does not hold on,
as they usually do. He lets my hand drop after a few minutes.

In the early afternoon a few days later, I am walking past the
Grand Mosque. I hear, "Mr. John! Mr. John!" It is Mustafa, on his
way to pray, he says, and then he will go to sleep. I offer to show
him my apartment first.

"Would you like some tea?" I ask, once inside.

"I'm fasting," he replies, with a look of incomprehension.

Of course. Why had I asked? It's impolite to tempt him during
Ramadan, and surely he must be thirsty by this time of day. "Sorry,
I forgot," I say.

He proposes walking around town with me later. I have an appointment at eight, I say, so perhaps after. He leaves, smiling and
giggling.

Mustafa calls around eleven that evening, while I am eating at the
restaurant Challal with a friend from the university. I tell him my
friend will soon want to return home. Meet me at the restaurant.

He calls again, several times—he cannot find the restaurant—and
arrives a half hour later, accompanied by a second cousin with whom
he works. Mustafa sells sweets; the cousin delivers them. Challal is
a very upscale place, not the kind Mustafa or his cousin are likely
to visit; still, it is a well-known restaurant in this largely Christian
neighborhood. They refuse an offer of food but agree to join me for
a drink—tea, that is. We move to a larger table, Mustafa sits across
from me, his cousin to the side. The cousin is quiet but pleasant
enough. Mustafa wears his hair greased down, a chic style that many

young men prefer; the cousin wears his sheared on the sides, longish on the top, also a popular style but one that makes his head look unflatteringly oblong.

I ask about fasting. Mustafa admits, with a grin, that he drank tea this morning, but he did not eat.

"If I did, I'd have to repeat the day again," he says. I note he is apparently rather relaxed—for a Sunni Muslim—about dietary rules. His cousin says that he himself abstained from both water and food this morning.

Mustafa is in good spirits. He flirts with me for a couple of hours, asking teasing questions about my marriage and divorce. Why not remarry? What do you think of me? He asks my age. I say guess. He guesses forty. I say fifty-one. And instead of saying, "Just as I thought," as do most young people, he exclaims, "You are old! You look much younger."

The two boys tell me about their families and their work. Mustafa misses Dara, his hometown near the Israeli border, and Damascus, where he has been living; he is in Aleppo only because of the work. His cousin shares no plans for the future other than to work for his father and uncles. We meander back to the souk, walking on the street three abreast, sometimes arms over shoulders, sometimes holding hands. It is around one o'clock in the morning, the humidity is gone, the city quiet, the moon lights our way. Mustafa comments that he is locked out of his hostel after midnight. I invite him to sleep in the extra bedroom in my apartment. "Maybe," he says, "but I can also stay over at my cousin's. He lives nearby."

As we near the souk, Mustafa suddenly announces, "Yes, I will stay with you tonight!"

"That will be nice," I reply, uncertain as to what he expects.

"I am very happy. I am very happy tonight!" he exclaims. "I feel as if I have known you for a long time."

I thank him for the compliment, and we keep walking.

"What do you think of me?" he asks, again.

"You are nice, nice—*jayid, jayid*—handsome, clever."

He laughs, "No, I am not clever." I put my arm around his shoulder as we walk on. His cousin splits when we reach the entrance to

Figure 20. The Sacred

the souk at the Grand Mosque. We all say goodbye; they kiss each other on the cheek.

After the intricate task of finding the right keys and opening all the locks on the doors to the khan and apartment, we step inside, take off our shoes, drink some water. Mustafa wants to eat—now is the time for his second meal—and he especially wants bread, Arabic bread, what Americans call pita bread, flat loaves which in the morning are laid out on blankets on the sidewalk to cool and dry before being stacked and put in plastic bags, ten or more to a bag. I rarely buy a bag because I can never eat more than one a day, and then I am tempted to throw the rest away, which I shouldn't, because Arabs think of bread as something precious. They never, never throw bread away, but put it out for the poor, or leave it in an open place for birds or other animals. I have no bread and, in fact, very little food on hand.

Mustafa is visibly disappointed that I have no bread. After he wakes he will not eat or drink the entire day, and he must work for ten hours. In the sitting room I put out everything I have: some nut-

and-honey pastries, dry cookies, pomegranates, raisins, nuts, olives, grapes. He does not touch the nuts, but eats pomegranate seeds, after adding a ton of sugar, and he wants to share them with me. Way too sweet for my tastes! I try to feed him some, but he says no, he likes to eat and drink on his own; nonetheless, we should eat out of the same bowl.

An hour is spent with him setting boundaries. We sit together, he stands and sits in the chair across from me, he returns to sit by me—but this time he crosses his legs so they point away from me, and, whereas initially he looked in my eyes as he talked, now he occasionally looks away. I have the distinct impression that he has an erection but is trying to cool it off. Maybe I am wrong.

He asks, again, "Why don't you want to remarry?"

"There are many forms of love," I say, "and everyone should experience marriage once. But why twice? You understand?"

"Yes, I understand," he says.

"And you, when do you want to marry?" I ask.

"I don't know," he says. "I am too young. Later. But I can get married four times."

"Will you?"

"Maybe."

I play some music on my Mac G4 laptop. He does not like the Swiss-born Julien Weiss and his al-Kindi Ensemble. (Julien lives down the street in the souk and plays the zither (*qanun*) and reinterprets classical Arabic melodies.) He does not like Joni Mitchell, or Bjork, or Mozart. There is not much music on my computer to choose from, but finally I find something to his taste: "Istampitta," a French recording of Medieval European dance music. After about five minutes, though, he says he is really tired.

"Can I kiss you?" I ask.

"No."

"No?"

"No."

His emphatic "no's" make me smile. Once in response to this question, another young man his age answers, "Just a little."

"Okay, then," I say, "let's go to bed," and I give him my last bottle of water from the refrigerator, in case he wants to drink before sunrise.

"Which room?" he asks.

"Whichever you want," I say, and I point to my bedroom, "I sleep in this room."

"Then I will go here," he says, taking the bedroom opposite across the hall.

"When do you want to get up?"

"Ten," he says. I can hear him trying to lock the door to his room, but it does not lock—it barely shuts.

I say, "Keep it open for a breeze. And open the window in your room."

He does, and keeps the light on the entire night as he smokes and tosses in the bed. I am a light sleeper and hear the repeated sound of a match lighting, before I eventually doze off.

The next morning, he gets up at nine instead of ten. I am already giving an English lesson to Ahmad, and we discuss the research he is doing for me. I introduce them to each other.

"Why couldn't you sleep?" I ask Mustafa.

"I don't know."

"You were so tired."

"Yes."

He joins us at the table, drinks some tea, smokes, and observes the English lesson and our interaction closely. And he looks me in the eyes, directly and friendly, as he interrupts us, first to ask for a comb (I have none), then to ask the meaning of "research."

I finish the lesson with Ahmad by introducing some new questions I want him to explore with merchants and workers.

Mustafa stands to leave, and says to me, "You are welcome in my shop anytime." We shake hands.

A few days later, I stop at his shop, and the new clerk says Mustafa is in Damascus.

Mustafa takes to calling me from Damascus—"whenever I feel like it," he explains—at noon, at midnight, at two in the morning. Because he has no money, he calls and hangs up before I answer.

Then even if I do not answer, I know he has called—my cell phone records this information—and I return his call when I am free.

A week later, he calls while I am eating dinner, coincidentally again at Challal. "Where have you been?" I ask.

He is in his hometown, Dara, near the Israeli border. "My grandmother died," he answers my question.

"I am sorry," I say. I explain that I inquired about him at the shop where he worked, but he is never there.

"I quit," he says. He got into a fight with the owner and hit him with his fist, something I have never witnessed.

"I want to see you," he says. "I want to work for you."

"But I am not an employer! I don't have employees! What would you do?"

"Anything," he says, "anything you want."

I do not know how to understand his request. What does he want? Care? Closeness? What work? The sudden infusion of money into our friendship makes me uneasy. Prostitution? Not to lose me? I tell him I will be traveling the next couple of weeks; when I return we can discuss his proposal. That same day two other young men I know call: a waiter and another young man who works for his father in the souk—both want me to join them with their families for *iftar*, the "breakfast" at dusk during Ramadan,

"Hello, do you know who this is?"

"No," I reply.

"This is Mohammed."

"Hello, Mohammed."

"Come soon," says Mohammed.

"Tomorrow morning," I say.

"I miss you. Goodbye, my love."

I suspect he calls out of boredom. Young people learn a standard English-language response to foreigners they have already seen: "I miss you." A kind of sincere twist to "Where ya been?" or "What's up?" As for "my love," he translates directly from *habibi*, which has as its root *hub*, meaning "to love," or merely, "to like." To close with "Goodbye, my love" most likely means to him simply "goodbye to my cherished friend" or "goodbye to you whom I like."

I visit Damascus for several days the next month, and tell Mustafa I will reserve one night for him. "You know where the juice bar Abu Shaker is?" I ask. "It is near the apartment of a friend where I am staying."

"Yes, yes," he says, in a tone that makes me think he does not really know where it is. I suggest instead the Cham Palace Hotel, on the far corner in front of the Cham Palace Cinema.

He is a quarter of an hour late, and greets me with a smile and a single kiss on the cheek. He is wearing a long black leather trench-coat, making him look like Count Dracula or a figure out of *Mad Max*. Exactly as he wants: tall, handsome, dashing. But Damascus is hot and humid, and when we sit down, he reluctantly takes the coat off, and he has a thin sweatshirt on underneath.

"I put everything aside to meet you," he says. "I think about you all the time."

"I think about you, too," I reply. I tell him I want to see Damascus through his eyes; he should lead. He seems pleased, but then takes me on a dull and busy street that I already know. We enter a park near the new, huge Meridien hotel—ostentatious Gulf wealth—and sit on a bench. Twice men offer to sell us coffee or tea. We decline. Mustafa holds a cigarette in one hand, my hand in the other. I squeeze his hand slightly. He likes this but does not reciprocate and is clearly alert to how other people in the park might see us. I tell him I want him to live, and therefore he should cut back on smoking. He says he does not want to live, but nonetheless agrees he will try not to chain smoke.

We eat nearby at Abu Kamal, a mediocre but pricey restaurant. In my experience, Aleppian restaurants are far better than those in Damascus. It serves no wine or beer, so after the meal we wander the streets to find an open liquor store; we ask people along the way. Half an hour later we find one very close to my apartment, and I buy, for about twelve dollars, what turns out be an excellent Ksara wine from Lebanon.

Once in the apartment, we make some tea before drinking wine. "I would like you to take me with you, . . . to America," Mustafa confides, a bit mournfully.

"So, Mustafa, when you look at me, what do you see?" I ask.

"A father, or perhaps a brother. Someone with lots of experience."

"You see me as a father?" I ask.

"Yes," he says.

"Then if I am your father, you have to do as I say," I joke.

"What?" he asks. Perhaps it is the language, switching from English to Arabic and back. He wants to make sure he understands. I repeat my statement.

"But I disagree with my father often; I don't do what he says if I do not want to."

I encourage Mustafa to tell me more about himself. On Tuesday he stayed up all night, he says, and then slept nineteen hours straight. On Thursday he got up at three, and stayed up until one the following morning, and only then was he tired again. After the army, which he will be forced to enter soon—it is compulsory service—he will go back to school. He dropped out because of some bad grades, he says, and also because he was young and not motivated at the time. He considers himself a very good chess player, excellent at most card games. He used to be good at soccer and swimming, also, but now that he smokes he is not. He confesses that he has lost his faith; he no longer believes in God. Neither his father nor mother pray regularly. I tell him that I am also not a believer.

I scroll through my music list again to find something he likes. This time he asks about Joni Mitchell; I translate some of her lyrics—"They paved paradise and put up a parking lot" and "Help me, I think I'm falling in love again. When I get that crazy feeling, I know I'm in trouble again." I try to explain the American love/hate relation with California modernity. I find the George Wassouf album that I recently downloaded. Mustafa loves Wassouf, "the King of Kings" for modern Syrian ballads, and he wonders how I acquired a taste for Wassouf. I say I hear him every day somewhere in some shop or private home. I ask him if he likes Um Kalthoum, the Egyptian diva that other people tell me sings the real language of the Arab, sings to the depth of the heart and makes them cry. He says yes, but unenthusiastically. I ask him to sing along with Wassouf, and he does, with his favorite song, one he says he sang daily as a child. Wassouf has a succulent, whining, pleading voice, and his lyrics are all about the pain of love. I find the sound of his voice pleasing, but the more I learn of the lyrics, the more schmaltzy his music sounds to me.

My screen saver begins showing some beautiful slides from a trip to Pompei, Naples, and Sicily. "Thank you, Steven," I say—my American friend who took most of the pictures. I have no idea how these slides made it onto my screen saver, but I am glad it is these slides instead of other photos on my computer. Once a young soldier visited me in my apartment and happened onto artistic photos taken of body parts, mostly my body parts, though you could hardly distinguish which body part, much less that they were mine. He quickly skipped over the shots of Thailand, India, and Sicily, and kept returning to one particularly ambiguous photo of a crevice. Not so with Mustafa and this slide slow, which, along with the music, relaxes him, as does the wine.

He says he is sad and worried about his younger brother, whom he loves more than anything. He's very ill and needs to go to the hospital tomorrow. He cannot reach his father. I begin to suspect that perhaps Mustafa is a stepson, or the son of his father's least favorite wife, but he says no. Then I realize that the three uncles for whom Mustafa worked were not his father's brothers but his mother's. These maternal uncles do not have the obligations to care for Mustafa, their sister's son, as they would for their brother's sons. Hence Mustafa often feels abused in his work, or relatively neglected in his living arrangements, though he does not complain. This experience of neglect explains some of Mustafa's generous care and boundless love for his own brother.

I ask Mustafa what his father does, but he does not know exactly. All he knows is that his father has many cars and works in Lebanon. So Mustafa will have to take his brother to the hospital, but he cannot pay for him; he has no money for tests. He does not ask me to help.

We talk more about love: his love for his brother, his distance from his father. He does not mention his mother or sister, and he never refers to a girlfriend.

"Is our relationship about love?" I ask.

"Yes," he says.

"What does it mean to love me?"

"Love never dies," he says, and refers again to his sick brother, who is only sixteen now. "I will love him forever. What do you think?"

"Love may never die, but it changes form. You cannot count on it staying the same. In any case, it never does stay the same."

"Why are you divorced? Did you quit loving her?" he asks.

"It has been a long time, more than twenty years. Love changes," I say.

"Why did you have no children?" he asks.

"I do not want children. If I had children, I probably would not be with you right now. I probably would not have even come to Syria."

We are both tired. I say I want to sleep, and welcome him to stay over, and to join me in my bed, but he wants his own bed. I point him to a room. He says, "Maybe I sleep with you tomorrow, or I'll come and visit you in Aleppo."

He sleeps for only a few hours, and leaves before sunrise. Shortly before I wake, the friend in whose apartment I am staying returns, and she finds that her cell phone is missing. She is very upset. I find my own phone and notice that Mustafa has been trying to call me—twelve attempts. I call back and tell him to return the phone immediately or I will report it to the police. "Will I forgive him?" he asks. "Yes," I say, "of course." An hour later he shows up wearing a stocking cap, despite the Damascene heat and humidity, with a close friend, Salim, and the cell phone, which he had "borrowed," he says, because his own lacked minutes and he thought he might need it to take his brother to the hospital.

I explain why I was upset, that the phone was not mine to lend, and I invite Mustafa and his friend for lunch. Mustafa says that what he has belongs to his friends, and vice versa. Salim is an engineering student and speaks excellent English, though, he says, he has not had the opportunity to speak English for the last couple of years. Mustafa is amused that Salim left his girlfriend standing on the streetcorner in order to come and meet me. "Just like that," he says, "she stands there and watches as we leave." He repeats this several times, enjoying it more with each retelling.

Salim explains, again, why Mustafa had taken the phone and says how angry he was that I threatened to call the police. He is extremely gracious and flirtatious; he offers to get me any computer programs I need. And he is openly critical of the regime. "Look at this," he points to the busy street, dismissively, "nothing going on here, disorganized, dirty, hopeless." I say that streets in the United States are not that different. He ignores my comment and says there is no opportunity in Syria. I ask him if either his girlfriend or Mustafa might not be jealous of all the attention he is giving me. Mustafa chuckles and says nothing. Salim smiles and says that Mustafa trusts him, and they would never be jealous of each other. He is the brains among his friends; he does the organizing. Mustafa is the brawn.

For about three months I do not see Mustafa though I talk to him on the phone. His brother is doing fine, he says, and he himself is postponing military service, which in January 2005 the regime shortened from thirty to twenty-four months. One can pay a fee to get an exemption, which also involves working outside the country for five years. Mustafa periodically reports to me that someone has offered to pay this fee for him, or someone has guaranteed work in Bahrain or Dubai, but these offers always prove fraudulent. Every young man I meet says he wants to avoid military service. Of those who have completed service, or are now completing it, most tell me of the typical army experiences of brutality, humiliation, and boredom.

On my final visit to Damascus, I call Mustafa, and, as he works an eleven- or twelve-hour day, from 10:00 a.m. to 9:00 or 10:00 p.m., he can meet only late at night. He pleads with me to visit him at work, in a shoe store owned by a maternal uncle in a souk about a twenty-minute taxi ride east of Damascus, and then he will accompany me back to my hotel. I agree. He sends me a text message. It is very difficult to read in Arabic script on my cell phone, but translates something like: "You are in my thoughts, always / Even when the eyelashes are sleeping / Don't say no until I see you / in my thoughts, always." A kind of love poem.

I arrange with the Hotel Sultan, where I am staying, for him to stay the night, just in case, though of course they always insist that Syrians not share rooms with tourists, or even visit us in our rooms. I ask the owner of the Sultan to explain how to get to Mustafa's workplace. "I have lived in this city for forty years," he laughs, "and I have no idea where this is." "Class," I think; he has never had a guest who visits people from the lower-class neighborhood where Mustafa works. I call Mustafa on my cell phone and he gives directions to the hotel owner, who writes them down for me to give to a taxi driver.

I arrive at eight. My driver says this is a poor and dangerous district; I should not stick around, but it looks to me like a normal lower-class souk. Mustafa tends a store with a cousin, selling women's shoes and purses. He greets me warmly, with a couple of pecks on the cheek, and he takes my hand and leads me into his shop and into the one next door, both owned by maternal kin, manned by himself and young cousins. His hair is slicked down and now parted in the middle, not on the side, as last time, making his face look wider than usual; without the waves in his hair, it simply looks dirty brown and greasy.

"Your hair looks better combed back, not parted in the middle," I say.

"But girls like it parted," he says, though no longer fully confident this is true. He grabs a mirror and dutifully combs it back. "How is this?"

"Better," I say, but I do not risk telling him it would be better if he washed it also. Syrian men generally take great pride in their appearances, and primp themselves in front of mirrors often and in front of me without much ado; they take care that their hair falls in exactly the right place, or that the curls are minimum, or the mustache is trimmed properly. Most men also care impeccably for their hands; regardless of the roughness that might result from the type of work they do, the fingernails are nearly always clean and uniformly trimmed. Today Mustafa insists on speaking mostly in English, inserting a few Arabic words or phrases that are difficult to translate, perhaps to impress his friends, perhaps because he finds it hard to always understand my American-accented Arabic. He offers to take me on a walking tour of the suburb, a mixed town that includes at least two Christian churches and one very large mosque. He says he has friends who are Kurdish, Christian, Druze, and Palestinian, and he will have Jewish friends in the future if any Jews come to reside in the places he lives and works. He takes me by the arm, or sometimes we hold hands, as we walk slowly, either on the six-lane street in the direction of automobile traffic, or, where possible, on the sidewalk competing with shoppers.

"Where do we come from?" he asks. This question pops up from nowhere, at least not from a place I have already visited with him. I am unprepared. Mustafa is usually very laid-back.

"I don't know," I say.

"From God."

"I don't know that. It's not a question I can answer."

"But God created everything," he asserts, gaining in confidence. After a pause, he asks, "Where do we go when we die?"

"That's it; it's over. We don't exist anymore."

"How do you know?" Mustafa is animated. He has obviously thought about what he wants to say. He switches completely to Arabic to make himself better understood.

"I have no evidence to the contrary; I see no evidence of life after death," I say.

"What about heaven and hell? Do you not believe in them?"

"No. I do not."

"But we cannot live without God. Mohammed is only a prophet. But Allah, he is everything."

"Have you been visiting a religious school recently?" I ask. "Last time we met you said you no longer believed. You broke your fast during Ramadan. And now you are going on about God. What has changed?"

He avoids my question, and instead pushes aggressively for my agreement to the existence of God, of an all-powerful creator who explains and is the explanation for everything that we do not know, and whose existence needs no sensual or empirical proof. I must believe in God, or my life is meaningless, our relationship is meaningless.

Our conversation frustrates Mustafa, partly because I will not agree, but also because neither of us can express ourselves clearly in the other's language. Then he asks, in English, "What do you want from me? Tell me."

"That should be clear," I say. "Friendship, love, sex, whatever is possible."

"Men cannot have sex. That is evil. If I have sex with a man, I kill him, I kill me." I am silent. Mustafa's internalized anger is all new to me.

"Could I fuck you?" he asks, in English. Never before had he used the word "fuck."

"Maybe," I say, startled at his question.

"Then you are a woman. You are not a man. And I cannot respect a woman."

"No, I am still a man, whether you fuck me or I fuck you. I am still the same person, and so are you."

"No!" he exclaims, and feigns a look of disgust as he asserts that he would never have "sex" with a man, that men cannot "fuck" each other, and if he did have sex or fuck—the two words he uses interchangeably—he would have to kill the other man, or himself.

"In Europe and America, and I am American," I say, trying to calm him some, "we do not think of sex so radically. It is not evil, and not such a big deal today, though it used to be."

"I want to be your friend but no sex," he asserts. "I will do everything for you. I love you. Others want your money. I do not want your money. All I have is yours; I will always be there for you. But no sex. If you fuck a man, you are a woman. You agree?"

"No," I say, truly astonished at his little polemic, and at the directness with which he seeks to reproach me.

"We cannot be friends if you do not agree. I am everything for you, but no sex with me, and no sex with other men," he states his conditions.

"I tell you what, Mustafa, I agree to no sex with you. That's fine. We are friends; we do not need to have sex. But I do not agree to your second demand, not to have sex with other men."

He does not respond to this, at least not verbally. We walk on without arguing further. He keeps hold of my hand throughout and leads me through the busy traffic back to his shop. The tension subsides; he has said what he wished to say.

Mustafa does not want to take a taxi—a waste of money, he says—so we catch a minibus back to the old city, where he lives with another uncle and aunt and their two children. We walk, hand-in-hand, past his uncle's apartment. He asks if I want to meet them. I decline, as it is dinnertime, and they would insist I eat, too. He asks about my wife again, "Did she leave because you sleep with men?"

"No," I say, "she went back to Sweden. She had her own boyfriend. It was not a problem for her." He registers this without comment.

Mustafa is back to his old self, relaxed, smiling, laughing. He tells me about working for his uncles; some are more demanding than others. He quit working for the last one because the hours were too long. "When people pass us on the street they look at us," he says, proudly. "When they look and hear us speaking English, they think that I am American also."

Fathers and Sons

It is not only Mustafa's relations with men but his relation to religion and politics that is to be explained, largely and at least initially, in terms of estranged relations with his father and thus dependence on the care of maternal uncles. He experiences a lack of discipline and love, both of which he wants more of but is also highly ambivalent about. It is into this vortex—the engulfing void created by the absence of the father—that I appear, and he seeks from me both employment and love. Or that is the initial, narrower interpretation of what Mustafa wants.

Though inexperienced emotionally and still fully dependent on kin networks, he is no longer a child. He has male friends and cousins his age who genuinely like him, some of whom I have met and who respect and care for him while granting him a high degree of

autonomy. Given these relations, it is safe to assume that he is somewhat aware of his desires, including the desire for "sex," which becomes named as such only in his relation to me, the American
stranger. He experiences a need to order these desires, a disciplinary
need in his case not coming from any particular institution, network,
or person. It is not Islam—though he does call on the omniscient
Allah as ultimate authority—nor is it the law of the secular state,
nor a particular controlling paternal figure, nor a familial-friendship
circle—that rings an alarm and alerts him to the danger of "sex." It
is, rather, within his own imagination that he reconfigures religion,
politics, and desire in order to deal with an awakened desire, in this
case the desire for "sex," which mandates he try to convince me, a
man thirty years his senior whom he "loves," to agree to a general
prohibition.

What, exactly, this general prohibition makes taboo are not the
practices—oral, anal, genital—that an American might associate
with sex, but a principle embodied in the English word "fuck." For
Mustafa, this principle is symbolized by a man losing respect if he
were fucked like a woman. The principle and its symbolization, the
"fuck," Mustafa says, is prohibited, at least between men. In this
case, "sex" between us is possible only if there is instantiation of a
taboo, including an agreement to keep the act unnamed. But Mustafa names the act, thereby instantiating the taboo in the name of
Allah, but this instantiation also makes thinkable its transgression.
The question, which in this context we cannot ask, is: if one, instead,
does not name the act, what power does the taboo have over what
one can do? With Mustafa, it is clear that "sex" does not preclude
love or affection, including intimate physical contact of a sort that
most Americans would associate with "sex." Not having had intimate physical contact with Mustafa, on what basis do I draw this
conclusion? Many Syrian and Lebanese men who have traveled in
the West and experienced the two intimate orders have explained to
me that the Arab prohibition is purely in the realm of speech. They
explain that sexual acts with men are usually possible only upon
showing a respect for the taboo, that is, a verbal affirmation that one
does not name practices of "sex" with men; *but* after that affirmation

Figure 21. First Cousins

of the taboo and the authority behind it—Allah—a wide range of
acts of physical intimacy, including intercourse, become possible,
depending on the person and situation.

Possibilities in the realm of affection present themselves as situations, largely undefined generically by gender, age, erotic type, or
exact relation of one person to another. This situational erotics is
not random, however, for traditional familial relations—with
mother, father, brother, sister, uncle, aunt, nephew, niece, and
cousin—provide the template. But templates are stereotypes and
they break down in practice, behavior being more nuanced and opportunistic than cultural models would predict. Cousins appear to
enjoy the largest degree of trust and erotic free play, especially in
childhood and through adolescence. One can also enjoy intimacy
with school friends and neighbors. None of this is considered "sex."

Relations with the father, while from birth affectionate and car-
ing, begin in earnest in late childhood, often as sons accompany
their fathers to work (and, incidentally, to the hammam). At that
point, sons experience a break of sorts with their mothers, who until

then had literally smothered them with love and esteem, drawing few physical boundaries. Then sons not only begin sleeping alone, but they are increasingly positioned between the parental interests, either as the mother's love-object who replaces her husband, or as the father's apprentice and double against the mother's interest. Mothers, even when cross-cousins of their husbands, retain their natal name and control of two forms of property: the *mehr*, or payment by the groom upon marriage, and the dowry, or, if it exists, the property they bring to the marriage. Both retentions—of name and property—serve as perpetual reminders that the wife's most important ties are to the authority of her own father rather than to her husband. The specter of the mother's loyalty as being elsewhere, to her father rather than to her husband and son, sustains a separation anxiety that men experience generally with women. To outsiders, such as myself, this anxiety may appear to be disrespect for women, whereas in fact it is a result of the theoretical power over care and intimacy that women might wield. As families become smaller, at times without sons, and as women move into employment, relations prove flexible and pragmatic. In Syria these matters are in fact changing, though it appears less so for men of Mustafa's class.

After men marry, nonerotic and frequently competitive relations with brothers often become more important because of employment through the father, the patriline, and the potential of co-inheriting property. Then also sex outside marriage with men, or in some cases with women, if it occurs, is quick, inconsequential, and most often with strangers. Men often retain a financial and emotional responsibility for their sisters, even if and after they marry. In the case of unmarried or divorced sisters, men often assume as part of their role of maternal uncle, as with Mustafa's uncles, the responsibility to care, to some degree, for the children of the sister. What tends to remain constant and taken for granted until death is the relation with the father and mother, the former as source of authority, the latter as template for relations with women. Increasingly in contemporary Syria, fathers can no longer provide employment or meet the material expectations of their sons, undermining their location as source of authority.

Still to be explained is Mustafa's appeal to Allah and turn to an Islamic register of thought as he tries to instantiate a taboo on "sex." Several months prior to this encounter he had been lackadaisical in following the fast of Ramadan, and had subsequently even declared himself faithless. Yet, in his search for an authority for a general prohibition to which I would agree, he appeals to a religious register. He could have, alternately, appealed to "custom" (the rule of his father, clan, or peer group) or even to secular law (Syrian law prohibits an undefined homosexuality). Instead, he appeals to Allah, suggesting that the alternatives—custom or paternal authority, secular law—lack the authority to instantiate a prohibition and they lack the authority to forgive its transgression. The family father and Allah are of different registers, the former a declining (or even absent) authority, the latter omniscient. The decline of the father's authority makes way for opportunistic authorities, in this specific instance, of Islam. In sum, the way in which Mustafa's desire results in an appeal to a general prohibition expresses both the lack of faith in or even respect for secular authority and the contemporary trend for Islam to fill the void of paternal authority in Syria.

"It is a blessing"

Syria does not have the elaborate tourist infrastructure to compete with many other Asian sites. It relies more than others solely on its ruins, on the imaginative histories connected to its place and peoples, on friendly and honest dealings with strangers, and on the stories all of this can generate for tourists to tell. Many of the tourists who come to Aleppo's souk come above all to collect stories, and to take them away. And for most, the story of stories is the one about love.

A friend asks me if I have heard the oft-quoted verse of the great Sufi philosopher, Ibn 'Arabi: "I follow the religion of love wherever its camels turn." Ibn 'Arabi may have been talking more narrowly about where to find the form of God, and asserting that this form is not exclusively the province of a particular faith. But I prefer to take his moral relativism more literally, and to think of what might be the "religions of love." Or what is peculiar to the way a camel, that totemic symbol of the Arab Middle East, turns? Unlike the horse, who is bridled through the mouth, with two reins to direct, camels are bridled through the nose, with one rein instead of two, giving the camel more freedom (or responsibility) and the rider less precise control. Moreover, the nose ring of the camel resembles a piece of traditional Indian wedding jewelry—a nose ring attached to a chain—called the *nath*, that Indians attribute to an Arab origin.

As for the "camels' turn," they are loyal herd animals, and would prefer to turn most likely to find other camels—hence the renowned "stupidity" that humans attribute to camels might be due to the fact that they seem to have a mind of their own, since their loyalty is oriented—through their highly developed sense of sight and smell— not to humans but to other camels.

When I think of the camel, I think romantically: of its sweet and open face, the large, unblinking eyes and flared nostrils, its peculiar hump (the dromedary or Arab camel has only one), its oversize knees and tall spindly legs. I think of its relation to the ancient overland Silk Road that used to extend, from the time of its origin around 100 B.C., from China through the Fertile Crescent to Rome. Beginning in the sixteenth century, the discovery of a sea route around the Cape of Good Hope reduced the importance of the Silk Road, and slowly the caravans of Aleppo and the camels that carried the goods from China to Europe and back, and the city of Aleppo itself, declined in importance. Today, the Syrian part of the Silk Road no longer exists except as an imaginative topos, a source of revenue for residents who can use its geographical and cultural history—evoking Marco Polo, Alexander the Great, the Crusades—to lure tourists to visit. The camels' turn parallels this larger history of material decline and displacement to imaginary sites.

Now and then, I see a camel on the road between Aleppo and Damascus, but for the most part I see them used only by Bedouins in the eastern part of the country, who offer me as part of the tourist experience the opportunity to ride, or at least sit on them, for a small fee, at many of the country's archaeological sites.

Jihad—his real name—is a tourist guide who arranges a camel ride on his tours. Upon returning from a month-long trip with twenty tourists in Egypt and Jordan, he is anxious to tell me about an accident on a camel. Jihad is the second of four brothers, and the only one who does not work for his father. The other three share the business with the father, which, Jihad says, will break apart once his father dies. All of them contribute to the care of the oldest brother, who is retarded.

"It is a blessing," is how he characterizes his father's decision to help him establish a business—and his own independence. Even though the family business in antiques was expanding at the time of his separation, it still could not support, so his father thought, all four brothers. Then Jihad was of two minds, but now, at the age of forty-four, married with three children, he is relieved not to be under the control of his father, and not to share in the daily bickering and fights about money and inheritance between his brothers. Jihad works for a Canadian company as a guide for English-speaking tourists to the Levant and Egypt. Nearly all of the tourists are elderly Americans and Canadians, for, he says, "young people don't have the time or money to take such tours."

I always smile when I think of the coincidence that a man named "Jihad," the one Arabic term with which all Americans are familiar, is now—post 9/11—responsible for the safety and comfort of North American tourists traveling abroad. Jihad says that some tourists are initially taken aback by his name, which in English is most often translated as "holy war" but in Arabic has multiple meanings and is more often understood ambiguously as "moral struggle." But, he says, they are reassured in person by his competence, thus enabling him to quickly defuse any anxiety they have.

"You wouldn't believe," he begins, "I had a group of twenty-five, and on the eighth day, in the desert in Egypt, right after we visited the Pyramids, one American woman, Peggy, had an accident. She fell off her camel, and I had to take her to the hospital, and then leave her there and rejoin the group for the rest of the trip. I made sure they knew that this part, a morning caravan ride on camels in the desert, was optional. Peggy is overweight, very heavy, and I warned her, and all the others: 'This is optional; you shouldn't do it if you are afraid, if you have any problems with balance.' But Peggy insisted she was game."

Jihad explains that from the start he was concerned because Peggy, though one of the youngest women in the group, was unfit. "Often, he says, in climbing stairs, or on long uphill walks in the heat, women and men in their seventies are the fittest of the group." He speaks of the new American elderly as those who have some money, are meticulous with their diet, exercise regularly every day, and remain adventurous into their retirement years. But Peggy was in another category, with some money but neither elderly nor particularly attentive to her diet, still adventurous though no longer athletic. The itinerary for the day was tight: the group was to mount the camels at 4:00 a.m. and ride for four hours, with a breakfast of porridge made with baked lentils and olive oil and lemon served along the way, and then return and check out of the hotel by noon.

While it was still dark outside, the Bedouin assistants hoisted Peggy onto the camel, and while they were waiting for the others to get seated, the young man in charge of Peggy's camel, in a moment of inattention, let go of his charge's rope. The camel began to move on his own, apparently to join some other camel he was attracted to elsewhere in the caravan. Peggy plopped, on her shoulder, on the ground, in the middle of the desert.

"We had no cell phones that worked, and this was a small, relatively isolated village," explains Jihad. "We had our driver take us— Peggy and me, I left the group, which I am told not to do—to a hospital in the next biggest village, about thirty kilometers away. There they would not even examine her unless she paid up front. But Peggy had left her money in the hotel, so I paid, about $350, to the hospital.

"She was so grateful, 'You are my sweet, I want to take you to America with me, you are like a husband to me. I could not survive without you.' All warm and thankful. She had broken her shoulder blade, nothing life-threatening but she was in a lot of pain—it took us several hours to get her to the hospital—and she could not continue to travel. But I had to go back to the others. I told Peggy, 'I am really sorry, but I have to return to the others. I've called the American Embassy, they will take care of you here, I've arranged everything. But one thing before I leave, I need a signature here, to confirm that you will reimburse me for the medical expenses.'

" 'No, I owe you nothing,' Peggy snapped back at me. 'It is your responsibility that the camel ran away with me. I refuse to sign anything.' "

Jihad was alarmed. That was his whole salary for the month.

He returned to the other tourists, who were supportive and told him he had done the right thing in abandoning them and taking Peggy to the hospital. They assured him that she would eventually pay. During the remainder of the trip, Jihad stayed in telephone contact with the hospital and the American embassy, which arranged to transport Peggy back to the States. When he returned to Aleppo, however, the tour company told him that Peggy had sued for damages, and that they would therefore withhold his pay until after an investigation.

The Rumor

The day before my official university appointment ends, a friend there offers me an alternative explanation to events. "Remember the member of parliament, the M.P., who called to find you in early September?"

"Oh yes," I say, "we since have become friends, and he also used my work in his teaching."

"Nobody knew where you were back then, even though the M.P. said you were teaching here at Aleppo University. That started a rumor: if nobody knows where or who he is, and a member of parliament wants to find out, then we better be careful about letting him teach."

"But the M.P. told the law school, where he teaches, that they should invite me to teach there. He is very enthusiastic about the directions of my research," I say.

"That doesn't matter. Nobody cares about what you taught or are teaching. And people in the humanities faculty do not talk to the people in the law faculty, so they do not know what the M.P. said later. They only know, and the dean is very cautious, that there was a call from Parliament asking about you. That's enough. But add to that Dr. Lababidi's resistance to having you teach in English, then you have an explanation for why the entire faculty, deans and department chairs, decided to decline your services."

"The odd thing is," I say, "that I came here hoping to study rumors in the souk. Souks are notorious for gossip. But I did not record a single rumor that seems significant to me, at least not until now. Yet it was a rumor about me, a false rumor, which framed my entire experience at the university. And I do not find this out until the night before I depart."

a

b

c

d

e

f

g

h

Figures 22a–22h. Faces of Syria

— Chapter III —

Syria

"These are my children"

In Aleppo, about a month of fall precedes winters, which are for the most part mild, rainy, and last about two months, and are followed by a month, or, if the inhabitants are lucky, by two months, of a brief and slightly demarcated spring. For the rest of the year, around nine months, Aleppo enjoys summer, including about five or six months of unbearably hot and humid weather. So I drink a lot of water, most often even carrying a bottle with me on the street, or, if I run out while walking downtown, I stop by one of the many water-filled coolers with plastic glasses attached outside shops. Initially, I am afraid to drink the cooler water, which comes from the Euphrates River, though people reassure me that it is free of harmful bacteria.

The Euphrates, which begins in Turkey and flows through Syria and Iraq, runs through the small town of Raqqa in north-central Syria, where I am invited to give a lecture at al-Adiyyat, the Society for Archeology and Literature. I arrive mid-afternoon by bus with an Aleppian doctor friend, who made the initial contact for me and agreed to translate. The president and other officers of the Society greet us at the bus station, and we walk to their offices nearby, in the most imposing building in the city, which resembles a European town hall. Raqqa is said to have been first established by Alexander the Great, though its heyday came much later, in the eighth century

Figure 23. Shadowless Banks of the Euphrates

under the Abbasid dynasty (remnants of the original walls survive), after which it went into terminal decline. Raqqa revived, on a much smaller scale, in the twentieth century, providing a home to refugees from other conflicts, most famously to Christian Armenians fleeing the Turkish genocide that began in 1915. The town retains a distinctly secular feel to it; there is an ethno-religious mix of Muslims, Kurds, and Christians, with few public signs of religious or political distinction, much less antagonism.

I offer the organizer several topics for lectures; he insists on the most political one, a comparison of the Iraqi and German occupations. The room seats about sixty, and is full, with most men dressed formally, some in suit and tie, as I am. The men range in age from late twenties to seventy; one introduces himself as a retired foreign diplomat, another as a human rights activist. Only one woman is present, a poet and novelist in her fifties, with long blonde hair worn on this evening in a thick braid pulled over her shoulder. She wears a once-fashionable leopard-patterned dress, which makes me think she must have been a siren in her younger days, and she still has a full sensual presence. She introduces herself as a poet and novelist.

In my lecture (which I also later give in Aleppo), I strongly criticize the American occupation of Iraq but also analyze elements of
the American occupation of Germany that made that one successful,
and discuss the conditions that might sabotage or make possible a
peaceful outcome to regime change in Iraq. If we regard the occupation and the imposition of democracy as a gift the United States
thinks it is bestowing on Iraq, what are the consequences if Iraqis
refuse this gift (i.e., engage in an insurgency), and what are their
options if they accept? My friend translates, precisely, word-for-
word the first three pages, which doubles the amount of time it takes
to deliver an idea, so for the rest I cut accordingly and simply summarize major arguments that I have elaborated in writing, making
his job—to succinctly summarize a succinct summary—even more
difficult.

The public listens attentively but seems above all eager to ask
questions and engage in an exchange with me: a rare opportunity
for them to query an American face-to-face about topics that affect
them directly. A couple of the men want to lecture me (and the
others in the room) rather than ask questions, and when the organizer cuts them off gently, they direct their anger at him. After the
discussion, others criticize him for not calling on them, or for ceding
control of the forum to the most aggressive questioners. The major
concern of most of the questions is to condemn the United States
and Israel, but also people take pleasure in merely being able to
express political opinions in such a public forum. About this I am
also pleased, for the organizer explains to me that this is the first
political lecture they have ever had at the Society. "We are hungry
for politics here," he says. On the other hand, nobody in the audience asks a question that takes seriously the conundrum of how,
given American power in the region and the reality of the occupation, they or we might help the Iraqis achieve a peaceful outcome.

Before dinner, the local cultural magazine for the Society interviews me. "Is dialogue possible between this American administration and Syrians?" they ask. This question is the standard one journalists are to ask foreigners like me. "No," I reply, unwilling to go
along and make believe, "not in the relations of the current govern-

ments with Bush and the Republicans in control of the U.S. government, but a dialogue between cultural organizations in civil society is possible, and I hope that is what we are engaged in here." The Society did publish a brief report of the lecture in their quarterly magazine.

For the evening meal, the organizer and two other men drive with me in a taxi to the home of the woman in the leopard-patterned dress who attended the lecture. A big meze, about ten distinct dishes, is spread out on a table, enough for ten or twenty people. We are only five. Her house is a 1970s four-room, single-floor dwelling with an open courtyard in the middle. She tells me that she has been married three times, but they were unlucky marriages; she has thought of leaving Raqqa for a larger city but never does. "Now I am growing old, without husband or children to share my life with. Only Allah knows why," she laments, and walks over to a cradle and rocks it gently. "These are my children," she says quietly, pointing to the books of poetry she has written and published, now resting in the cradle. She is a strong woman, but I cannot help feeling some pity for her: divorced and unmarried in a society that stigmatizes such status.

I ask how it is possible for a single woman to be entertaining men alone at night. The men present explain that people in Raqqa are more liberal than elsewhere in Syria. Ten years ago nobody went to the mosque, they explain, and today only a few go, though their numbers are growing. But in this region, even in the small villages when men visit other men, women can serve them in the absence of their husbands. If the husbands or brothers return home, it is no problem that strange men are already there. Economically Raqqa is depressed, as is much of Syria, and most of the young men have left. But residents no longer experience consumer shortages, as under Hafez el-Assad, though even then they had what was necessary, simply few Western goods. Today a well-stocked corner store, their version of an American 7/11, is open all night.

That evening, I sleep over at the home of the organizer, an economist by profession but most proud of his writing as a poet. He is a recently married man in his forties, and he explodes with joy at the

Figure 24. The Birth of Poetry

sight of his two-year-old daughter, who runs to the door to jump in his arms. He tells me he has a brother who is a grocer in Manhattan. We chat some about the lecture and audience, but by then it is past midnight; I am very tired and no longer able to speak anything resembling coherent Arabic. The child, however, is full of energy and does not want to sleep. "When do you put her to bed?" I ask. Mother and father look at me with incomprehension. "She goes to sleep when she is tired," he says. Aha, I think, and counsel myself to be patient. Eventually, they take note of my state and take her into their bedroom; I sleep on the sofa. This time of year Raqqa has freezing temperatures at night, and they turn the *mazout* (a light fuel oil that resembles diesel) heater off and give me two extremely heavy cotton blankets. I usually toss and turn some in my sleep, but have difficulty turning over even once under this weight.

The following morning I meet several men who attended the lecture; they give me a private tour of the town, of the local archaeological museum, the ruins of the old city walls, and the Grand Mosque. For lunch we take a taxi to a restaurant directly on the Euphrates River. In Arabic, the river is called al-Furat, originally an adjective meaning "sweetest water." The river's appearance is modest and does not conjure up its mythical stature. Still, I cannot help but think of Assyrian, Babylonian, and Sumerian civilizations, of the ancient Mesopotamian cultures. Some accounts even link the Euphrates to the Garden of Eden. But this is all a very distant past, a mythical time, an evocation provoked by the world of literature and museums in which I am a frequent guest. And it is misleading to try to appreciate or understand the present with reference to this mythical time. Today, they tell me, the use of its waters for irrigation and hydroelectric power make the Euphrates a source of political tension, which will likely increase as water challenges oil for the commodity most in demand in the Middle East.

Back in Aleppo, armed with the assurance of the owner of my apartment that its tap water, which also comes from the Euphrates, is drinkable, I brush aside my worries about bacteria, and drink it whenever I run out of bottled water. I prefer mineral water with gas, in the European tradition, but that is not available in markets around the souk, and Syrian bottled water is very flat, sufficient to quench thirst but practically tasteless. So I go with the water of the Euphrates, which is indeed sweet, with a rich, deep taste. To be sure, notwithstanding the reassurances of locals, it contains some bacteria that my system is unused to, and I intermittently suffer through a mild diarrhea.

Aleppian Food, in Public

Rumor has it that Aleppian food is the best in Syria, the Eastern Mediterranean, or even the Arab world and the Middle East. In my limited experience, that rumor is true. The conservatism of Aleppo finds its most positive expression in its cuisine, which tends to assimilate foreign tastes while rigorously preserving the quality of the familiar. Its food combines elements of the cuisine of Arabs, Armenians, Greeks, Assyrians, Jews, Kurds, and Turks—the other peoples united with Syrians for nearly five hundred years under the rule of the Ottoman Empire. Then there is the matter of freshness: most produce is grown nearby. Within a couple hours' drive from Aleppo are olive, fruit, and nut orchards; nowhere in the world have I tasted better figs, pomegranates, or pistachio nuts. Lamb is the basis for most meat dishes (though chicken is also often served), and the city is surrounded by flocks of mild-mannered Awassi sheep, with brown faces and legs, fat tails, and floppy ears.

Aleppian food resembles other regional cuisines—cold and hot appetizers; main dishes of kebab, kibbeh, stuffed vegetables, lamb, rice, and pita, served with water, coke, or arak (grape spirits distilled with anise); desserts and Turkish coffee. But it is distinguished by an insistence on freshness, attention to detail, and the variety and delicacy of seasonings. Not much effort is put into presentation: the platters, bowls, dishes, silverware differ only by quality of silver, tin, or glass; placement of the food—each dish gets its own plate—is completely standardized. Many people prefer pita bread to scoop up food over forks and knives that jab, pick, and cut.

I usually eat a pastry and drink tea for breakfast, but most people eat olives, cucumbers, tomatoes, *labneh* (a thick strained yoghurt), and pita bread. Although I have a kitchen in my apartment, I use the gas burners only for boiling water for tea. I do not want to eat much fried food (also a token gesture to keeping my weight down), and I cannot figure out how to use the new electric oven in the kitchen. For lunch and dinner, therefore, I dine out and sample the cuisine in all of the best restaurants of the city. Lunch is between noon and three. Dinner out normally begins after nine o'clock. I eat most frequently at a group of renovated villas in the old walled quarter of Jdaideh: Jasmine, Martini Dar Zamaria, Kan Zaman, Sissy House, and Beit Wakil; and in two restaurants in the newer Christian Assizier district, Challal and Wanes. There are a few restaurants downtown (like Al-Andalib) and near the Souk al-Medina (Bazaar al-Chark, Khan al-Harir) where I also eat often. I never do understand why all of the best restaurants are in two adjacent Christian quarters of the city, even though customers are indistinguishable by confession and sect. Perhaps it is that the elites often drink alcohol—arak, wine, beer, and even scotch and whiskey—which Christian restaurants can serve in public in their neighborhoods without provoking any protest, as might be the case in predominately Muslim neighborhoods.

Many of the owners and waiters get to know me well, and the guests I occasionally bring along are surprised by how friendly and enthusiastically I am greeted. They are also irritated, as I am at times, by how the waiters in some places hover over the customers, removing plates from the table while one is still chewing a last forkful. Most restaurants offer the same menu, the very best in three languages (Arabic, French, English), valid for both lunch and dinner. Prices are rarely noted for particular items (though this is changing); the total cost at each place is remarkably consistent, somewhere around $5–$7, irrespective of what I eat—excluding beer or wine. Most tourists I meet are uncomfortable with this lack of detail in pricing, and occasionally insist on itemization, to my embarrassment even when I do not share their table. I adjust easily to the local pricing, ultimately feeling liberated from the ubiquitous price rationalization of the American economy. That I can afford this food, of course, is the precondition for my comfort. My normal meal consists of meze: appetizers (usually cold) followed by something hot with meat, though all food tends to arrive at the same, or nearly the same, time; therefore most hot meat is room temperature before eaten.

I always begin with a salad, and they are plentiful: plain large leafs of romaine lettuce with whole radishes, onions, jalapeño-like peppers, and tomatoes on the side (as a specialty, sometimes pickled beets); watercress or a sweet thymelike herb in a balsamic vinaigrette, or with fetalike cheese bits and whole lemon chunks and raw garlic; *salata jarjir*—arugula seasoned with lemon and olive oil, flavored with *sumac* (a tart, red spice); *fattoush*—torn romaine lettuce, tomatoes, parsley, mint, radishes, and cucumbers, mixed with small pieces of deep-fried pita, in olive oil and vinegar, with *sumac*; tabouleh—finely chopped parsley, tomato, onion, and cucumber. Sometimes salads are sprinkled with *zatar*, a zesty wild thyme spice. The most exquisitely unusual taste for me is *muhammara*, a spicy rust-colored paste made of hot peppers, tangy pomegranates, and ground walnuts.

Although most restaurants share the same menus, local cooks fashion even the most standard dishes to their own taste. At Jasmine, for instance, traditional hummus (chickpeas, garlic, olive oil, lemon juice, cumin, and tahini), baba ghanoush (eggplant, garlic, tahini, lemon juice, parsley, and hot pepper), or *moutabbel* (pureed eggplant, garlic, tahini, yoghurt, lemon juice, parsley, tomato, and olive oil) are topped with pomegranate paste, or even with fresh pomegranate seeds. Or the hummus is made creamier, as at al-Andalib, a smokey rooftop restaurant frequented by intellectuals, and also topped with pomegranate seeds; or the eggplant in baba ghanoush can be chopped instead of blended as at Challal, a high-end restaurant in the Christian quarter with full-length glass windows that open to the street; or more varied, with diced sweet onion and tomato chunks added. Then there is Challal's competitor down the street, Wanes, same décor and same feel, which offers incomparable chicken wings in lemon garlic sauce and a heavenly hummus.

Restaurants offer a seemingly endless variety of kebabs and kibbeh (ground lamb and bulgur mixed, then poached, steamed, fried, grilled, or baked). Most kebabs are marinated with olive oil, salt and pepper, perhaps tomato juice, before being grilled over a wood fire. One variation served throughout Syria and Lebanon is named after Aleppo, kebab Halebi, a simply seasoned ground lamb with onions and parsley. Shish kebab is perhaps the most well-known: ground lamb with dried mint, cumin, tomato paste, mashed garlic, olive oil, and lemon juice. It is usually served with grilled onions and tomatoes.

I dine most at the five renovated villas with restaurants in Jdaideh, largely because I love the aesthetics of the places—tables around a central fountain, canvas ceiling over the second floor (meaning smoke from the narghile does not settle), rough stone walls, Mamluke-style windows and arched doorways. Kan Zaman has a very modern all-glass elevator and offers its own Kan Zaman kebab: a crushed pistachio crust around ground lamb with cumin and pine nuts, baked. Beit Wakil, where President Assad and his wife have stayed several times, offers a very rich version of the kebab karaz, ground lamb in a sauce of freshly stewed cherries. Sissy House, perhaps the fanciest of the villas, across the road from Beit Wakil, offers the most succulent rack of lamb in town, a bit thicker than in other establishments. Most of the time, lamb chops or the rack of lack is served very well done, at its worst grilled to a leathery toughness. Given the high quality of the meat and care taken in butchering, I can only attribute this preference to taste and local custom. My favorite of the kibbeh is the raw lamb, called kibbeh nayyeh, which at its best in Challal or Sissy House or Wanes has the finest quality lamb ground with onion, parsley, and mint, with garlic olive oil and *sumac* seasoning on the side. The only raw meat I normally eat in the United States or Europe is *carpaccio* (thinly sliced raw beef), so kibbeh nayyeh is for me a revelation of sorts. I especially like eating it alongside french fries and *muhammara*.

Most meals in restaurants do not end with dessert; everyone stops simply because they are full. Sometimes pastries arrive anyway, compliments of the restaurant. There is nearly always food left on the table, which is then given to the poor. More than half of the customers in most places end their meal by ordering a narghile—they choose from different flavors of tobacco—and toke away for another hour after the meal. Desserts, when desired, are usually eaten at home, purchased beforehand in pastry shops, but there are also public ice cream stands and pastry shops where one can have dessert. The cafés rarely serve pastries. Aleppian pastries are, again, renowned, and justly so, and the quality hardly varies throughout the city. My favorites combine, in some fashion, roasted sesame seeds with pistachios or almonds and honey or rose water. One buys them in bakeries not by the type or piece but by weight alone.

I consider myself a very good cook, so about two months into my stay I invite friends from the city, the university, and the souk for a dinner. A gathering of difference that only an anthropologist would be bold enough to venture. I decide to treat them with Mexican cuisine, and make enchiladas. My creativity is challenged: I do find several avocados, but I substitute cumin for cilantro, pita bread for tortillas, deep-fried pita for corn chips. In fact, nothing tastes Mexican. I salt the beans too heavily, and two of the guests appear suspicious of my roasted chicken (which I purchase from a stand nearby), so they stick to the vegetables. After this experience, I cook no more, neither for myself nor for others.

Obtaining an Exit Visa

After three months, I try to obtain an exit visa that will allow me to reenter Syria after I leave for a week to attend two conferences in the United States: one on truth and justice at Harvard and one on anti-Americanism at Stanford. My current visa expires on November 4, and I plan to return on November 8, which means I need only a four-day extension. Friends say there is no problem obtaining a three-month extension. I take a taxi to the Department of Immigration, where I pay a small fee for the proper forms for visa extension and hand them to someone in a row of six officers. I am directed to another man, who tells me that in order to process the form I have to return with the owner of the apartment I am renting.

"But she has nothing to do with this. I am waiting for a residency permit through the university," I say.

He pulls my file and finds the permit, which looks like it had been sitting there in pristine form since the university submitted it seven weeks ago. He hands it to a colleague. Then this colleague and three other men behind the counter take turns leafing through my file and typing data in computers. They send me from one to the other, back and forth, back and forth, to initial documents. The goal seems to be a particular sequence of signatures. After another hour and a second signature from "the General" in a separate office at the end of the hall, they put a new stamp in my passport and replace the white piece of paper that said I was employed by the university, and which was to serve as my temporary residency permit, with another white piece of paper with even less written on it and no mention of the university. When I get home, I try to decipher the scribbled numbers in the several large stamps in my passport. The crucial number, the new date my visa is to expire, seems to be "2.11.2004," in other words, my new visa now expires not four days later, as I wanted, but two days earlier than its original date. I check with a professor who used to teach in the United States but now resides permanently and teaches part-time in Syria, and he confirms my suspicions: instead of adding four days, they subtracted two. If it were not so absurd, I would have been angry.

This professor knows "the General" personally though he had not seen him in several years. He returns with me to the Immigration Office. The reason they are so inefficient here, he explains, is that they get paid a piddly $150 a month. If they paid them better, they'd work better. We talk first with Mohammed, the man in charge of the group of soldiers who process my form. He does not budge; they had cancelled my residency permit, he explains, because I was leaving the country, and it was up to me to decide how to return.

"But he is teaching at the university," my friend explains, and then appeals to status: "he is a professor at Princeton University, with a degree from Harvard University."

Upon hearing these references to status, Mohammed's unexpressive face morphs into a sneer.

"And he needs to go to conferences at Harvard and Stanford," continues the professor.

Mohammed is unimpressed. He tosses my passport on the desktop, "See the General if you like." The professor politely thanks him.

We visit the General, who acknowledges our presence and quietly sends an assistant to fetch my file. There was an error by the university, he explains, where they listed me as "tourist," which is why my residency permit was cancelled. Everything can be corrected, however, if I get a letter from the university stating I need to leave to fulfill my teaching duties. We return to the counter and the row of men, where, upon request, Mohammed scribbles a couple of sentences for the letter we are to obtain. The professor rewrites them in legible Arabic, and holds the note up for Mohammed to read, "Is that the wording you need?" He rewrites it one more time, and gives it to me to take to the University.

I call a professor at the university who has been supportive, and we meet at the office of public affairs, where a man types the letter that we then take to four different offices—for signatures, stamps, registration, and copies. I return to Immigration, again pay the same minor fee for a visa extension, and leave victorious but also flattened, weary, unamused. This experience is minor and trivial, of course, especially compared to what happens when Syrians themselves try to obtain documents to leave Syria and enter other countries. Syrian friends have told me of waiting years for approval to travel, the delay most often caused not by Syrian authorities but by the country they wish to visit. Things have gotten worse for them since 9/11.

On November 9, I return from the United States, uneventfully, by taxi via Beirut. My driver pays the usual baksheesh—the equivalent of $1.00 to each officer who supplies a signature—and he delivers me, at 4:10 p.m., to the front of the souk, three days before the end of Ramadan. My first lecture is still more than two weeks away, but I rush back in order to experience the end of the month-long fast, the build-up of tension as people engage in a buying frenzy in preparation for the release of Eid.

Toward the end of December, I return to Immigration once more to inquire about my residency permit. An employee of the University had spent two hours the previous day attempting to clarify my status. I take with me a professor who had dealt with this office frequently on behalf of others. Mohammed, the officer in charge, is charming and personable today. He explains how to expedite my permit: an elaborate procedure of faxing my passport and papers to Damascus and then back again. My papers are held up because my actual Fulbright residency is for only six months, whereas they always request full-year residencies for the visa. If I only stay for six months, I cannot officially get an exit visa to leave in this period. Mohammed proposes to change the application to a one-year residency, even though the university is employing me for only six months. Great, I think. Mohammed approaches me and asks what I am teaching. "Anthropology," I say. He says he heard that my lectures were very good. "How?" I ask.

"I talked to some of your students." He pauses, then asks, "What about the American Indians, where did they come from?"

I smile. "From eastern Asia, across the Bering Strait from Siberia to Alaska when they were still connected."

"When was that?" he asks.

"I am not an archaeologist," I say, "and I am bad with numbers. My professor friend suggests four thousand years. I say, "More like twenty thousand, probably even fifty thousand."

Mohammed gives me a form to fill out. While I fill out the English parts, I am impressed by how my professor friend first holds Mohammed's hand warmly and then reassures the other employees, chats, and jokes with them in a quiet voice. When they say the computer is slow because it has to heat up, he jokes, "Bring it to the radiator here; it'll warm up faster." My residency permit apparently does finally show up in Aleppo, in April during my second stay, but the employees at the university are too busy to pick it up. I ultimately leave without obtaining it, and return the next time as my Syrian friends direct me to, with a totally new tourist visa.

The Ba'ath Party

Early on in my stay, I ask to arrange an interview with the leading official of the Ba'ath Party at the University. Out of fear that I will misspeak or that the interview would go wrong, the people I ask to arrange this keep putting it off. Two days before I leave, an interview is scheduled with the Secretary General of the Ba'ath Party, Dr. Hoboo (the Arabic root of his name is "love"), a historian of Semitic languages by training, and former dean of the Faculty of Arts and Sciences at Aleppo University. He had left for about five years to work in Yemen before returning to Aleppo and assuming this position, meaning, I am told, that he is above all valued by the Party as loyal and trustworthy. Initially I want to bring along a student to interpret, figuring that Dr. Hoboo will ignore the student and that way our conversation will not be mediated by a strong interpreter. But at the last minute Dr. Hoboo arranges for the leading linguist at the university, Dr. K., to accompany me. At the last minute I also leave my tape recorder at home, as I am advised it would simply put everyone on guard.

We wait about ten minutes in a large office in the campus Party headquarters. A man sits behind a big desk, signing and organizing papers, and I assume he is Dr. Hoboo. After ten minutes of silence, I speak and say I have four questions, which the linguist begins to answer. To the first—"What is the role of the party in the university?"—he gives a long, historical answer that I could have read out of any Party platform. The man behind the desk, who I thought was to answer me, is quiet. We get stuck on my second question—"I've talked to perhaps a hundred students, and not one has said something positive about the role of the Party in the university; how are you responding to this?" The linguist says, "You're not going to ask him that!"

"Yes, I am."

"That's like saying you've lost the rank and file!"

"Well, I want to know what he thinks. He can refuse to answer it if he likes."

The man behind the desk had wandered in and out several times already; he suddenly stands up and leaves. "Why is he always leaving?" I ask. "I want *him* answering the questions."

"That's not the Secretary General," the linguist corrects me, "Dr. Hoboo is in the other office, and he points to the signs on the doors: a white board for the assistant; an embossed copper plate for Dr. Hoboo. I am paying insufficient attention to the obvious signs of rank; I feel like a fool.

The assistant escorts us into the other office, where Dr. Hoboo is wearing a grey suit. He greets me and directs me to sit in a very large chair on one side of the room; he and the linguist sit on the other side, slightly obliquely from Hoboo's oversize desk, which seems a mile apart from me. At least we are facing each other! Dr. Hoboo is a nondescript man, neither fat nor thin, tall nor short, average in every way, about sixty years old.

As the linguist already answered my first question, I start with a follow-up, about changes in the way the Party sees itself at the university. With pen and paper in hand, I take copious notes on what is said. "Article Eight of the Constitution says the Party leads the way," Dr. Hoboo begins. "It leads the 'state and society.' That is, in theory, the Party drafts policy and strategies, but it is not in charge of implementation. In practice, of course, it is also involved in policy and oversees the nitty-gritty of administration. The president of the university needs to consult the party, and there are meetings on Monday afternoons at the university." (In fact, no classes may be scheduled on Monday afternoons to avoid conflict with the Party meetings).

I ask, "If the Party checks the president, as someone must, who checks the leadership of the Party?"

Dr. Hoboo explains, "There is a regional and national Party leadership that checks the Party, and ultimately President Assad directs the Party and comes up with strategy."

"So the Party checks the Party," I summarize.

Dr. Hoboo smiles.

"What about the two or three private universities that were recently started?"

"They are different, they are excluded from this. There is no branch of the Party there, though they are subject to the Ministry of Education, which is ultimately subject to the Party."

"It still seems circular to me," I say.

Dr. Hoboo is giving me standard answers, which the linguist is translating exactly. He seems to have an inner monologue prepared, and stops my questions momentarily by giving me a short lecture on what he calls "anthropology," by which he means the long history of Syria, focusing on how it was once filled with city-states that ultimately united. The Ba'ath Party slogan is crucial to its role: one party, one people, pan-Arab—and secular. The Party's ultimate goal remains pan-Arab unification, the uniting of all Arabs in one state, like from the eighth to the thirteenth century under the Umayyad dynasty and the secular Abassid caliphate. But they are aware how difficult it is to unify the Arabs. Moreover, the Party's mission is more than just Arab unity; it also wants to contribute to world civilization. Arabs want to unify among themselves but also to unify the world. Under secular principles. Those principles are stable, but the methods have changed.

"What are these methods?" I ask.

Here at the University of Aleppo, he explains, professors can choose to supplement the standard textbooks with their own material. Also, Syria's leaders have graduated from many different schools in different countries: for example, France, England, Russia, the United States. The current Minister of Economics studied in Belgium, for example, and did his doctorate on the transformation of the economy from a Communist to a market system. He was a member of the Party leadership at Aleppo University before taking on this role. The Party today seeks a gradual political and economic opening; it sees itself as merely supervising this process, helping to organize and implement changes, as part of a regional command structure, linked to Damascus.

I ask my second question, which Dr. K. thought impertinent, about the massive student disapproval of the Party on campus.

"That depends on your sample. Who have you talked with here?" he asks.

"Let's assume I talked to all the wrong people. And that only the people I talked to, let's say a hundred students, disapprove of the Party's role on campus. Do you have a strategy to win them over, or are you unconcerned with their opinions?"

Dr. Hoboo responds by citing the large numbers of students, nearly twenty thousand of the seventy thousand enrolled students, formally involved in Party activities, with six thousand full members.

"What about student participation?" I ask. "I see so little student activity here. There is no film society, I have heard no public debates, attended no forums for discussion. I showed a film series here on American culture, and most students didn't even know there was a cinema on campus where one could show films."

Dr. Hoboo claims there are many activities on campus, though I may have not seen any, such as public debates, meetings, and lectures. Above all, the student union exists, and it focuses on political lectures, though participation tends to be confined to political activists. If students want to organize something new, they must submit a list to the Party of their activities. But they are always active on Revolution Day, the Eighth of May, the Anniversary of the October War, the Israeli War of '67—he rattles off a list of official or quasi-official holidays. There is also a film society, he says, though not active now.

My own impression does not confirm what he says. Students are extremely passive, for good reason—because self-initiative is punished, and compared to their fathers, they have become largely apoliticized. I frequently hear the complaint from other teachers that students learn how to memorize but are unable to think independently, to interpret, to make connections between disparate events. From what adults tell me, each succeeding generation in the last forty years takes less initiative. Even the festivals that used to have little to do with the Party and state now suffer from lack of enthusiasm and participation generally. The one student demonstration in recent memory of which I am aware—a campus sit-in resulting in the arrest and suspension of several students—occurred two years ago; it involved engineering students only, and they were protesting the withdrawal of job guarantees upon completion of the degree.

I move on, and for my third question begin with a connection between Dr. Hoboo and myself. He had studied in East Germany, where I initially did fieldwork. I tell him that we both, based on our knowledge of East German socialism, are aware of problems legitimating revolutionary authority over time. In East Germany and throughout Eastern Europe, the ruling socialist parties used the revolutionary generation, *jeel al-thawra* in Arabic, in schools and public discussions as a public face of why the government acted in their interests and had legitimacy. But in Syria, I never see members of that generation in public or at the university, and the Party does not seem to pay them any attention. Is the Party distancing itself from the idealism of this founding generation of the Ba'ath Party?

Dr. Hoboo replies that as time goes on, generations succeed each other, and the Party today no longer needs to utilize these elders. The Party is neither isolated nor static. Revolution continues through peaceful dialogue, and is not dependent on the initial founding members. Through open dialogue the Party contributes to thinking, but it does not control all the nitty-gritty. They meet, discuss issues; there are military camps for students, scientific camps; new blood is brought into the Party. There is no gap with the people, no hiatus with the older generation. Yet the principles of Ba'athism will never die; they remain the same.

The Party itself has a charter, but also has think tanks that adjust its strategies. It tries to think in parallel to developments in the world, and knows one needs new methods. But the basic principles are constant: Arab unity, socialism (not Communism), and liberty. Socialism is not Communism, he emphasizes, and there is no firm socialist ideology. Unity, also, cannot be imposed by force, overnight, but must be achieved gradually through the exchange of ideas and cooperation among Arabs. The Syrian leadership does not desire to be isolated from the rest of the world. It recognizes economic blocs and deals with them openly. There is, for example, a "partnership with Europe." On economic policy, the goal is to create a single Arab market, in a democratic way, by convening meetings, having debates, creating consensus. And there is a progressive front; there are other political parties, and a new law governing all parties will soon be issued, encouraging more citizen participation. But the principles do not change. For example, there will be no parties representing minorities alone, nor a Syrian nationalist party.

My final question concerns control over the reform process, and comparisons with the break-up of the Soviet Union and dissolution of Yugoslavia. I explain that in the attempt to reform in these other contexts, two major problems presented themselves: one, the organization of minorities and intergroup tensions (between ethnic and religious groups); two, tensions of modernization, such as the rationalization of industry (resulting in the firing of workers), elimination of state subsidies (resulting in increased poverty), and the opening of a more dynamic political arena (resulting in increased social tension and challenges to the authority of the government).

Dr. Hoboo replies that Syria was always one state and will remain one state. It is a mosaic of minorities, with unstable majorities and minorities. But the one majority is Arab. In the past, Iraq always lived in peace with differences before external intervention. Religious differences in Syria will not be a problem unless there is external intervention.

"External intervention is a norm in this part of the world," I state, "so I wish you well in dealing with it. Nobody here that I have talked to desires the Iraqi outcome."

I ask Dr. Hoboo if he has questions for me, and he asks about my teaching and research in Syria. I mention the lecture I recently gave in Damascus on American secularism, which was to have been the basis of my course at the university (parts of which were later translated into Arabic and published in the Lebanese newspaper *an-Nahar*). He says that lecture interests him and if I return, he would be pleased to organize an audience. I agree, only on the condition that the linguist serve as my translator.

The week after I leave, the Mukhabarrat interviewed many of the students whom I met at the university. They were aware of the dinners I had at student homes, of the other guests, and even of some of the food that was served. They asked the students about the content of our conversations, and they asked them to submit a detailed written protocol of what was discussed. I tell the students, when I see them three months later, that I would love to read how they represented our talk, to compare perspectives, for I, too, have written up our conversations.

Student Radicals

I meet two of the eleven students who helped organize a demonstration on February 25, 2002, at Aleppo University, to protest a new law that ended guaranteed employment for engineering graduates. One has a daily rendezvous with friends in the university cafeteria near the medical school; I join his table several times. The other I meet only once at his home.

Both identify themselves as "leftists" and "human rights activists"; others at the university identify these young men as "student radicals." Both are eager to discuss politics, unlike nearly all other students I meet, and I assume that is what other students find most radical about them, in addition to, as I soon learn, a willingness to act on their political beliefs. For me, in neither appearance nor belief do they distinguish themselves from most other students I have met. One, a mechanical engineering student, is husky with refined features, and exudes a pleasant, quiet stolidity. Suspended from his advanced degree program for organizing a sit-in in protest of the new law, he has nonetheless since been able to secure a job. The other, who continues to pursue his degree in engineering, is built like a rock, but unlike his friend, quite emotional and tense. His warmth and friendliness turn into an aggressive masculinity when political topics arise; he argues passionately, points his index finger, spreads his knees apart, leans forward for emphasis.

Once, the student who is still enrolled invites his uncle along to translate, so we can have a more philosophical discussion. The uncle has been living in France for fifteen years, with his German wife and daughter. He speaks with a deep, seductive voice that betrays the abuse of a chain smoker, and soon upon meeting me he confides he is also fighting an alcohol addiction, and that he drank too much arak the night before. I tell him he probably has to go cold turkey. He smiles and repeats the phrase fondly, "Cold turkey? Cold turkey. Cold turkey." His ability to translate is unrivaled, but he bothers with only some of what is said, often inserting himself into the discussion. And the other men present speak too fast, and switch topics too often, for me to understand most of what they say in Arabic.

The student who had been suspended explains, in response to my questions, what the two weeks he spent in prison were like. He was not tortured or treated abusively, he says, though some of the other students reportedly were. The student union should have defended him, he complains, but instead built a case to kick him out of the university.

The translator tells me he is worried about his nephew, who is risking too much for too little reward; Syrian society may not be ready for his sacrifice. He fears his nephew is experiencing a personal crisis, too, as his father was a Communist but has now begun praying. (The idea of "the Communist" pops up in many of my conversations with people. Hafez el-Assad systematically persecuted them, and I meet a surprising number of people, always accidentally, who themselves had been imprisoned, as they put it, "for being Communist," or who have a close friend or relative who was.) I ask the translator what he does when he visits family here. He says he returns to Aleppo yearly for the warmth of interaction with relatives, for the exquisite food, and for the pleasure of engaging in custom—for example, to be able to eat with his hands. On the basis of his yearly visits he concludes that there is a tendency towards more public and more aggressive religious expression, and he points as illustration to a recent incident in the village where he grew up, fifteen miles from Aleppo. He was sharing a taxi with three other men, who smelled arak on his breath. "Have you had something to drink?" one asked. He admitted he did; they stopped the taxi and insisted he get out. "That would have never happened five years ago," he says.

I ask the young men what kind of society they want, specifically if they see Syrian society as secular, and what role they foresee for the Ba'ath Party. They insist they want rights, above all, not the arbitrary administration of law. Like many Syrians, they see the violence resulting from the American attempt to force democracy on Iraq, and have become skeptical of the concept of "freedom." They want rights like freedom of speech and assembly, freedom from arbitrary arrest. They would like the Party to give up its monopoly, but that is not the major issue, since they do not want a leadership vacuum and a repeat of the violence in Iraq. They do not agree with each other about the issues of Alawite dominance, abuse of power, and corruption. The enrolled student has an Alawite girlfriend, and the others kid him for being prejudiced on the issue. They agree that a Muslim party would probably win any free election. But then, I ask, what rights would minorities have? The suspended student replies that if this government collapses, and a Muslim party rules, it will result in civil war.

Subsequent discussions with other students confirm my earlier observation about the unique political vision of these two young men, its special character being simply that they have a vision and are willing to articulate it. Others have different priorities; some of which I heard include democracy over rights, the right to be free of Israeli or American occupation over free speech, economic over political reform, national sovereignty over a free press, national self-sufficiency over wealth, theocratic over secular rule, and un-restricted religious practice over political freedoms. The conflict with Lebanon in 2005, which led to the assassination of former Leb-anese Prime Minister Rafik Hariri, the withdrawal of Syrian forces, and an international investigation (led by Detlev Mehlis) that came perilously close to indicting members of the Assad clan, undoubt-edly reinforced conservative tendencies to hold onto the familiar as well as onto Syrian nationalism. As another student put it, citing an Arab proverb: "My brother and I against my cousin, my brother and cousin and I against our neighbor, we all against the foreigner."

Teaching Anthropology and American Culture

My first lecture and film screening take place about twelve weeks after my arrival, plenty of time, I think, for all of us to prepare. Be-cause half the semester is over and because of the lack of exposure in Syria to contemporary anthropology, I jettison my original idea of giving a seminar on American secularism and instead decide to lecture about anthropology and American culture. The lectures are entitled: American Anthropology before World War II, American Anthropology and the Humanities, American Anthropology and the Social Sciences, Topics in American Anthropology Today. The screenings are of four feature films, from 1958 to 1997, which exam-ine key characteristics of American culture, specifically the meanings of love, marriage, family, divorce, and history. I hope to demonstrate how certain everyday practices in the United States relate to an official secular state ideology, and then to elicit reactions from Syrians that might help me understand the parameters of secularism in Syria.

Several days before my first lecture, Dr. Lababidi, the head of the English Department who had instigated the resistance to my teaching, calls me, and we set a time to meet in her office. The university vice president had taken over organizing my lectures, and he appointed her—a kind of ironic reprimand—to introduce me and to translate, if needed, during the lecture.

I was told she would apologize, but of course she did not. "Have you been here before?" she smiles innocently and extends me her hand.

"Before?" I ask incredulously.

She is about forty, with round, rosy-red, plump cheeks that make her look perpetually youthful, absolutely cherubic, I think, certainly not devious or cunning. A chic blue-and-white headscarf frames her face but is loosely, seductively draped, so that much of her brown hair escapes, and though she dresses modestly, there is nothing conservative about her appearance. Light pink lipstick and blue eyeliner suggest a careful management of impression, a feminization that would be appealing to many men.

"Why didn't anybody contact me?" she asks in a high-pitched, desperate voice. "All of this at the last minute."

"You must ask them," I say.

"Why hasn't the American Cultural Center called? I haven't heard from Stephanie or Sahar in months. Would you like to meet . . . ?" and she names all the deans, the president, the vice president, the department heads.

"I wonder, too," I decide to be as mendacious as she is and play along with her feigned ignorance. "I have been here many times, and I have met them all—the president, the vice president, all the deans, the heads of several departments. You are the only one I haven't met! I am so sorry it took so long for me to be able to extend American hospitality to you, to invite you to lunch or dinner. Why did it take so long, you think? Nearly three months."

She giggles and flashes me a smile, making her round cheeks even rounder, and mutters something about the difficulty of fitting anthropology into the curriculum of the English Department. I wait for her to set the tone. She decides to chitchat, and mentions her study in Nottingham, England. Her advisor there was American, she says, and he was very nice and supportive, not like the British, who are cold by comparison. Some are racist, she adds.

I take that as an opening, "That's why I decided to lecture on American anthropology, because it has been involved in fighting racism in the United States, and people seem to know so little about it here, and when they think they know what anthropology is, they mention only colonialism and Orientalism, or the Dead Cities and archaeology."

She returns to talking about herself, "Yes, Nottingham, I was there for seven years. I got my degree in an American cultural studies program."

"When was that?"

"Guess," she says in a girlish voice.

"About fifteen years ago?"

She looks disappointed. "Eight."

"Was there any anthropology in the program?" I ask.

"No," she says, and adds, "I am really not qualified to translate in this field."

I reassure her that my lectures will be broad, one even on the relation of anthropology to literature, which may interest her, given that she teaches American literature. She asks me for my notes. I give her a copy, but ask that she translate key terms only, the rest are incomplete sentences from which it is difficult to infer what I will be saying. She skims the notes, and zeroes in on two phrases: "Picture of Bush" and "Boas was a German-Jew." I intend on showing a *New Yorker* cover from 2002 where Bush, wearing a blinker on one eye to prevent any peripheral vision, is riding a horse galloping crazily out of control in a barren landscape.

"What is this, politics? Who is this BO-SE? These are hot topics here."

"Bo-Az," I correct her, "Boas, the founder of American anthropology."

"People here get very excited about these things. These are hot topics."

"If so, perhaps then we should discuss them." She pauses, and I try to joke, "If you prefer cold climates so much, you should go live with the Eskimos in Alaska. Syria *IS* a hot country."

My joke doesn't work, but she giggles nonetheless and continues, in a kind of stream-of-consciousness, on the theme of heat, "It took a couple of years to get used to living in England. It is so cold there! I always had an extra breath there, you know," and she demonstrates how one's breath precedes you in the cold. "I like the warmth of Syria, though it took a while to readjust."

She asks about my impressions of Syria. I mention how in traffic people seem calm even when there is general bedlam, and confess I would have hypertension if I lived in Aleppo permanently. She says she learned to drive after returning from England, and now has no problem with Aleppo's traffic. "Everything is solvable here," she concludes, "one just needs patience."

"Yes, lots of patience," I mumble. "Perhaps that is the function of faith here, it teaches patience, and here you cannot live without it; nothing else seems to work."

"Americans are hot-blooded," she returns to the hot/cold theme, "unlike the English."

"Really only the Hispanics," I say, "if we are talking stereotypes; most Americans are pretty cool."

"Americans are not as cold as the British," she corrects me, "but also not too excitable."

One of the vice deans enters, and I feel relieved, hoping the conversation will turn to the organization of my lectures. Instead, Dr. Labibidi talks again about the University of Nottingham, and what a good education she got there.

"Can you bring your CV along so I can introduce you?" she asks. "Is it twenty pages?"

At one level I would like to reassure her. I realize she is insecure, hence both mocking me and seriously overwhelmed by the flashiness of an American resume. She had obviously seen mine: too many publications, too many talks, too many honors. But she has done everything she could to make my lectures impossible. I am not so easily placated, "I will bring along a shortened version, just four lines, that's all you'll need."

She asks what I am doing in Aleppo. I say the Fulbright Commission surely sent her my proposal—she denies having seen it. I tell her about living in the souk. "What are you doing there?" she asks, clearly puzzled.

"I just hang out with people, sit and drink coffee and tea, talk to them."

"What do you talk about? Politics?"

"Surprisingly seldom," I reply, "People in the souk do not discuss politics with me."

She raises her eyebrows but says nothing. An older student enters the office, and she gives him my notes to copy. He returns and gives one copy to Dr. Lababidi's M.A. student, a quiet (also veiled) woman, and keeps one for himself. I begin to suspect something fishy. For some reason, Dr. Lababidi does not want me to leave. I have my second cup of coffee, from a man who circulates between offices.

Eventually someone appears and says the dean wants to see me again. We go to his regular office—not there. We go to the office he keeps as his private library—not there. We go back to his regular office—he is attending a seminar on archaeology and history. Dr. Lababidi shows me the visitor's room where I can sit with students and order coffee or tea. We pass the other deans in the hall. A student, Omar, calls on my cell phone and asks if they are invited to the lecture. Of course, I say. He puts Abdella on the line, who apologizes for not having called recently and promises to come to the lectures.

Finally, the dean returns to his office and seats us in the large armchairs in front of his desk. He talks as if reading a formal statement, looking straight ahead. Dr. Lababidi translates, "I welcome you to Aleppo University. We are very pleased to have you give lectures here. But they cannot be about politics; this is not political science or law, this is humanities."

"But why does he think I am lecturing about politics?" I ask.

"The picture of Bush," says Dr. Lababidi.

"How did he get that picture?" I ask, clearly at the end of whatever patience I cultivated. She looks at me, silently, innocently, but clearly aware that I am upset.

"How did he get it? I gave it only to you. No one else. Did you give it to him? Why? Why did you do this?"

It obviously had landed on his desk along with my notes while we were visiting the other offices. The dean says something about this being a humanities faculty and not politics, and he would not authorize political lectures here.

"Translate for me," I insist to Dr. Lababidi. "Translate every word I say: This is an image, a representation from the *New Yorker*, the leading American literary magazine. I repeat, LITERARY MAGAZINE. Most famous major American writers—the ones you teach here—have had initial publications in this journal. It is not a political journal, but a literary one."

"But he insists you omit the politics from your talk, no mention of Bush," she translates the dean's response.

"The vice president has already approved my talk," I reply. "Call him. Here"—I hand them my cell phone—"I have his number. Or call the president. Or the Ministry of Education." We reach the number, but the vice president is in a meeting.

"We are trying to protect you here," says Dr. Lababidi.

"From what? I have had no problems here, neither with the students nor the community," I say.

"There are other groups here that might cause trouble; he does not want responsibility for that," she says. "There were demonstrations outside the American Embassy last year."

"This is not the American Embassy," I say. "Who is causing this problem? Who is making a problem out of this? How does he even know about the picture?"

"We want you to be happy. We want things to go well," she says, quietly, and the sympathetic vice dean who is present repeats this reassurance.

"But you are doing the exact opposite," I say, exasperated. "Why is this of concern to you? It is a literary representation of a figure in

American culture. The drawing does not discuss policy, and neither does my talk."

"Is it necessary for your talk?" Dr. Lababidi asks.

"What is necessary in a talk?" I ask. One frames a problem a certain way. This is a humorous framing; it helps the public understand."

"Just leave it out and then everything will be okay," she says.

"My first talk is about pre–World War II anthropology," I explain, choosing my words carefully, "which is involved in debates on race and immigration; these are of course political debates, but they cannot be excised from the American political context to talk about culture. I also mention important Supreme Court decisions that were based on anthropological research. You're a literary critic. This drawing is a metaphor for something in American culture. You know the importance of metaphors. Are they necessary?"

The frustrated dean's face remains cold, perhaps angry, strangely vacant except for a tightly closed mouth, as if he had tasted a raw olive. Nearly three months ago in this very same room he had welcomed me to the university. Shortly after, he had signed a letter saying, in effect, that I was unqualified to teach any course, in any department, in the Human Sciences Faculty at Aleppo University. He had just recited a welcome statement similar to the one he initially delivered, performing like he was giving a forced confession, until the twist at the end—"no picture of Bush." "He will not take responsibility for your talk," Dr. Lababidi repeats; "he needs a written statement from the president." I say, "I will omit the picture only if ordered to do so personally by the president or vice president." Eventually, they reach the vice president, who authorizes showing the image. He calls me later that night and says I should not worry, just say what I want to say; he will write the letter for the dean if necessary.

The next morning, I arrive early and find at the entrance to the Humanities Building only two copies of the poster announcing the lecture series, and they are small copies, on eight by ten pieces of paper, hardly visible. The lecture is to begin at 10:00. At 9:30, the door to the lecture room is still locked, but Dr. Lababidi is already in her office working to correct a PowerPoint presentation of my talk, in Arabic, prepared by her M.A. student, who had stayed up all night translating my notes. "I should have translated it myself," she reprimands the student in front of me.

"You shouldn't have bothered," I say. "Please just summarize briefly what I say every five minutes, with the help of key words."

The room is full, about 120 people, including the vice president, the head dean, the two vice deans, department chairs, students, people from downtown. About ten people have to stand. The head dean yawns his way through about two-thirds of the lecture before departing early; the others present listen closely. Dr. Lababidi insists on not following the PowerPoint presentation that her student had completed but instead translates anew every sentence from my text, even breaking into the middle of my sentences—we both have microphones—and talking over me. I ask her to stop. "I will forget what you say," she pleads. Several students complain that they cannot switch between the two languages easily, and encourage us to drop the translation altogether; they can read the PowerPoint projected on a screen above us. Several more times I ask Dr. Labibidi to stop. She does not. "It's not my specialty," she says, and continues talking. Once I even warn, "I'll skip this," in order to save time, but she still translates the notes on which I had elaborated the sentences that I now omit. Later, the vice president tells me that from the questions after it appears some people thought this was about politics. I say it doesn't matter to me what they think it was about; I am pleased that (almost) everyone stayed alert and engaged me with questions.

In the talk, I set up a tension within American culture between two visions: the antisecular, missionary vision of America as a special land, of "God's country" (which Bush represents), and an Enlightenment-inspired vision with secular understandings, in which an appreciation of facts leads to a questioning of dogma and superstition, truths are subject to critical scrutiny, and an official agnosticism is affirmed about the various visions of a "good life" or the proper expression of religiosity. The antisecular vision values certainty, belief, and conviction over knowledge, doubt, and science. Anthropology is a child of Enlightenment science, and thus has worked to foster a critical understanding of difference, to question dogma and prejudice, and to unsettle understandings of human behavior that have no scientific or factual basis.

Questions after the talk continue for forty minutes. Several professors ask about anthropology and Edward Said's *Orientalism*. They appear to understand Orientalism as a longterm process whereby the West represents the East as unchanging, backward, authoritarian, feminine, inferior, repressive—and in its passivity needing to be colonized by the superior West. As I also later get questions about Orientalism in lectures in Damascus and Latakia, I conclude that this line of questioning serves as an anchor for deeply felt sentiments and allows people to be formulaic in analysis of problems in the Middle East. The specific role of other factors, for example, Arab educational systems, authoritarian governments, oil wealth, Saudi hypocrisy, and the politicization of Islam, are thereby rendered unimportant. In Syria, Said's study of Western representations of the Middle East serves less as he intended, to open up questions, than to entomb thinking. From the secure resting point of *Orientalism*, further thought appears unnecessary; everything in the present appears to be a repetition of early patterns of Oriental representation and Western domination.

A professor of philosophy asks me to explain what Bush thinks he is doing in Iraq; a professor of literature asks if the knowledge of American anthropology is not being misused, against its Enlightenment intent, to dominate and conquer instead of to understand Arabs; another professor adds that their experience in the Middle East has been of domination and colonization. Students ask whether the American stereotypes of black and savage have not been replaced by stereotypes of Arabs.

Only one question is based on a false understanding of what I said (one listener told me that this was, I regret to say, due to Dr. Lababidi's mistranslation). I had mentioned that in the 1893 World Columbian Exposition in Chicago, Franz Boas had helped organize the anthropology exhibit, called the "assembly of peoples," which involved "living exhibits" (whole villages imported and rebuilt) of American Indian, native Africans, Germans, Egyptians, Labrador Eskimos—with actual representatives of these cultures living in

Syria

187

them. I had also mentioned that Boas's support for the integrity of American Indian and African American cultures was much more progressive than the general intellectual climate in the United States at the time, as in 1902, a visiting Pygmy from the Belgian Congo was still displayed for weeks in a cage in the primate house of the Bronx Zoo in New York. Dr. Lababidi apparently translated this to mean Boas supported the display of the Pygmy in the zoo, as a living exhibit. In response to a student question, I try to distinguish between the progressive intent of "living exhibits" and the demeaning nature of exhibiting humans from anywhere alongside other animals in a zoo.

On their way out, students—male and female, advanced and beginner—gather around the lectern where I sit, and I agree to meet them in the cafeteria, though first I am obligated to go back to the dean's office—for coffee and, it seems, just to sit together in the same room. We hardly chat about anything; there is much silence. Students and secretaries come in to get signatures. All this takes another half hour, or longer. While I am there, the students call me twice on my cell phone to reassure themselves I am in fact coming. I finally stand up and excuse myself, awkwardly, for it probably appears strange to want to meet with students rather than spend time like this—empty time for me but a dimension of sociability, hence meaningful, for those present. I spend an hour with the students, and encourage them to come to the film.

Cat on a Hot Tin Roof

The film that night is *Cat on a Hot Tin Roof* (1958, directed by Richard Brooks). Assuming that Syria was not as technologically advanced as the United States, I bring with me four films in reel-based, magnetic tape videos that play on VCR machines. I purposely choose these instead of digital videos for CD or DVD players, but soon discover that most Syrians probably never owned VCRs; instead they jumped directly to digital recordings for television or computers. In addition, they all have satellite dishes on their rooftops to get TV reception from four continents; cable is not regulated by the government and thus totally free after one purchases the satellite. Hence I cannot play my films without first getting them converted to DVDs, which is costly, takes several weeks, and results in very poor quality recordings. Not only do some of the images blur and colors blend but the voices are often distorted.

Twelve students attend the first screening; two men there at the beginning leave during my introduction (I assume they work for the Mukhabarrat and are to write a report). Four of the women present are veiled, and two approach me after to thank me for my modesty and kindness.

I introduce the video with the following summary: "*Cat on a Hot Tin Roof*, directed by Peter Brooks in 1958 and based on a 1955 play by the renowned playwright Tennessee Williams, is a story about frustrated sexual desire in the 1950s. It takes place in an American family in the South, where love between husband and wife, played by Paul Newman and Elizabeth Taylor, follows unpredictable paths. 'I'm not living with you,' snaps Maggie at Brick. 'We occupy the same cage, that's all.' Even the powerful and confident Big Daddy, Taylor's father, cannot keep the marriage going and make his daughter happy. Both Taylor and Newman were nominated for Academy Awards as was the film for Best Picture."

Within minutes of the film's start, a student seated to my right says it is difficult to understand the dialect, especially Elizabeth Taylor's faux-Southern accent. A bit later, he asks another question after the voluptuous and catlike Maggie (Elizabeth Taylor) fails, again, to seduce her husband Brick (Paul Newman). Brick explains it is "because you disgust me." The student asks, in English, "Why does he disgust her? Is Brick gay, like Tennessee Williams?" About a quarter of the way through, the same student encourages me to fast forward, "This is too much, the others will walk out"—at the scene where Maggie, always trying to be ever-so-seductive, approaches her husband Brick, who lies prone on the bed, drinking. She is dressed in a revealing white slip and flits around for about five minutes, before she puts something equally revealing of her perfect hourglass figure over it. "Don't worry," I say, "she doesn't take her clothes off. Anyway, I cannot fast forward because she stays this way most of the rest of the film."

My intent is to get them to think of how frustrated desire works in interfamilial dynamics. They do not find this point strange, at least not those who ask questions, perhaps because many Syrians think of frustrated desire and constant deferral as its normal state. Why don't Maggie and Brick simply accept their fate: a stalemate in ongoing marital struggle (which they in fact do at the end of the film)? Only one student, a beautiful girl of mixed Kurdish and Sunni parentage, attends all my lectures and films, and she asks the first question. She begins by apologizing for the absence of her fellow students and then asks, "Are all American families so dysfunctional?" Others follow up on this theme. I respond by pointing out how this is a representation of a 1950s family in the South, and the death of Big Daddy (Burl Ives) in the film signals the decline of many of the larger family clans; I discuss the power of inheritance and property, and point to the most important relationship for the film: that of Brick with his dead friend, a fellow football player whom Brick obviously loved so much that now, in his absence, he is the omnipresent ghost structuring (and frustrating) the desire of the living.

The next day, a man from the city who attended the lecture and film calls me and asks, "The lecture was wonderful, but who was that woman who introduced you?"

I ask students in several settings if there are any films they particularly like. The universal response of Muslim students: Mel Gibson's film *The Passion of the Christ*. Christian students, by contrast, are divided about this film; several say to me that there was too much brutality, and that there are other aspects of Christ that are more important to them. I ask people for explanations of this Muslim/Christian difference, and they offer two general arguments: one is that the film's demonization of Jews has particular resonance among Muslims here; the other is that the appeal is in the theme of martyrdom and the sado-masochistic atmosphere in the persecution of Christ.

Wild Dog Attack

The night before my second lecture, I eat late in the restaurant Kan Zaman with a friend visiting from Damascus, and we return home at midnight. A taxi drops us off at the entrance to the souk outside the Grand Mosque, and after we turn left at the corner in the first long, narrow corridor inside the souk, three yellow-haired dogs about the size of Labradors come around the corner facing us, barking and wagging their tails, which they hold high in the air. Their loud barks echo off the stone walls. Initially, I think the tail wagging is a sign of friendliness, and we keep walking toward the dogs. We are blocking their exit from the souk, so as they approach we flatten our bodies against the wall so they can pass. The smallest and undoubtedly youngest one passes, but the other two retreat instead, and we are suddenly caught between two adults on one side, a pup on the other. I am a dog lover and know farm animals well from my youth, so I tend to trust my instincts with animals, but I quickly realize these are not domesticated dogs. Up to this point, I had seen only one dog in Aleppo, a tiny Chihuahua owned by an architect who lives in what he calls a "phantasmagoric Mexican village" outside the city. Syrians love cats, but they detest dogs. The only Syrian dogs I am familiar with are the wild jackals I have seen in films about Syria and heard on a visit to the desert.

The barking gets louder and louder, and the dogs snarl and begin lunging at us from both directions. My friend is carrying a camera bag; I take it from her and swing it first in one direction, after which the dogs or pup in front of us would back up, then in the other direction, after which the dogs or pup behind us would lunge forward again. My friend and I scream, and we pound our shoes on the corrugated tin doors to the shop on our side, hoping to scare them into running away, but our noise merely adds to the feel of pandemonium, driving the dogs into an even greater frenzy. I say, "Let's stop making noise; we should get the dogs to relax." We quietly hold out a hand, palm flat facing the dogs, to signal to them to keep their distance, and very slowly we back up in the direction of the pup toward the entrance. At one point there is a narrow alley on the side, and when we reach that we sneak in; the dogs happily exit, still barking. Once in the apartment, we hear them return, barking loudly again, and wonder whether they have cornered someone else, some stray person wandering the souk at night.

The next day I tell friends about the dogs, and I call Jenny, the owner of my apartment. Everybody in the souk says they have never heard such a story. Jenny says the last time dogs entered the souk was in 1982, when the army came to Aleppo and set up blockades around the city to corner members of the Muslim Brotherhood, who had been carrying out a series of public attacks and assassinations against the secular regime and its friends (including moderate Sunni Muslim clergy). One can still see buildings damaged where tanks had entered parts of the city. Then the wild dogs which had escaped into the souk at night were trapped there, and in response, people in Aleppo massacred most of them. But some had obviously survived, including these three brave souls. I love dogs, and often show a picture of my whippet, Spot, to Syrian friends, knowing that it might be difficult to convince them of the worthiness of this love. But at the moment of the near attack, I agree with them and want these particular dogs shot. For weeks after I use other entrances into the souk.

Chapter IV

Reflections on Teaching and Learning in Syria

Pedagogy

Even under the best of circumstances, such as at Princeton, teaching is difficult. Not only is it impossible to measure effectiveness, but there is no one way to teach. Most learning occurs outside the classroom—in arguments within families, in play among peers, in listening to music or viewing television alone—and professors have little control or influence over these activities. So even when students learn, professors cannot usually ascertain the specific contributions of their own teaching. This book or exercise, that lecture or question—which, if any, makes a difference? And when? Most of what we know about our effectiveness as teachers comes as delayed satisfaction (or disappointment), as rumor or bits of information many years after a classroom experience. Asking students to evaluate the teaching of their professors, which they are compelled to do at most American universities, is a farcical exercise in democratic self-deception; for ten or twenty minutes, the power is reversed. Students do not and cannot know immediately after a class what they have learned, and, despite widespread confidence among American students in their ability to evaluate, they lack the experience necessary to understand and measure the effectiveness of the pedagogy of their professors. At most, student evaluations provide immediate impressions, which may be useful if interpreted carefully, but also tend to be based on the most superficial criteria—style of clothes, manners, public relations skills, clarity, simplicity in explanation— all of which have their place. But that is the point: how can one place and evaluate each factor? The best teachers develop their own style, and somehow make the material they use in speaking, lecturing, and arguing into a voice that is indelibly, unmistakably their own. To be effective teachers must especially both inspire and engage with the motivations of students—their horizon of expectations—what they want to learn and why.

What did the students in Aleppo want from me? Surely they did not want anthropology, since none had yet been introduced to this form of knowledge, how it is produced, or what insight it might yield. Yet they did want something, and, like all young people still largely unformed and unself-conscious, their desires were highly ambiguous to them. Initially, some wanted a mere conversation, a sense of the unknown in their midst, status from association, insight into the West, or perhaps even help to facilitate a trip there. But after several interactions, as they got to know me, experienced my strange answers to their questions, but also sensed my genuine interest in and sympathy for their plights, they sought me out for an alternative perspective, a jolt, a contradiction, an opposition, an adventure, an ally or friend, someone who did not just leave them be but who took their ambiguous desires seriously. That I might unsettle their understandings of the world as they knew it, both through my disciplinary knowledge (that is what anthropology, at its best, does) but also through my own personal form of engagement and their transferential relation to me, became not simply a condition of interaction but a want, a wish, a desire.

And what did I want from them? Also an alternative perspective, a jolt, an adventure, an ally or friend; more specifically, as much as I am aware, I wanted to know their wants, wishes, and desires. In order to arrive at this knowledge, I had to learn as well as teach, or teach as well as learn, and, as in much traditional anthropology, I engaged with a horizon of expectations radically different than my own. This did not mean submission to their norms and expectations (in the largely discredited sense of "going native") but making clear exactly where our relative horizons might meet, their delimitations and points of expansion, and the terms of engagement. The many modes of association I availed myself of—listening, alerting, provoking, empathizing, criticizing, teasing, flirting, discussing, sharing, serving, lecturing, arguing, reading—attest to the experimental and improvisational aspect of learning through fieldwork. Teaching was, for me, then, both a sharing of what I know as well as another opportunity to learn.

Lectures

My decision, as part of my Fulbright obligations, to lecture Syrian students about the interaction between American anthropology and American culture was, for me, a form of self-disclosure: of where I come from, at least intellectually, and how my intellectual field interacts in debates and controversies with the culture and politics of the United States. Although I did not, as initially planned, give a seminar on the theme of American secularism over the course of the semester, I nonetheless introduced it in my lectures, and therefore was still able to use my teaching on the topic as a learning tool as initially planned. By disclosing the complex and peculiar form of secular authority in the United States—which I framed as conflicts between Enlightenment and anti-Enlightenment thought—I could prompt my audience to reflect upon secularism and forms of authority in Syria.

The public lecture at universities, largely a nineteenth-century mode of imparting knowledge—imperial, all-knowing, distant—still has its place in transmitting general forms of knowledge to mass audiences, but it tends to work only one-way. In most settings it limits interaction with the audience to short questions and answers after a presentation. Therefore, I insisted at Aleppo University on what was a very unusual format for them: close to a full hour for questions after each lecture. Because of scheduling conflicts with regular classes, my audience decreased by about half for each subsequent lecture. I still met students outside of the classrooms, but then the discussion was only tangentially if at all related to the topic about which I had lectured.

After my first general lecture on the history of anthropology, I focused my second on the reciprocal relations of anthropology to the humanities, specifically history and literature. Using the work of Paul Ricouer, Tsvetan Todorov, Clifford Geertz, and Marshall Sahlins, I discussed how literary study and historical study had changed in interaction with anthropology, and anthropology, in turn, took up literary modes of analysis and became more historical, studying changes in discursive practices and symbolic forms. The most probing questions were by students, not faculty: What is the relation of spirituality to science? What about the U.S. role in using its science to support violence abroad? In our relatively lengthy discussion, I argued that spirituality might be better achieved with the use of and not against science. As example, I talked about pollution and Islamic belief, how in Islam the body should not be polluted because it is a site of spirituality, and how this thought might be extended to think of the whole environment as infused with spirituality (which in anthropology resembles what is known as "animism"); therefore one uses science to understand the sources of pollution—such as how to dispose of plastic water bottles (I lifted the one from my podium)—in order to serve a larger spirituality. Students wanted me, however, to deal with situations where spirituality and science are in conflict, where anthropology is in conflict with spiritual beliefs, or where spirituality might help to overcome civilizational differences. They also wanted more moral evaluation on my part, and one student, who prefaced her question with, "You may not want to comment on this," even sought a specific judgment from me on the exclusion of women from realms of activity in Syria.

My third lecture, on anthropology and the social sciences, focused on the contributions of anthropology to explanations for some of the larger existential questions—about freedom, domination, consciousness, society, religion, capitalism—posed by the great foundational social theorists: Hegel, Marx, Weber, Durkheim, and Freud. I then presented the work on New Guinea of the French anthropologist Maurice Godelier, who went to a so-called primitive society to study relations of domination structured by class and the system of production and found instead that domination was initially located in systems of sex and gender. I further used this lecture to show how we might understand "tradition" not as preceding the present but something produced in reaction to what we call "modern" conditions. The moderator did not leave time for questions after, but many students and a few faculty requested copies of my notes, and in the café later students told me merely that this was all new; they'd had little exposure to social science.

My final lecture was on some of the questions and projects pursued in contemporary anthropology, with a focus on two: studies of economic "development" that questioned the terms and even possibilities of third world development, and studies of changes in kinship, marriage, and sexuality in Europe where the logic of prohibitions and prescriptions was increasingly challenged by one of pleasure and bodies. Questions after focused solely on European kinship, and concerned the life of singles, the meanings of serial marriage, multiple parenting, and the separation of sex from marriage. As I sat in the café with students, some of the young women talked generally about how the lectures stimulated them to think of their own lives in many new ways. Abdulla and Omar, whom I had met before my very first lecture, said they had an argument about American students they wanted to clear up: is it true that most American students do not want to leave the United States? Since nearly all Syrian students want to leave Syria and study or work elsewhere, they found it mind-boggling that the entire American student body were so uncritical of their home, and that they all saw possibilities for a future without leaving the United States.

Films

The evening before the screening of my second film, I had dinner with my friend Majid from the souk and a visiting British journalist, and together we made up humorous introductions for the last three films:

Kramer vs. Kramer is a 1970s New York story of a bitter divorce of a couple played by Meryl Streep and Dustin Hoffman, and of the problems and joys of parenting alone. You need a heart of stone not to laugh, but get your buckets and mops out because the tears will be flowing.

The Apostle portrays a gifted Southern preacher of the 1990s, played by Robert Duvall, a man of faith and a man of the flesh in the search for redemption. It shows the brutality of organized religion in contemporary America through the conflicts of a marriage, where the husband increases his experience and strays far afield. Because of tit-for-tat, the wife also strays, and they tumble in a downward spiral of infidelity to a surprise ending.

Forrest Gump is a 1990s story of lovable stupidity where one man relives the major American events of this century. U.S. history is shown through the eyes of an innocent moron as he loses his innocence. As the moviemaker says, "Life is a box of chocolates, you never know what you're gonna get."

My first attempt to screen *Kramer vs. Kramer* (1979, directed by Robert Benton) was a disaster. The auditorium was closed, and in very cold weather about fifty people followed me around from room to room in the same building to find someone to let us in. The man in charge had gone home early, to his village one and a half hour's drive from Aleppo. Twelve people attended the screening the following week. The company that converted the VCR cassette into a DVD noticed a nude scene in the middle (when the divorced father Ted [Dustin Hoffman], begins an affair with Margaret [Jane Alexander], who stays overnight and leaves her bed, naked, to go to the toilet; she runs into the five-year-old son in the hallway, and covers herself with her hands). An employee at the company makes two DVDs for me, with the "nude scene" at the beginning of the second. I am told beforehand that some students may be offended, so I should fast-forward at the beginning of the second tape. I considered this, but when the time of the "nude scene" approached I found it too cumbersome to stop the film. As that scene came on screen, the student seated next to me says, "You should fast-forward, the others will all leave."

"It's only a few seconds," I reassure him. Not only does nobody leave, but in fact for most of the audience tears were in fact flowing at the intended humor. After, the questions revolve around the problems of divorce, and the expectations in a marriage.

For my third and fourth films, the audience had shrunk to around ten. I had hoped that *The Apostle* (director, Robert Duvall, 1997) would stimulate a discussion of the role of religion and evangelical sects in the United States, and of the changing relations between men and women. The students in attendance—all Muslim—seemed to have little or no knowledge of the internal political and cultural movements within American Christianity—the topic of the film— though they were well informed of the alliance between fundamentalist Christians and Orthodox Jews. Their questions focused on sects generally, and about the relation of politics to race. Several confided that they were surprised I showed a film so critical of Christianity, and this comment (and reaction) alone for me justified its showing.

Forrest Gump (director, Robert Zemeckis, 1994), my final film, was, I thought, a quintessentially American story, showing American optimism and belief in good luck in the face of a dreadful political history. I tied it in with my introductory lecture and the picture of Bush on the wild horse, and it was clear that students saw it as an allegory for American ideology: Forrest Gump in the movie and the horse ridden by Bush in that photo both symbolized America running. But why is it running? Initially Gump runs from mean children, to save his life as they seem intent on beating him up. But he keeps on running, just because it is something to do; neither God nor larger historical forces are brought in to explain his motivation or place. History always happens to Gump; he never makes history, and he is so dumb that he never comprehends what is going on. Yet all historical misfortune is ultimately rectified: the boy who cannot walk ends up running and winning in college football, the boy who is dumb gets the most beautiful girl, the man who loses his legs in Vietnam gets a new pair and walks, the man who loses his wife gets a son in return, the dumb man fathers a son who is brilliant. Violence, political assassinations, and racial hatred leave no real scars on Gump, and when he is given the opportunity, he ends up redressing some of the larger historical harm done to others by the nation.

America is innocent, yet the site of much violence and the site of redemption. In questions, students asked about anthropology's political orientation. And since my general theme was kinship, they asked if I approved or was critical of American kinship patterns.

What I might conclude generally from student questions is that they have a strong desire for an evaluation before inquiring into the nature of the facts offered or the questions asked. In other words, a foregrounded moral position precedes any general desire to learn, and the lack of such a clear position might even effectively foreclose an inquiry. Yet there is also evidence that the students wanted more to understand schemes of evaluation, alternative perspectives, than to reach a judgment. They did, in fact, listen closely to what I said and often tried to provoke me into saying things they themselves had thought but were unwilling or unable to articulate. At the same time they had to struggle to assert a significance for our exchanges in the context of Syrian education where learning by rote remains the standard mode of acquiring knowledge. In all of my lectures and in my use of films there was nothing to be learned through drill or memorization, which made my teaching of minimal relevance to the students' formal education. This lack of fit was, after all, the formal reason given by Dr. Lababidi for blocking my teaching in the first place.

One of the challenges for me pedagogically, therefore, was relevance itself: by not giving the students something to memorize for their courses and exams, but instead encouraging them to think in terms of questions, problems, connections, culture, and politics, they may have genuinely come to doubt the relevance for them of what I had to say. As I've written elsewhere in *Syrian Episodes*, however, one of my major pedagogical goals, in the United States as well as in Syria, is to introduce doubt or skepticism not only as a mode of scientific inquiry but also as a philosophical attitude to authority. Doubt may or may not be compatible with certain religious doctrines, but it is essential to any secular philosophy worthy of that name.

⟶ Coda: January 2006 ⟵

I

Thick fog promptly settles in Damascus as my flight lands in Beirut. A twenty-minute stop turns into an interminable delay, and it proves impossible to complete the last leg of a journey that began in Princeton and is to end in Aleppo—for three final weeks of fieldwork. The Damascus airport closes to all incoming flights. Rumors circulate among us passengers that the British Airways plane in which we were flying is equipped with antiquated navigation equipment, unable to handle this density of fog. Our dear aging airplanes! Almost as an afterthought I recall that BA called me in Princeton twelve hours before the transatlantic portion of my scheduled flight—from Newark to London—to cancel; unspecified mechanical problems, they said, and I flew out the next day instead. By the time the fog in Damascus lifts, our crew has been on duty longer than its legally permitted time; no other crew is available. Alas, we wait another eight hours in the airport before forcing a BA official to secure a bus for us for a trip that, if it had gone on schedule, would have been twenty minutes by air, less than three hours by road. My first planned day in Damascus—a waste.

Upon arrival in the early evening, however, a message from a friend, my only acquaintance who is also a member of Parliament, awaits me. He asks that I meet him at his home, and I take a taxi, a twenty-minute drive up the mountain on edge of the city. The taxi driver finds the area but drops me off on the wrong street. I walk by foot to a local store, call G., and he gets in his car and drives the two blocks to pick me up.

He asks about my Beiruti friend, Chibli Mallat, a law professor, human rights activist, and declared candidate for the presidency of Lebanon. I express admiration for Chibli's courageous, even outrageous act of declaring his candidacy. (I need not mention the string of recent assassinations of Lebanese journalists and political figures, and that Chibli is certainly on someone's hit list.) In the Middle East, offices are filled by persons selected through a local doctrine of predestination: inherited by patriline, allotted by sect or network, certainly not to be sought by an individual. I ask about G's own attempt to declare candidacy—for Secretary General of the United Nations, also one of these positions for which candidates are largely predestined. The next candidate is to come from Asia, he says, and Syria is in Asia. He has made no headway since we last talked, though he is still working on it.

He is curious about this book, *Syrian Episodes*, and asks me to include in it a reference to his wife, who on each of my visits generously serves us coffee and sweets. We avoid mention of the UN Mehlis Report, which accuses Syrian officials of involvement in the assassination of the former Lebanese Prime Minister, Rafik Hariri. Though it is obviously on my mind, and as I soon discover, on everybody else's mind, what can we—an American to a Syrian, or a Syrian who sits in the government to an American—say? The atmosphere between our countries is severely strained, and neither of us wants to get caught up in personally defending official positions. Just before I left the United States, the American government again singled out Syria as a hostile country, and many Syrians suspect that the United States is behind the UN investigation of Hariri's murder and determined to obtain a specific result: condemnation and isolation of Syria.

Back in Princeton, a mutual acquaintance who is currently teaching there told me to advise G. to stop giving interviews to the press where he speaks in vague generalities; he only embarrasses himself because he really knows nothing. "No one among us in Syria knows, because everything is being decided high up and in secret, and it is impossible to say anything without being attacked." Instead, I just say he sends warm greetings. But my friend responds, in turn, by giving me a copy of a Syrian newspaper article from this week attacking him for making statements critical of the government. "And he is my friend!" he exclaims. I ask if the dire economic prognoses for Syria—stagnant exports, rising youth unemployment, declining energy reserves—that I had been reading were true. He agrees with these, on the whole, but says the government has revised its oil estimates, and with new conservation measures the reserves will last until 2020. I ask if ethnic or religious violence would result should there be political instability. He dismisses both kinds of division and insists that conflicts in Syria today arise due to deep historical antagonisms within single local communities and therefore are not likely to spread to other villages or regions—or they are nonexistent.

II

The next night I visit the sister-in-law of the wife of my Princeton acquaintance. She and her husband are Druze and live in a poor, religiously mixed neighborhood north of Damascus. Though they are already in their early forties, they have two very young children, a boy and a girl of about five and seven, whom they handle with extreme gentleness and react to with such spontaneous joy that, although I am not particularly fond of the disturbance of children when among adults, I cannot help but take pleasure in watching the interaction. They tell me that they both spent time in prison for being Communists, she three years, he seven. Serving time in the women's prison was not that bad, she says, because she was not separated from the other prisoners, so she could read, knit, sew, work, and play with all the others; he, on the other hand, like other male political prisoners, was isolated from those jailed for nonpolitical crimes, so he was allowed to read only, and the material was highly controlled. A very elegant Palestinian woman soon joins us. She is a social worker, and we discuss patterns of divorce (increasing slowly), adoption (rare), and family conflict in Syria, most of which she says are specific to socioeconomic class membership and do not vary by sect or religion.

III

The bus to Aleppo takes three detours before finding a station with gas; the last and ultimately successful attempt involves backing up a quarter of a mile and crossing the freeway, all in busy traffic, to get to the station we passed on the other side of the road. The government had just increased gas prices by 25 percent (people tell me 30) and apparently there are shortages. We make our scheduled stop in Homs, and a ten-minute wait turns into nearly an hour. (I assume the driver is, again, looking for gas.) While waiting in the cold, a handsome young man wearing a baseball cap and sweatpants smiles at me, and we begin talking while waiting for our bus to return. M. is a soldier, he says, on a five-day furlough, going to visit his family who live close to the Souk al-Medina, the grand old bazaar where I lived the year before while teaching at Aleppo University. He is studying to be an imam at al-Azhar University in Cairo, the oldest Islamic institution for higher studies (founded around 970 CE) and considered by Sunni Muslims the most prestigious. Because of this study at a religious school, he says, and because he is Sunni Muslim, he has just spent two months in the brig. "But what was the actual offense?" I ask. M. explains: they discovered some email addresses of foreigners in his address book. Soldiers are forbidden contact with foreigners, and he reminds me, jokingly, that our conversation is prohibited. I ask him about the school, and he says he likes it very much; the authorities are very relaxed, he can travel a lot in Egypt, and the students call Pamela Anderson "our greatest temptation."

IV

In Aleppo, I ask people about their economic prospects. The floor and ceiling of the part of the old Souk al-Atarin around the corner from where I had lived is being reconstructed, making it hard to walk down the aisle (mud everywhere), and everything in the shops—spices, jewelry, textiles, clothing, shoes—is doubly dirty.

Merchants have more or less stopped cleaning. Though there are very few customers, the shops are still open every day, six days a week. Merchants hope for the one customer who may stop in. They were promised the renovation would take two months; it has been seven already. Yet they are optimistic. The large Marriott Hotel a block away is nearly complete, and they expect it will bring a new class of tourists to the city, and to this part of the city in particular. External renovation of the Great Mosque of Aleppo, which borders on this part of the souk, was just completed, and the garden area outside is beautiful, with small pools and fountains and benches for sitting. Internal renovations will take another year at least.

Adorning Jabri Square in the center of the old city is a huge new billboard four stories high appealing to patriotism (*wataniyya*) with masses of people waving Syrian flags. Aleppo, I am told, is gearing up to celebrate its designation as the "Cultural Capital of Islamic Culture 2006" (Damascus will be the site in 2008), but the only manifestation of this that I can see is an ugly inflated balloon representing the iconic architecture of a mosque. Two days after my arrival, I witness a ceremony with a large security detail around this balloon in Jabri Square. A taxi driver tells me it is Bashar el-Assad himself, but other people tell me it is only the Minister of Culture. The driver also takes the opportunity to affirm to me—in a totally unsolicited and unprovoked comment—his commitment to Bashar; the Syrian people love him, he says. I did not hear such ostentatious praise last year. With the specter of Iraq as their potential future, nearly all people unite behind Bashar el-Assad as the only hope to avoid the violent sectarian alternative.

V

When I meet Ziyad, the pious student I know very well, he says, "There are lots of vibes about you." "What do you mean?" I ask, and he tells me of his last meeting with the Mukhabarrat, and insists I promise not to tell anyone he told me. His mother informed them that I had arrived. Early in 2005, they had interviewed many of the students whom I had taught, and most of the merchants in the souk whom I knew, and also asked them to call back should I return. To ask for this call is a formality, of course; very few people actually call back. Against the advice of her husband, Ziyad's mother called in. "The fool," I think, and I have to control my anger. It is like calling Homeland Security in the United States and telling them about the arrival of a Syrian. Now the police will be obligated to keep close tabs on me. They make Ziyad promise to write detailed reports about our meetings, about whom I meet, what I want to know, and if I am corrupting the youth. To the last charge, I plead guilty. But I tell him to write the truth about what I say; I am doing nothing wrong or illegal. I'd in fact love to see how Ziyad manages to summarize our conversations. But at all costs, I admonish him, do not reveal the identities of other people, which is now my major concern. How do I learn anything without getting people in trouble for merely talking to me?

I ask about Ziyad's mother's fears. He says his mother—I have met both his parents—has family members who were active in the Muslim Brotherhood, and some were imprisoned for a long time in the eighties. They were assassinating government officials back then, I remind him. His parents say, Ziyad tells me, that today the Brothers talk ideologically about Islam but do not intend to install an Islamic state. I ask whether he truly believes that they are so moderate as they represent themselves. He has no opinion, but does confirm that he agrees with the Brothers in rejecting secularism. "You know I am secular," I say, and he says, "Yes." I wonder what exactly this rejection means to him.

Ziyad helps his father with plumbing and painting, but he has off the two weeks I am here. "Twenty-four/seven," he says, "I am free for you." I suggest he might do some simultaneous translating in situations where I want to do detailed interviews. Often I find myself in conversations where I understand about half of what is said, and when discussions turn philosophical, I am lost. While in Belgium this past summer, a friend had purchased the 2002 film *September 11*, composed of eleven segments directed by eleven different international film directors, and he intends to show it in public somewhere and have a discussion. I tell S. I'd like him to come along and translate some of the comments for me. He is eager to do so, but the screening never comes to pass, as those with access to public places for such viewings are hesitant to commit themselves to anything public, anything that might attract the attention of the authorities; they do not say no but simply procrastinate.

I bring along two CDs of new American pop/rock music, which I had my partner select for understandable lyrics, and I play some tunes on my computer. Ziyad and I translate some of the more difficult English. He has problems understanding what is sung, less the actual words than how they are used. Most of the songs are about love. "May I ask you a personal question?" asks Ziyad "Are you gay?" I hate being coy or disingenuous, but I have learned a direct affirmative answer shocks people, so I say, "Sometimes." "I am not," he declares, and then brings up his worries about AIDS, and we have a long discussion about the virus and the ways it is transmitted. I try to explode the rumors he believes, without dismissing his anxiety. Ziyad tells me that about a year ago when we went to the hammam with a group of students, an acquaintance I had brought along named Jihad told the students privately that I am homosexual. I had never had a conversation about sex with Jihad, so I wonder where he picked this information up, and with whom and why he talks about it. On that outing to the hammam, the students were alarmed by Jihad's presence; they strongly suspected he was there to inform on them for the Mukhabarrat. I had dismissed their worries at the time. "How did the security know this?" Ziyad asks me now. I really don't know, I reply. I invite Ziyad to a meal at Sissy House (named after Empress Elisabeth of Austria), which usually serves wondrously refined Aleppian cuisine. This time, however the lamb was way overdone, the pickled stuffed peppers could have been spicier, and the watercress salad mediocre; only the baba ghanoush was up to their standard.

A few days later I see Jihad on the street, we say hello and affirm we should meet, but this time I do not follow up. He asks friends about me, but I avoid him.

VI

The weather is alternately sunny and cool or rainy and cold. I catch a horrible cold, which begins in the chest, migrates to the head, then back again to deep in the chest. A doctor friend suggests first that I take an extralarge vitamin C and aspirin tablet twice a day, and on second thought, antibiotics. He borrows the small pad of paper on which the waiter in the café where we are sitting tallies up our bill, and writes a prescription on the back of a sheet. I pick up the medicine the next day.

It is Sunday and my friend Saad Yagan, whose pictures are the basis for the cover of this book, invites me to dinner at the restaurant Challal. The owner always has a table reserved for him, where he has coffee at noon and eats dinner nearly every Sunday. Saad is a genial man (in addition to being a supremely skilled and confident painter), and he has exhibited paintings in Europe and the United States. His work has made him a local celebrity, so the restaurant prepares exceptional dishes for him, everything just a twist different, more raw pomegranates in the *muhammara*, the kibbeh nayyeh from the very best raw lamb, a special kebab with an unusual combination of nuts and spices. Two architect friends join him, and the meal is by any measure absolutely fabulous; everything done perfectly and presented aesthetically: two glistening lettuce leafs standing on the hummus, warm pita sprinkled with sesame seeds. The older of the two architects, a warm and friendly man in his seventies, is wearing a deep grey-colored shirt and matching tie, and I compliment him on the colors. He says I have a nice presence, and later that I resemble in profile the national minister of transportation. Out of nowhere, he announces, "I love women." He does have a wife, and he has said in the past that they get along well and he loves her very much, but he never invites her to dinners with us. On evenings like this, he once explained to me, she eats with the family or with other women friends. There are some women in our restaurant, wives and daughters of other men. I cannot help thinking this statement an incongruity: at my table sit four men, no women, and suddenly one announces, "I love women."

VII

Majid, my best friend from the Souk al-Atarin where I had lived, has a birthday but delays planning a party as his oldest brother is recovering from a heart operation in Jordan; he does not want to celebrate amid so much anxiety in the family. I invite him to a restaurant, but in order to be alone with him, I have at the same time to promise three of his nephews who also work in the souk and whom I know well that I will also take them out for dinner the following week. Majid tells me he will soon be traveling for three months—to Australia, perhaps also to Indonesia or Malaysia—his first vacation in three years. Next month his brother returns from three years in Australia, having successfully acquired citizenship there, and he can now take over Majid's shop. His nephews tell me privately they are very jealous that he can take off; they do not enjoy any such prospects.

Majid says that some of the other merchants have declared war on his family's business. They resent the competitive advantage of the seven brothers and their sons, as well as their ability to expand in the souk. Some merchants have begun to engage in systematic price cutting, which of course pleases the customers, most of whom could care less about whether merchants actually recover their costs. But now, says Majid, many merchants sell below cost just to prevent him and his family from making sales. "They hate us," he adds worriedly, "they forget how hard we work to get where we are."

I ask Majid about a man with whom he had an affair, and later lent money to, a sum large enough to finance his entire three months of vacation. Immediately after receiving the loan, this man began to ignore him. His requests for repayment went unanswered, and he was initially truly distressed about losing the money. Now, however, without a trace of bitterness in his voice, Majid says that their paths have not crossed for nine months; he now counts his blessings that the affair ended, and he did not lend him even more.

VIII

In the early evening I join Majid in his shop in the souk. We gather his nephews together and walk to a new restaurant in an old villa that has been renovated on the edge of the souk. Actually, I very much enjoy the nephews, but more so one-on-one than as a group, when their behavior is ritualized and inevitably directed toward each other. All of them got new cell phones in the last year, and one shares with me the video clips he has downloaded onto his. His latest find is of a woman wearing high heels stomping on the genitals of a naked man lying on his stomach. "Aaayyy," I say, "please keep it for yourself. It pains me just to watch." He chuckles and pushes another, similar clip in my face. I ask him if he identifies with the man or the woman in the video. He simply laughs.

The restaurant has several large public rooms along with some smaller, private rooms. My friends choose the one in the basement, with pillows and carpets instead of tables and chairs. The food is excellent, and after eating, even before we are done, everyone anticipates smoking a narghile. We all lay on our sides on the pillows, and I open my computer and play some pop and rock music (Rickie Lee Jones, Joan Armatrading, Red Hot Chili Peppers, U2), which they do not particularly like. Then I switch to modern Arabic jazz fusion and set up my computer to show slides of pictures of them and others in the souk, and of a trip to Sicily. These they enjoy immensely, and comment irreverently about pictures of themselves or those they know. "Ugly!" "Butch!" "Queen!" "Gorgeous!" Our young Kurdish waiter senses that we are a lively bunch and joins us as often as he can sneak downstairs. We exchange telephone numbers, and he asks us to come back for breakfast. Darling as he is, I decline his invitation; not only do I rarely eat much for breakfast, but I do not have the energy or time to play this ambiguous, flirtatious game with him.

IX

M., the soldier I had met on the bus, calls twice to get together, but I cancel both times because of my cold. He wants me to come to his home; his mother will cook for us. Usually I accept such invitations, but first I would like to meet him alone, without his family, so he can be more frank. We agree to meet in front of the Tourist Hotel on Jabri Square. I ask Ziyad to come along and translate. It is lunchtime. We walk two blocks away to the Restaurant al-Andalib, and initially we are the only customers. The four waiters on hand recognize me, as I have eaten there many times (my two friends have never been there), but they say nothing and seat us alone next to the *mazout* heater at the other end of the room.

I ask the soldier about his military service. He heartily dislikes it. I ask about life at the religious school, al-Azhar. He loves it, and he enjoys the freedom of Egypt. And I ask about his teachers. "Not controlling." I ask what they are not controlling about. He smiles but says nothing. (Later, he brings up the "Great Temptation" Pamela Anderson again, and Ziyad asks me, in English, if she is the one with the "big knockers.") "Any women at the university?" "No." "Do you think there should be?" "Yes."

I ask him about topics of debate among students and in classes, and it takes some time to make him understand that I want to know about their disagreements. He assumes I want to know what they agree on (e.g., Israeli illegitimacy, American imperialism). He delves into what I consider esoteric topics, such as disagreements about the status of Jesus as Prophet and about his resurrection, how to understand contradictions in the Hadith, or about the nature of Allah. I ask him if they disagree about the role of the United States in Iraq. "No."

In the middle of this exchange a middle-aged man enters the restaurant and sits behind us, alone. I ask Ziyad why he thinks this man has picked a seat next to us. I suspect he is there solely to listen in; they pay no attention to him.

"You certainly want to know a lot about me," says M. "Every-thing," I say, and laugh. "Would you like to know more about me," I ask, "about my studies, what I teach, or about the United States?" "No," he says quietly and, after a pause, asks, "Why would I?" "Oh," I reply, "if I know more about you I can appreciate and understand you better, who you are and why you think and act like you do." M. smiles and asks nothing, perhaps out of politeness, deference to the authority of a professor. As we leave, he again requests that I come to eat with his family. He will stay in the city two more days. I say I think it might not be a good idea for me to visit him in his home; given that the police seem to be following me, I might get him in trouble. He seems unfazed by this worry, shrugs his shoulders, and says I should visit him anyway. He gives me his hand, and I give him the traditional three-peat kiss on the cheeks. His eyes open wide; he smiles, nods in my direction, and says to Ziyad, "He has learned, hasn't he?"

X

When I see Ziyad two days later, he says the police had visited him at home and asked him about our meeting at al-Andalib. They in fact showed him pictures, taken with a cell phone camera, of the three of us standing outside Tourist Hotel, and asked him to identify the third man, his address and telephone number. I hope you did not tell them, I say, my worst fears heightened. I gave them his first name only, Ziyad says. But the rest of that afternoon, he is totally paranoid. As we walk along a busy street, he thinks every man get-ting out of or into a car is following us. We go to the train station, a quaint, beautiful sandstone building with socialist realist art on the walls inside the entrance and a very large, modern flat-screen television in the waiting room. I take some pictures. Ziyad is very apprehensive and thinks everyone is looking at us. Perhaps they are, I say, but we are doing nothing wrong.

XI

Basil, the young law student who had translated essays of mine on accountability into Arabic, sets up an appointment with the dean of the Law School of the University of Aleppo. The Law School has a budget for publishing foreign legal scholarship in Arabic that goes unused. Nobody seems interested in foreign legal scholarship. But faculty and students at the school had closely followed the Mehlis investigation into the Lebanese prime minister's murder, which involved gathering the testimony of Syrian witnesses. They realized that they lacked sufficient theoretical knowledge of those aspects of international law or politics to understand how to respond to the issues of the case. Hence there is a renewed emphasis on publishing foreign literature. I submit the Arabic translation of my manuscript to the dean, who promises to read it with great interest. They are very interested in publishing it, he says.

Basil and I take a bus to Homs, two hours south of Aleppo, to visit the quiet Alawite village nearby where he lives. About ten thousand people live in this village, which has one main street of two city blocks with a couple of vegetable and fruit stores, a butcher, a liquor store, two small general stores (one where I buy some extra minutes for my cell phone), and a mosque. There is nothing that I would recognize as public "entertainment"—no clubs or bars or wild youths roaming the streets—just a few men in shops smoking, a few playing cards or backgammon. Everyone has a satellite dish on their roofs, and there is no government or private regulation, so perhaps that is where most of them are, in front of the television. Yet here I have intense and open discussions about everything—with televisions usually droning in the background. Perhaps I know the only intellectual residents, but I think not; other men keep dropping by to take part or just listen in. I ask about where the money comes from for all the foreign bank accounts of members of the Syrian ruling elite, and mention the key name—Bashar's cousin Rami Makhlouf, the Assad clan insider who controls several lucrative monopolies, including the "Ya Halla" cell phone network. This causes them to pause, thoughtfully, but briefly. They see defense of the present regime as their only choice and do not waiver in their loyalty.

XII

A young student who attended all of my lectures last year and I meet in one of my favorite cafés near the city center. Her shiny, dark brown hair matches her doelike brown eyes. H. is a beautiful and spirited young woman. Last summer her father died, and now she tells me the details: a traffic accident in a car late at night caused him to go into a coma and die the day after, but the driver and passenger behind him escaped unscathed. "I loved my father so much," she says. Referring to an email I had sent offering condolences, H. adds, "I was so moved that you understood my pain. Now I am just going through the motions. I am completing my studies just for him. I have no motivation."

H. studies English at the university, and is the only Syrian student I know who loves literature. Others read because they have to, or they are only interested in linguistic competency, but H. reads out of pleasure, and she reads widely. Her favorite novels are Russian and Latin American epics. We talk about her plans after graduation. She has an uncle with contacts at the United Nations, and she is exploring training and employment possibilities at other international organizations. She confides in me that she refused a marriage offer with a Syrian medical student studying in France. "He didn't want to grant me freedom," she says. "This must not have been easy," I say, knowing that her father was alive at the time and knew well the family of the potential husband. "I will wait," she says, and I encourage her to be selective. "You will have many opportunities," I say, "you can do better and need not choose now."

Last year H. lived in a student dorm, but has since moved to an apartment that she shares with several other students. "I could not live among the students anymore, after my father died," she says, "I do not want the contact, the conversations. I live in a Christian house, in a Christian neighborhood, and they think I am Christian, too. I do not correct them; it would just create suspicion. They are so racist; they hate the Muslims and talk bad about us all the time."

We talk about her studies and the other students whom I know. H. sees them all often but never talks to them and they do not approach her. Since she is both very beautiful and Muslim, I would think she is someone they desire and talk about. From my own conversations with the young men, I know they all want to marry and hence are very aware of the female students around them. I ask her why there is no contact, and she says, "They respect me, I think."

I ask if the Mukhabarrat contacted her last spring, as they had other students I taught. "No," she says, "my last contact was when I was fourteen. Then, the Ba'ath Party chapter in my school asked me to join, and I said vehemently in front of the whole class that I would not. Two agents came to my home. My father let them in, was polite, served them coffee. They asked to talk to me. He called me, but I refused to talk to them. He told them, 'That's her opinion, she has a mind of her own, I cannot force her.' Since then, they have left me alone."

I see H. a few days later; she brings along another female student whom I had met several times, a Christian friend. The first thing she says is: "They followed me from the café the last time we met, and wanted to talk to me. I said, 'No, I will not talk to you in public, and not on the street. I am a Syrian citizen, you are a Syrian citizen, we have the same rights. I know Mr. John will not hurt me and I will not hurt him. I have nothing to say to you about him. You can call me,' I told them, and I gave them my telephone number, and they called."

I tell her to write the reports of our conversations that they want, but she refuses to cooperate with them in any way. I ask H. and her friend about the Danish publication of cartoons depicting the Prophet Mohammed. They both condemn the comics: an insult to religion, they say, and one should not insult religion. I mention that European governments have limited control over the press, which is largely granted the freedom to report without censorship, and I ask if they have any sympathy for this position. They say they have never heard it articulated before.

XIII

An election for board members to the local chapter of the Red Crescent takes place while I am in Aleppo. T., an openly secular Muslim who is active in public health issues, has been asked to be a candidate. The organization used to be called the Red Cross and was dominated by Aleppo's Christian elite. Currently more than half of the members of the board are Muslim, but they are all relatively inactive elder statesmen. T. loses the election, he thinks because of a rumor that circulates claiming he is a Communist, even though he has never been politically active, much less a Communist. Since there is no word for "liberal" in Arabic, "Communist," in this instance, stands in for any secular persuasion. Among the newly elected members, several are religiously conservative Muslims. In the last several years, religious conservatism among doctors has expressed itself in demands such as insisting that only female doctors treat female patients and that surgeons, whether male or female, have restricted contact with female bodies. T. interprets this election to mean that the majority of members feel less threatened by a religiously motivated board member than a secular one.

One evening while dining with me, T. receives a call asking for advice. A girl of sixteen is pregnant and wants an abortion. T. says it is rare but possible to impregnate a woman without breaking her hymen. If this girl were not a virgin, the abortion would not be a problem. The doctors would perform it secretly and there would, if all went well, be no trace of its effects. But in this case, to abort they, the doctors, must break the hymen, meaning the girl will become unmarriageable, or, upon the point of marriage, the potential husband's family will discover that she had already lost her virginity and—he looks pained and draws his hand across his neck. "Her brothers?" I ask. He nods yes. "And who was it?" I ask, assuming it was her father who got her pregnant. "An uncle," he says.

The family would of course not kill the uncle, perhaps not even dare accuse him of rape; no, should it become public, the girl must be sacrificed to preserve the family's honor. So instead, T. explains, the doctors will do a cesarean section, leaving visible scars on the girl's stomach. But those scars can be explained away, as complications from an operation having to do with stomach or intestinal problems. Doctors do perform abortions in Syria, but with great secrecy (for abortion is illegal, and there have been prosecutions, though rare). They perform them in hospitals late at night when few people are present, keeping the circle of those who know to a minimum, and they charge the patient a great deal of money. But to amass that kind of money requires a girl to tell someone, at least her mother, or perhaps some other family members, for how are they going to account for the disappearance of such a sum from the family budget? In order to pay the costs, the circle of complicity in the family, at least, must be widened, which then increases the risk of discovery.

In 1967 in my own family, also, such a ruse was created surrounding a first cousin, an only child on my mother's side. I was twelve at the time, Maryann was sixteen and wildly in love with a handsome, rebellious young man named Terry, also her age, who liked to get into fights and to race other boys in his car. My uncle's opinion of Terry was that he would come to nothing, so he refused to let his daughter even date him. One day, it was announced out of the blue that they were moving to Arizona. Arizona? We knew nobody there. Back then people stayed put, and their children stayed put. My earliest memories of dreams involved a desire to leave home, not knowing how or exactly why, but now the act of leaving took on mystery. So sudden, so quick, is it possible? My parents did not discuss the matter, though their silence hardly normalized the event.

My uncle and aunt sold their idyllic little Wisconsin dairy farm, which had a creek running below the front lawn, and about eighty acres of forests with trails for horseback riding. Two years later, they returned, with Maryann, and rebought the farm. Maryann, now eighteen, had finished high school and began to work as a grocery clerk in the nearest town. With a bit of grumbling but not much fanfare, she began to date Terry again and soon became pregnant. They married in a small wedding. The only detail I still remember is Maryann's white wedding dress, a fact never discussed but which preoccupied my mother—the scandal of it all!

XIV

After my return to Princeton, J., an American whom I had met in Syria in 2004, calls me to say she received an alarming email from a mutual acquaintance in Latakia, a city on the coast. He is a man I introduced her to, a well-known poet—seductive, irreverent, warm, very funny—and he was so taken by J.'s beauty that he charmed her into an affair, a rocky affair, as these things go, with problems in translation and many misunderstandings. But it was not without its special moments; for example, he would spontaneously translate his poetry into English, or send clever text-messages from his cell phone. J. sent me his email to her, dated early January, about seven months after I had already been absent from Syria and before my last visit:

> Thank you . . . tender J.
> hope to see you too . . . BUT PLEASE I hope you can help me in this . . . without any anger . . . please I'm these days very worry about something . . . was there any chance to get HIV from contacting you!!! because a doctor from Aleppo called Samir Nissaaneh said that john have it and a friend of him from usa!!?? how does he know . . . I think he lies!!?? Sorry J . . . but truly I'm really very worry. please laugh and say you are not . . .

Her tart response to him:

> This doctor sounds like an absurd anti-gay, anti-westerner extremist. Neither John nor myself have any STDs . . . anyway HIV cannot be contracted by talking, eating and listening to music together.
> J.

I send emails to several people in Aleppo to ask if they had heard this rumor, and whether they knew who this doctor Samir was, and if I had ever met him without learning his name. Such rumors, I write, have a life of their own and can effectively make people fear me, spelling the death of any future fieldwork. Two friends write back, unable to identify the doctor, and they reassure me that I should ignore the rumor and in any case return soon.

The following week, by chance I hear the poet being interviewed on National Public Radio. He does not equivocate in discussing Syrian censorship and policing. I contact him by email. Arab friends in the States advise me to use the Arab literary convention of coding the information or rumor as a dream:

Dear ———,

I don't know if you remember me, but I introduced you to J. I hope this finds you doing well, writing more poems, happy, and enjoying life. I am back at Princeton, teaching full time. I recently had a dream, and you were in it, and somebody told you that I had AIDS. Of course, on dreaming this I woke up. I hope you have not had the same dream! All the best,

John

The poet never did reply to my email, but his initial response to the rumor deserves more attention, for, as I described in several earlier chapters, it was also a rumor about me at the beginning of my teaching at Aleppo University that did much to structure my experience among students and teachers there. "I think he lies!!?" is an ambiguous statement. The poet follows what is in fact an assertion with two exclamation points and a question mark, suggesting that he truly wants to dispel the rumor (!!), but nonetheless is unsure (?); hence he must immediately question his assertion. One could rewrite this sentence as a thought sequence: "I think he lies! I think he lies! But does he lie?" The poet's anxiety rests in the possible truth that is concealed behind what appears to be a lie.

His response—an inquiry into the source and veracity of a rumor that I might have AIDS—is a tempting way to deal with the rumor, most likely spread by the Mukhabarrat (though I have no evidence for my suspicion), but it could never effectively put the rumor to rest. On the surface, the poet turns to the technique of verification employed by Arabs to authenticate Hadith, the prophetic dictums or utterances of the Prophet Mohammed passed on in an oral tradition for a century before being written in the Abassid period, one hundred years after the Prophet's death. Verification of a Hadith required a chain of witnesses whose credibility was scrutinized; they must cite their sources and furnish proof of their own integrity. Urinating in the street or eating in the marketplace, for example, were acts that in themselves might impugn the dignity of a witness and result in the disqualification of an entire collection of Hadith. A single imprecision in the chain of transmission was sufficient to question the moral integrity of the transmitter's reputation (see Abdelfattah Kilito, *The Author and His Doubles: Essays on Classical Arabic Culture* [Syracuse: Syracuse University Press, 2001]).

No comparable procedure exists to verify the authenticity of rumors; they spread by means of another logic. Many of the activities of agents of state security involve appropriating the power of rumor, which works like Freud's explanation of *fort und da* (the game of peek-a-boo): through the universal social logic and power inherent in moving from presence to absence and back again. Security agents disseminate plausible lies in ever wider circles, which ultimately gain a momentum and a factuality independent of any process of verification. Over time, the dissemination requires less and less effort by the original agent, whose identity, in fact, becomes secret—for the time being. Direct refutation or denial is useless, as the efficacy of rumor is not dependent on its truth but merely on its periodic repetition. The secrecy or unlocatability of the source removes the major impediment to the repetition. Silence, on the other hand, can also be an ineffective strategy to defuse a rumor, as it would facilitate unconscious registration without the possibility of negation. In other words, in order to negate a rumor one must first tell it, but the telling guarantees the rumor's efficacy by keeping the information in it circulating. I draw the inspiration for this line of inquiry from my close friend Parvis Ghassem-Fachandi, whose research on the use of rumors about abducted women in the Gujarati pogrom of 2002 confirms exactly this process by which rumors acquire power through being told and heard.

I go on at length about the poet's response to a rumor about me, for it demonstrates a conundrum analogous to one running through this book: How can I as an ethnographer resignify stereotypes without unintentionally affirming, defensively contradicting, or remaining silent about them? What is the best strategy to deal with plausible but quite deceptive stereotypes about Arabs generally, and Syrians specifically? These stereotypes abound in the realm of culture (e.g., patriarchy, tyrannical fathers, and oppressed women; the prevalence of revenge motives; the tribal nature of belonging), politics (e.g., backward, corrupt authoritarian regimes), and sex (e.g., coerced veiling of women; vulgar sexual expression and passion). In this book I have tried to avoid the circumlocution that characterizes the writing of many scholars today in what is called the field of "postcoloniality," who prefer critical deconstruction or genealogical tracking to the daunting task of resignifying representations in and of empirical encounters: I was there; I saw things; I felt things; he said this, I said that; I understand. At the same time, I wish to sustain in writing the productive ambiguity inherent in my interactions with Syrians, in which polymorphous desires and ambivalent identifications evolve and do not result in the fixing of identities or the deployment of cultural meanings to shield one from mutual intelligibility.

In many of my encounters, Syrians were torn between a desire for me to declare an identity—married or unmarried, gay or not, professor, father, brother, friend, or stranger—and an equally strong desire not to eliminate the ambiguity that made possible a cultural encounter in the first place, where an experience that is not predefined unfolds. Readers of this book, too, may yearn for the assertion and security of identities and definitive conclusions—theirs and mine, the tying up of loose ends, and the satisfaction of the single or multiple determinants that theory often provides. To this end, much theory is used to reduce the ambiguity of experience and quickly substitute in its place an explanation. By this, I do not mean to oppose explanation to experience, but rather to draw attention to those forms of theorizing that foreclose discovery by not taking into account the internal ambivalence of the subjects of inquiry, by reducing persons to preassigned cultural roles, by isolating single factors to then incorporate with other disparate facts metonymically into a general hypothesis, or by subsuming scenes into a delineated habitus. Instead, in trying to take seriously what people actually do and what they mean—to themselves, to me, and to the others around them— I write episodically so as to splinter theory (I thank Abdellah Hammoudi for this felicitous phrase). This splintering is perhaps most poignantly manifested in how I write about my encounters as experiences of sense-seeking bodies, less determined by learned techniques (Mauss), the organized system of production (Deleuze), or disciplinary technologies (Foucault), and less motivated by socialization (Douglas, Bourdieu), than much theory would lead us to believe.

The focus of my inquiry here has been more specifically on my relations with sons and fathers: the question of the authority of the father and his changing relation to his sons, in which our bodies in interaction are not only primary indexes of sociopolitical processes, but also actively desiring and moving in a world of ambiguous (and ambivalently experienced) erotic—that is, life-affirming—possibilities. During fieldwork I cultivated a methodological ambiguity so as not to foreclose the transferential process whereby people project onto me their own wishes and try to "please" the projection and where I, in turn, try to "please" them. That our encounters were primarily about "knowledge" (and Syrians did want to *know* about me as much as I did about them) did not lessen our emotional investments.

The ethnographer's relation to people in the field setting has sometimes been compared to that of a colonial administrator to the subjects of his empire, where the pursuit of knowledge is an extractive process of information retrieval and accumulation. This likeness may in fact ring true for some anthropologists, and all Syrians I met were aware that I, as an American citizen, am part of an assertive empire, and that during the time of my fieldwork the United States government was actively seeking to bring about a collapse of the Syrian government. The parallels of the current American occupation in Iraq to the early twentieth-century British and French Mandates in the Near East are all too real to deny. Indeed, I readily admitted this parallel when talking with Syrians, but I also sought to create scenes where Syrians would not see in me the ghost of their colonial pasts. My hope was that by foregrounding our ongoing encounters, I would affirm my desire not to extract from Syrians what they know but rather to understand something about their experience of authority by engaging in that experience with them. Whereas colonial administrators often interpreted their own encounters as unavoidable obstacles in the path to truth (experience was therefore to be overcome or put in private diaries), I saw my encounters—everyday sensory experiences, listening to stories, embarrassments, impasses, and mutual exchanges—as the most ethical mode of engagement. The major work of resignifying, then, entailed less changing the representation of myself or the Syrians than opening myself up to relationships with them. From this transference and countertransference, I discovered a range of communicative and relational possibilities, some of which, such as the father-son or father-daughter, I could, to my surprise, embody.

"Father" was projected onto me in two senses: the *genitor* who inseminates and begets children, and the *pater* or source of authority that to some degree always represents independence from the attachment to the mother. I completely frustrated the projection of *genitor* by refusing to acknowledge a desire for procreation (which, to be sure, did not stop the projection—the questions about marriage and children continued), while pleasing, to some degree, the second sense. This projection of the *pater* contains within it acute tensions that result in a highly ambivalent identification. Namely, the father not only stands in for the loss of the separation from the mother (who herself never disappears, never loses the loyalty or total love of her children, especially of her sons), but he also symbolizes freedom and an unknown, unpredictable kind of love. The separation from the father is, therefore, unimaginable, as he represents freedom and the risk of an open love. Yet the precondition for freedom is also the father's death, for only upon his death can the son become his own source of authority, that is, to have authority over others and become subject only to himself: to choose his own wife, keep his own bank account, construct his own household. While the father is still living, the son can procreate as much as he pleases, but having children of his own does not release him from his duties and obligations to his father; only the father's death can free a son from this authority. So, young men are caught, needing the father to realize their freedom but unable to be autonomous until his death.

For many young men in Syria, I was, as in the "Kiss Daddy" episode or in confrontations with tradition, incorporated into a family not as a substitute for the source of authority but as a prop to renew the father, an instrument to reproduce an authority that was in need of support. And, as I've suggested, over the last half-century the Syrian political leadership generally, certainly with the active complicity of the entire oil-guzzling West, has undermined the father's authority within the family. In the wake of this loss, the authority of Islam often steps in to fill the void. There are, of course, alternative processes of authority construction, including some that are democratizing—such as new pan-Arab televisual practices, or old forms of culinary standardization. That said, however, crises in the authority of the father are not unique to Syria or to the modern world generally, meaning that the problem of the father is in fact not resolvable, theoretically or otherwise, except perhaps in fantasy. The best I can do, for now, is to mimic the game of *fort und da* at another level, and in this to mimic the *mullathamun*, medieval Muslim poets so renowned for their beauty that they veiled in order to distract women from them. To cite an Arab poem by Dhu'l-Rumma (loosely translated by Omar Pound) in *Arabic and Persian Poems* (Washington, DC: Three Continents Press, 1986):

> Of all garments
> God blast the veil
> It hides beauty
> to incite the young
>
> and masks the vile
> to urge us on.
> God blast the veil.

That is, I move from the fullness of description to the austerity of theoretical insight, and back again; I depart from the known into an encounter with beauty and ugliness whose end—for knowledge, secrets, love, friendship, status, or merely touch—is unknown.

— Further Reading —

This work is informed by an extensive literature, without which I would have been hopelessly lost in the field, but its authority is based solely on the experiential encounter, not on the academic practice of literature review. There are only two short citations in the text. Yet both to acknowledge my debts and to direct the reader to more scholastic reading, I include this essay on suggestions for further reading. My suggestions (and acknowledgment of debt) are nonetheless selective, with my major concerns being readability and direct relevance to the questions I ask; I omit the excellent work of many authors. I list only English-language works, though on Syria specifically there is a large literature in French and German, and, of course, in Arabic; and I list only published books (omitting journal articles or unpublished dissertations), most of which have longer reading lists that refer the reader to other scholarly and journalistic publications. Among Arab countries, only in Lebanon and Egypt is there much support for social science—anthropology, sociology, politics—though many Arab scholars publish in European languages; their work is included without distinguishing country of origin or residence.

Only three books exist with an anthropological focus similar to mine: the relation of fathers to sons, and how, in turn, this relation generates a certain form of political authority. For how the model of the authoritarian father is transposed into the political sphere, see the work of my colleague, Abdellah Hammoudi, *Master and Disciple: The Cultural Foundation of Moroccan Authoritarianism* (Chicago: University of Chicago Press, 1997). For a focus on how hierarchy is

expressed in ironic language about idealized masculinity and violence, and how it is reproduced under conditions of civil war in Lebanon, see Michael Gilsenan, *Lords of the Lebanese Marches: Violence
and Narrative in an Arab Society* (Berkeley: University of California
Press, 1996). Or, for a comparison of father-son relations under pastoral and nomadic modes of production, see Michael Meeker, *The
Pastoral Son and the Spirit of Patriarchy* (Madison: University of Wisconsin Press, 1989). For the theoretical and comparative anthropological background that informs and motivates my focus in *Syrian
Episodes*, see the essays in a book I edited, *Death of the Father: An
Anthropology of the End in Political Authority* (New York: Berghahn
Press, 2004). For a superb anthropological-historical account of the
transformation of the imperial Ottoman state into the modern na-
tion-state of Turkey, see Michael Meeker, *A Nation of Empire: The
Ottoman Legacy of Turkish Modernity* (Berkeley: University of California Press, 2002). For an ethnographic work on Turkey focusing
solely on secularism, see Yael Navaro-Yashin, *Faces of the State: Secularism and Public Life in Turkey* (Princeton: Princeton University
Press, 2002).

The importance of the souk—symbolically, economically, socially—to people in the Middle East is undisputed, but only one
long essay, a brilliant, Weberian-inspired ethnography and analysis,
attempts to theorize the souk as a "bazaar economy"; see Clifford
Geertz, "Suq: The Bazaar Economy in Sefrou," in *Meaning and
Order in Moroccan Society: Three Essays in Cultural Analysis*, ed. Clifford Geertz, Hildred Geertz, and Lawrence Rosen (Cambridge:
Cambridge University Press, 1979), 123–314. The quotation I cite
is on p. 123; see also his ideal-typical characterization of the souk
on pp. 214–15. On the Aleppian souk and its environs, see the valu-
able study by Annika Rabbo, *A Shop of One's Own: Independence and
Reputation among Traders in Aleppo* (London: I. B. Tauris, 2005).

For the only ethnographic account of political symbolism and its
reception in Syria, specifically looking at the cult of Hafez el-Assad,
see Lisa Wedeen, *Ambiguities of Domination: Politics, Rhetoric, and
Symbols in Contemporary Syria* (Chicago: University of Chicago
Press, 1999). Her argument about the effect of the Assad cult is that

people act as if they revered him, which in turns leads to forms of depoliticization and political compliance. More than a decade after her research, and after the death of Assad-the-father, it appears that the depoliticization holds but that the father is also, in retrospect, appreciated; he, and the authoritarian regime he personally stamped, have changed not merely how people act but also how they think about authority. For an attempt to theorize new ways of thinking prompted by an engagement with new media in the Muslim world, see Dale Eickelman and Jon W. Anderson, eds. *New Media in the Muslim World: The Emerging Public Sphere* (Bloomington: Indiana University Press, 2003).

For a general overview of anthropological topics on the Middle East (with an extensive set of references to the literature), see Dale F. Eickelman, *The Middle East: An Anthropological Approach*, 3rd ed. (Englewood Cliffs, NJ: Prentice-Hall, 1997). For a comparative historical approach to a similar wide range of questions, see Roger Owen, *State, Power and Politics in the Making of the Modern Middle East* (London: Routledge, 1992). For a sociological perspective, see Halim Barakat, *The Arab World: Society, Culture, and State* (Berkeley: University of California Press, 1993).

Two British travelogues from the 1970s present lively and personal tourist perspectives on Syria. On cultural differences among Arabs generally, see Jonathan Raban, *Arabia: A Journey through the Labyrinth* (New York: Simon and Schuster, 1979); on travels in Syria, see Robert Moss, *Cleopatra's Wedding Present: Travels through Syria* (Madison: University of Wisconsin Press, 1997). For a more contemporary and historicized account by an American journalist, with a focus on the Levant, see Charles Glass, *Tribes with Flags: A Journey Curtailed* (London: Secker and Warburg, 1990). Although his focus is on Lebanon, the British journalist Robert Fisk offers undoubtedly the best eyewitness accounts and analysis of Lebanese and Syrian political events over the last thirty years. See *Pity the Nation: The Abduction of Lebanon* (New York: Thunder's Mouth Press / Nation Books, 2000).

The foundational political and cultural history of Arab peoples remains that of Albert Hourani, *A History of the Arab Peoples* (Cam-

bridge, MA: Harvard University Press, 1991). Hourani also wrote
the only comprehensive history of Syria, though it is now a half-
century old: see Albert Hourani, *Syria and Lebanon: A Political Essay*
(Oxford: Oxford University Press, 1946). On Syria in the early part
of the twentieth century, see Philip S. Khoury, *Syria and the French
Mandate* (Princeton: Princeton University Press, 1987). A contemporary history of Syria is forthcoming: see Joshua Landis, *Democracy
in Syria* (New York: Palgrave MacMillan, 2007). For an excellent
history of Lebanon, which has historically been part of Syria and
therefore illuminates this relation, see Kamal Salibi, *A House of Many
Mansions: The History of Lebanon Reconsidered* (Berkeley: University
of California Press, 1988).

Much more has been written on the politics of Syria. For an indispensable analysis of Hafez el-Assad's government and Middle East
politics generally up to the mid-1980s, see Patrick Seale, *Asad: The
Struggle for the Middle East* (Oxford: Oxford University Press, 1988).
On the political economy under Assad, see the detailed and highly
informative work by Volker Perthes, *The Political Economy of Syria
under Asad* (London: I. B. Tauris, 1995). On the most recent developments in Syria, see Alan George, *Syria: Neither Bread nor Freedom*
(New York: Zed Books, 2003). For a longer and more specific historical analysis of Syria's political economy, which also includes basic research on the sources of authority in contemporary Syria, see Hanna
Batatu, *Syria's Peasantry, the Descendants of Its Lesser Rural Notables, and
Their Politics* (Princeton: Princeton University Press, 1990).

On Arab nationalism, which historically and still today directly
influences the politics and sentiments of belonging in Syria, see Ra-
shid Khalidi, ed., *The Origins of Arab Nationalism* (New York: St.
Martin's Press, 1979); and Philip S. Khoury, *Urban Notables and Arab
Nationalism* (New York: Columbia University Press, 1991).

There is a great deal of work on Islam, though none specifically
on Islam in Syria, and I am skeptical about the degree to which the
global reach of Islam informs the relation between secularism and
religion in Syria specifically. For an authoritative work on Islam also
informed by research in the Levant, see Michael Gilsenan, *Recogniz-
ing Islam: Religion and Society in the Modern Middle East* (I. B. Taurus,

2000). See also the wide-ranging theoretical essay on the topic by Clifford Geertz, *Islam Observed* (Chicago: University of Chicago Press, 1971). On historical shifts in secular sensibilities in the modern West and Middle East, see Talal Asad, *Formations of the Secular: Christianity, Islam, Modernity* (Stanford: Stanford University Press, 2003). For a bold and insightful attempt to define "Muslim culture" generally, focused specifically on law and political culture and based on ethnographic research in Morocco, see the work of my colleague Lawrence Rosen, *The Culture of Islam: Changing Aspects of Contemporary Muslim Life* (Chicago: University of Chicago Press, 2002). For a more popular, though nonetheless rigorous and erudite work on the entire modern Muslim world from Morocco to Indonesia, see Malise Ruthven, *Islam in the World* (Oxford: Oxford University Press, 1984). For a less conventional approach to understanding Islam, see the conversation about the meaning of Islamic practices, specifically their adaptability and relation to context, in Michael Fischer and Mehdi Abedi, *Debating Muslims: Cultural Dialogues in Postmodernity and Tradition* (Madison: University of Wisconsin Press, 1990). And finally, for a brilliant study on the experience of the hajj, where the different national and regional versions of being Muslim meet in Mecca and intersect with Islam's Saudi-dominated global reach, see Abdellah Hammoudi, *A Season in Mecca: Narrative of a Pilgrimage* (New York: Hill and Wang, 2006).

The citation on camp is taken from the classic essay on this topic by Susan Sontag, "Notes on Camp," *Partisan Review* 31 (Fall 1964): 515–30. On Arab masculinity, see the insightful essay by Frederic Lagrange, "Male Homosexuality in Modern Arabic Literature," in *Imagined Masculinities*, ed. Mai Ghoussub and Emma Sinclair-Webb (London: Saqi Books, 2000).

Research on the position of Muslim women, inspired partly by Western feminism and gender studies is very deep. See (on Syrian women, specifically) Bouthaina Sha'ban, *Both Right and Left-Handed: Arab Women Talk about their Lives* (Bloomington: Indiana University Press, 1991). Among the many anthropologists writing, see work by two of the pioneers: Elizabeth Fernea, *Middle Eastern Muslim Women Speak* (Austin: University of Texas Press, 1978); *Guests of the Sheik:*

An Ethnography of an Iraqi Village (New York: Anchor Books 1965); Robert Fernea and Elizabeth Fernea, *Arab World: Personal Encounters* (New York: Anchor Books, 1985); and see Lila Abu-Lughod, *Veiled Sentiments: Honor and Poetry in a Bedouin Society* (Berkeley: University of California Press, 1990); and *Writing Women's Worlds: Bedouin Stories* (Berkeley: University of California Press, 1993). For important work outside anthropology, see Lois Beck and Nikki Keddie, eds., *Women in the Muslim World* (Cambridge: Cambridge University Press, 1978); Judith Tucker, ed., *Arab Women: Old Boundaries, New Frontiers* (Bloomington: Indiana University Press, 1993); Fatima Mernissi, *Beyond the Veil: Male-Female Dynamics in Modern Muslim Society* (Bloomington: Indiana University Press, 1987); Leslie P. Peirce, *The Imperial Harem: Women and Sovereignty in the Ottoman Empire* (Oxford: Oxford University Press, 1993).

Finally, there has been much study of the intersection of feminism, gender, politics, and Islam, though none on Syria specifically. The most relevant to my study (and the only ethnographically based work) is Saba Mahmood, *Politics of Piety: The Islamic Revival and the Feminist Subject* (Princeton: Princeton University Press, 2004), which, as the title suggests, seeks to understand forms of patriarchy and piety in Egypt by looking at women's participation in Islamist movements there. See also Karen Armstrong, *The Battle for God* (New York: Random House, 2000); Asma Barlas, *"Believing Woman" in Islam: Unreading Patriarchal Interpretations of the Qu'ran* (Austin: University of Texas Press, 2002). Amina Wadud, *Qur'an and Woman: Rereading the Sacred Text from a Woman's Perspective* (Oxford: Oxford University Press, 1999), gives the Koran a more gender-inclusive reading. On Iran, for a study of nineteenth-century Iran through the lens of gender and sexuality, see Afsaneh Najmabadi, *Women with Mustaches and Men without Beards: Gender and Sexual Anxieties of Iranian Modernity* (Berkeley: University of California Press, 2005). See also Minoo Moallem, *Between Warrior Brother and Veiled Sister: Islamic Fundamentalism and the Politics of Patriarchy in Iran* (Berkeley: University of California Press, 2005); for gendered notions of siblings as the key to understanding the modern fraternal community, see Nilufar Gole, *The Forbidden Modern: Civilization and Veiling* (Ann

Arbor: University of Michigan Press, 1996); for the bold attempt by Fatima Mernissi to reconcile feminism and views of the "progressive Muslim" with the Koran, see her reading of literary sources going back to the seventh century, *Women and Islam* (Columbia, MO: South Asia Book, 2002); see also Mernissi's *Islam and Democracy: Fear of the Modern World* (Cambridge, MA: Perseus Book Group, 2002).

~ Index ~